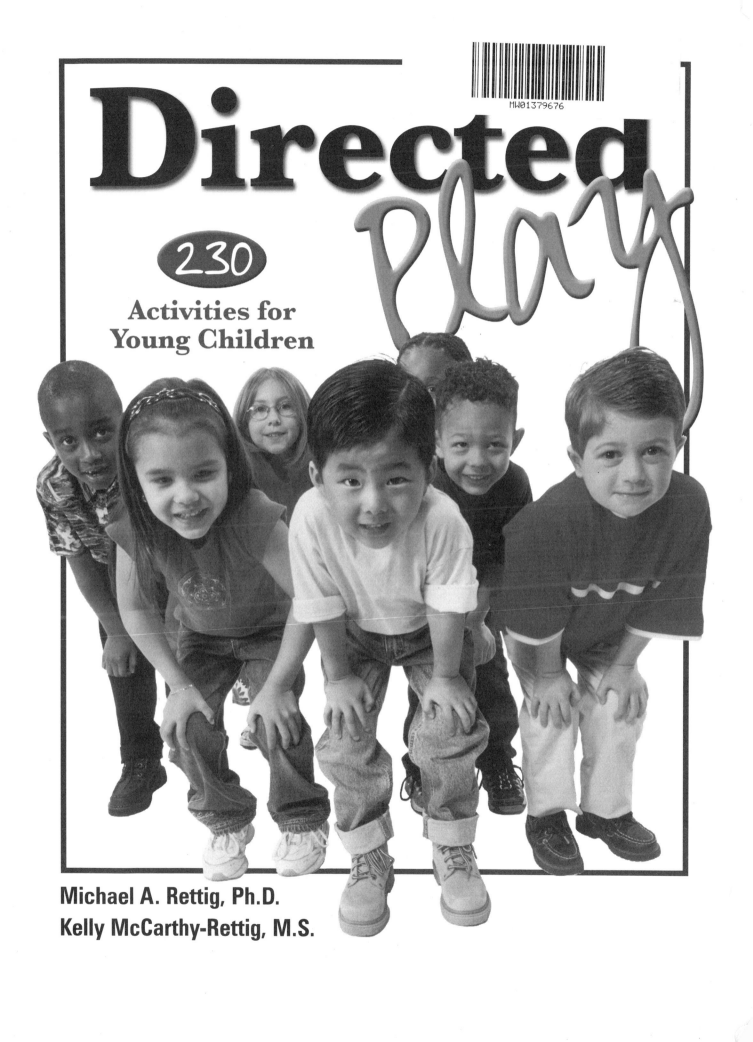

Copyright 2003 by Sopris West Educational Services. All rights reserved.
07 06 05 04 03 02   6 5 4 3 2 1

Developmental Editing by Claudia Manz
Copy Editing by Mitchell Duval
Cover and text layout/design by Sherri Rowe
Illustrations by Steve Clark

Permission is granted to the pruchaser to reproduce the forms for use with his or her students only. No other portion of this work may be reproduced or transmitted in any form or by any means, electronic or mechanical, including photocopying or recording, or by any information storage and retrieval system, without the express written permission of the publisher.

The following activities: Cooperative Drawing, Cooperative Towers, Roller Ball, Back Stand, Partner Kick Ball, and What You Wear are adapted from *The Peaceful Classroom* by Dr. Charles A. Smith, 1993, and are reprinted with permission from Gryphon House, P.O. Box 207, Beltsville, MD, 20704-0207.

Velcro is a registered trademark of Velcro Industries B.V.
Lego is a registered trademark of Interlego A.G.
Duplo is a registered trademark of Interlego A.G.
Little Tikes is a registered trademark of The Little Tikes Company
Candy Land is a registered trademark of Hasbro, Inc.
Nerf is a registered trademark of Hasbro, Inc.
Hula-Hoop is a registered trademark of Wham-O Mfg. Co.
Koosh is a registered trademark of ODDZON, Inc.
Hungry Hungry Hippos is a registered trademark of Hasbro, Inc.
Barbie is a registered trademark of Mattel, Inc.
Popsicle is a registered trademark of Good Humor-Breyers Ice Cream
Wikki Stix is a registered trademark of Omnicor, Inc.

ISBN 1-57035-526-6

Printed in the United States of America

Published and Distributed by

SOPRIS WEST
EDUCATIONAL SERVICES

4093 Specialty Place • Longmont, CO 80504
(303) 651-2829 • www.**sopriswest**.com

161DP/10-02/BAN/2M/417

About the Authors

 **Dr. Michael A. Rettig** is an associate professor in the Department of Education at Washburn University in Topeka, Kansas. Dr. Rettig specializes in early childhood and elementary special education and earned a doctorate in early childhood special education from the University of Kansas in 1984. He served for many years as a teacher of young children with disabilities and also has extensive experience with children's computer applications, in addition to publishing software for young children.

 **Kelly McCarthy-Rettig** is a kindergarten resource teacher in the Desoto, Kansas, school district. She has a master's degree in early childhood special education and certification in special education and elementary education. She has been teaching young children with disabilities for the past ten years and before that she served as a second grade teacher. She was honored as the Kansas Division for Early Childhood's distinguished service provider in 1995 and as the teacher of the year in the Desoto school district in 1999. She enjoys walking, yoga, and caring for our active two-year-old daughter Kate Li.

Acknowledgments

For Kate, Ryan, Megan, and Michael and all they have taught us about play.

Thank you to all of the professionals we have worked with over the years for all we have learned from them. Special thanks to Dr. Nancy Peterson. Special recognition and gratitude goes out to Sandy Hubbard, Diane Meyer, Diane Byerlay, Jana Flannigan, and Holly Buser for their limitless support and efforts in helping young children with special needs and their families. Thanks also to the staff at Sopris West for their assistance and the opportunity to share our experiences.

Contents

Introduction
What Is Directed Play? 1

Chapter 1
Foundations for Directed Play 7

Chapter 2
Toys and Play Materials 17

Chapter 3
Play and Children With Disabilities 25

Chapter 4
Observation and Assessment of Play 39

Chapter 5
Strategies for Successful Classroom Management 63

Chapter 6
Personal/Social Skills Activities 69

Chapter 7
Motor and Movement Activities 133

Chapter 8
Fine Motor and Perceptual Activities 179

Chapter 9
Readiness and Preacademic Activities 251

Chapter 10
Thematic Units 309

Appendix A: Multiple Intelligences and Play 381

Appendix B: State Technology Projects 393

Appendix C: Activity List 397

References 399

What Is Directed Play?

Directed Play is a teaching curriculum developed by the authors during their 30 years of combined experience working with young children, both with and without disabilities. Its foundation—that young children learn best through play—is based on proven techniques and current empirical research into the learning styles of children. Play is a fun and natural way for children to learn about the world and to practice the skills they will need as adults. More important, Directed Play is an appropriate way for children to learn about another and to interact in positive ways.

In Directed Play, strong emphasis is placed on increasing and enhancing interactions among children, three to six years of age, in a fun and natural way. Children must learn to socialize with one another in a positive manner in order for mainstreaming and inclusion to be fully realized. Children with disabilities may need special assistance in social situations, so teachers should be prepared to help these children in knowing what to do and what to say.

In Directed Play, a teacher or caregiver needs to be thought of as a director in a theater production. Just as a theater director "sets the stage" for a production and helps actors learn their lines and follow a script, Directed Play teachers and caregivers set up the play environment with proper materials and then assist children in what to do and say. Children are guided through a play episode before direct adult involvement is gradually withdrawn.

Directed Play makes use of "structured free-play." This means that children participate in free-play activities that have a specific focus or target objective. Toys or learning materials are set up or "staged" for children, and adults guide or direct children through the activity. An adequate amount of appropriate materials ensures that every child can participate, and children are free to use the toys and materials while teachers monitor and observe the activity. Teachers "direct" children by:

- Setting up and preparing the learning activity

- Organizing them into play groups of three to five children

- Introducing the play activity and showing children what to do and say

- Encouraging and increasing child-to-child interaction

- Being present in the play setting and assuming a role in the play episode

- Encouraging children to play with and help one another

- Asking open-ended questions, such as "Tell me about the truck" rather than "Do you like the truck?"

- Adding words or ideas to what the children are saying

- Pointing out similarities or differences between people, objects, and events

- Making sure children are on-task and engaged in the activity

- Giving children "Extended Time" to play

- Exposing children to real objects and places whenever possible, for example, taking children to a farm to see real animals

- Providing disability awareness activities

- Observing children to monitor and keep data on their performance

- Providing instruction on new concepts or skills and providing opportunities to practice these skills

Directed Play activities are best suited for small groups of three to five children. However, the size of the Directed Play group depends on the age of the children, the type and severity of any handicaps, and the specific play activity being carried out. Early childhood educators will need to make decisions on group size and composition based on their knowledge and experience with the children in their classrooms. However, children should, whenever possible, be paired with peers of the same age and sex. Adults will want to ensure that children talk with one another during play, and some younger or lower-functioning children may need considerable intervention from the teacher to know what to say and do in play activities. Peers may also need assistance in interpreting what these children are saying.

Teachers using the Directed Play approach are encouraged to talk to children throughout the learning activities, pointing out the name or use of objects, or noting similarities and differences in things. Teachers should make statements or comments to children instead of asking direct questions, and they should assume a role in the play to guide or direct the activity. For example, instead of asking a child what color an object is, the teacher should just name the color, as in "You picked up the red ball." Instead of asking a child to identify objects in farm play, such as "Show me all the cows," the teacher could ask children to "Line up all the cows to go in the barn." Adults should speak clearly, use language children understand, and speak in short sentences.

Extended Time

Another important component of Directed Play is "Extended Time." Extended Time means that children engage in play activities for longer periods of time each day. Further, they engage in activities over several days to ensure that they understand the concepts being presented. This leads to a sense of familiarity with the concepts and allows the children to engage in higher-order forms of play. Over several play sessions, a target objective can be addressed through developmental domains and across multiple intelligences. Material developed in one activity can be saved and incorporated into other related activities.

Directed Play　　2

Extended Time means also that you give children the time and opportunity to complete tasks themselves and not do things for them. Montessori (1967) concluded that children should be given the time they need to complete tasks. What may seem trivial to us is important to them. Giving them the time they need to complete tasks increases both their independence and self-esteem.

Learning activities have also been included in Directed Play to foster pre-academic skills. They are targeted at kindergarten-age children, and although many of these activities may not be thought of as "play" to adults, they should all be done in a play-like way for preschool to kindergarten-age children.

Organization of Directed Play Activities

Directed Play Activities described in this book are consistently organized in the following manner:

Activity
The name and general focus of the activity.

Target Objective
Specifies the target objective(s) for the children.

Developmental Domains
Which developmental domains (gross motor, fine motor, language, social, cognitive, or self-help) are addressed by the target objective.

Multiple Intelligences
Which multiple intelligences (interpersonal, intrapersonal, linguistic, logical-mathematical, spatial, musical, bodily, and naturalist) are addressed by the target objective. These are explained in Chapter 1.

Materials
Materials needed to carry out the play episode.

Preparation/Set-Up
What is needed to "set up" the play activity.

Procedures
The procedures necessary to carry out the activity and suggestions for what to say and what to do.

Adaptations for Children With Disabilities
Suggestions for how the play activity might be adapted for children with disabilities.

Components and Advantages of Directed Play

We have included a wide range of curriculum activities, grouped into five broad areas: Personal/Social, Motor and Movement, Fine Motor and Perceptual, Readiness, and Thematic Units. Individual activities usually address more than one developmental domain and type of intelligence. The activities are listed in a general developmental sequence, with the activities at the beginning of each section more suitable for younger children.

Directed Play compiles nearly 230 specific activities that we have found to be useful and fun for children, with descriptions of materials and procedures. We have also provided more than 225 suggestions for additional activities, as well as narrative information throughout the curriculum on such topics as sensory stimulation, blocks, mazes, pre-reading and prewriting, yoga, and computers. This information is provided to help guide activities and to increase the understanding and importance of the activities described.

In Chapter 1 we discuss the importance of play, foundations of the Directed Play philosophy, information on multiple intelligences, and ecological theory. This information provides a foundation for setting up and implementing Directed Play activities.

Chapter 2 gives some basic information about toys and playthings. This chapter contains suggestions of what play materials should be available and how to adapt toys. It also includes contact information for organizations that provide quality toys for children.

Chapter 3 discusses the impact of disabilities on the play of young children. We provide information on nine different disability categories, including mental retardation, autism, Asperger syndrome and pervasive developmental disorders, attention deficit disorder, developmental delay and learning disabilities, behavior disorders and emotional disturbances, visual impairments, language and hearing impairments, and physical and health impairments. When working with children with disabilities, it is important to know how a specific disability will affect a child's play. For each of these exceptionalities information is presented on the general play characteristics of children with the disability, as well as specific play behaviors and deficits.

Strategies for assessment and data collection are provided in Chapter 4. This chapter contains information on play assessments and includes sample observation and data collection forms that can be used in various activities.

General guidelines for successful classroom management are described in Chapter 5. These guidelines help to ensure that Directed Play activities are conducted in a fun and meaningful way.

Chapter 6 includes Personal and Social Directed Play activities that include body parts, self-help skills, emotions, home, family, dramatic play, cooperative play, disability awareness, and buddies.

Chapter 7 has activities that focus on gross motor skills, including indoor and outdoor activities, games with rules, and yoga movements for young children.

Directed *Play*

Chapter 8 contains Directed Play activities that focus on fine motor and perceptual skills. Activities in this section include blocks, sand, play-dough, coloring, mazes, easels, scissor crafts, and murals.

Readiness activities are described in Chapter 9. These include cognitive skills, prereading, prewriting, and premath activities, as well as time and computers.

Activities organized into thematic units are described in Chapter 10. A number of activities that are suitable for different times of the year are explained and include community awareness, occupations, post office, safety, and farms.

Foundations for Directed Play

This chapter provides information on the importance of play and the foundations of Directed Play, as well as descriptions of the multiple intelligences and information on "ecological" theory as it is applied to the play of young children. Reviewing this chapter will help you understand and implement Directed Play activities.

The Importance of Play

Many educators and theorists stress the importance of play in the development of children. Play is seen not only as an enjoyable activity but one in which children learn new skills and practice existing ones. Play incorporates all of the developmental domains: language, social, cognitive, and motor skills. Froebel (1894), the father of the kindergarten, felt that play was a way for children to gain insight into their world and their means of creative self-expression. Play, according to Piaget (1962), involves both assimilation and accommodation, the major ways in which children learn.

More recent research places an even greater value on play. Vygotsky (1976) suggested that play was useful in the development of language and thought. There are also indications that certain types of play, such as constructive or sociodramatic, may increase a child's IQ (Johnson, Ershler, & Lawton, 1982).

Play is a way of taking information from the world and organizing it. It has been shown that play can increase role-playing and social problem solving. Feeney and Magarick (1984) view play as a way for children to learn about the world around them, to talk and share and learn about themselves. Play is seen as a way to foster cognitive and social development and promote cultural diversity awareness. Through play and games children can learn about the similarities and differences in others. In addition, play allows for the practice and generalization of skills learned in structured lessons. There is a circular relationship with learning and play. As children play, they hone new learning skills that in turn lead to higher-quality play behavior.

Play is also a way to help children communicate and work through emotional problems. Virginia Axline (1947) was an early pioneer in Play Therapy, a technique in which a child is allowed to play with materials while a therapist helps the child deal with his or her feelings. Many of the toys and activities in Directed Play are consistent with those used in Play Therapy sessions; however, specific training is required to conduct Play Therapy.

Play is a natural way to promote the inclusion of children with disabilities and awareness of cultural diversity. Children playing together learn about one another and become more accepting of their individual differences. Research has shown that, without intervention, young children often segregate themselves in play (Peterson & Haralick, 1977; Peterson & Rettig, 1982). Children, like adults, seek out peers who are similar. For inclusion and cultural diversity efforts to work, children must interact with one another. Directed Play focuses on such child-child interactions.

Different Types of Play

There are many different types of play. These include functional play, exploratory play, constructive play, and dramatic play. Children need opportunities each day to engage in these different types of play because such opportunities allow children to practice new and varied skills. We have included activities that cross all of these types of play. See Chapter Four for more information on levels of play.

Foundations

Directed Play is based on proven teaching techniques and on our direct experience teaching young children, both with and without disabilities. It integrates several approaches to the education of young children, among them the work of Edward Sequin in the 1800s and Maria Montessori in the early 1900s. Sequin stressed that we must focus on the whole child—mind, body, and spirit—and that children need hands-on exposure to real objects during play. Montessori's work with children was based on the premise that the play environment should be "set up" for children. She believed in the use of child-sized materials and sensory stimulation, and rather than directly teaching children concepts, the Montessori method was based on the idea that children should be free to use and manipulate self-teaching materials independently.

Directed Play also makes use of current educational approaches, including the Preschool Integrated Curriculum (Odom, et al., 1988), and Joint Action Routines (Snyder-McLean, Solomonson, McLean, & Sack, 1984). There is an emphasis on curricular integration, the practice of addressing more than one developmental area at a time. Directed Play emphasizes cooperative learning and peer tutoring and incorporates these into daily activities, an approach similar to that used in the Peaceful Classroom (Smith, 1993), which focuses on teaching children acceptance, belonging, and cooperation. In addition, we have reviewed developmental assessments used with young children and have provided activities that address developmental milestones.

Multiple Intelligences

In recent years the concept of multiple intelligences has gained popularity. There is a growing appreciation for the idea that each of us possesses eight different types of intelligence, all of which we are able to develop and use to some degree. The concept of multiple intelligences derives from the work of Howard Gardner (Gardner, 1993). He identified seven different intelligences: Linguistic, Logical-Mathematical, Spatial, Musical, Bodily-Kinesthetic, Interpersonal, and Intrapersonal. And recently, a new type of intelligence, Naturalist, has been identified. **Table 1.1** provides a summary of the eight different intelligences. Each of us has certain intelligences that are more pronounced than others. We learn best when we are provided instruction directed toward those intelligences, but we still need to challenge and explore the others.

Teachers are encouraged to provide activities across all eight intelligences every day. Some children will naturally be good at and enjoy some of these activities and will not others. For example, a preschool class recently went on a short hike in the "forest" area of a park. This activity fits nicely with the Naturalist intelligence as well as the Bodily-Kinesthetic intelligence. The teacher reported after the activity that about half of the children really enjoyed the outing while the other half did not. After the hike, the class divided into groups to play Candy Land®, an activity that addresses Linguistic and Interpersonal intelligences. Following this, the children had an option to choose music or building with blocks, which address Musical or Spatial intelligences.

Some games and activities relate to two or more of the intelligences, whereas others tend to focus on only one. For example, playing pattern games or lotto games fits nicely under Linguistic or Logical-Mathematical intelligences but not so well under any of the other categories. Activities or games that concentrate on sorting and classifying objects or counting incorporate the Logical-Mathematical as well as the Linguistic intelligences. Children who favor Bodily-Kinesthetic and Naturalist activities enjoy playing in sand and water. Painting, drawing, and play-dough creations would be considered Spatial and Bodily-Kinesthetic.

Games for the Linguistic and Interpersonal domains may be combined in the form of group projects and cooperative learning or in various dramatic play activities. Smith (1993) describes a variety of activities designed to promote cooperation. Linguistic and Musical play activities might include finger plays, nursery rhymes, and singing. Doing the "Hokey Pokey" combines Musical and Bodily-Kinesthetic domains.

Games or activities for Intrapersonal and Interpersonal intelligences can be similar. Both of these intelligences center on an understanding of people, emotions, etc. Activities to promote belonging, acceptance, and an understanding of emotions would relate to both of these intelligences.

Table 1.1

Eight Different Intelligences

Linguistic

Children who have strong linguistic abilities are good with words. They tend to enjoy listening to and playing with the sounds of words. They may like to have books read to them, tell jokes or stories, have good memories for words, and will likely learn to spell words easily.

Logical-Mathematical

Children with Logical-Mathematical intelligence will be good at logical thinking activities. They may enjoy puzzles, or other board games where they have to think logically and clearly. They will likely be good at math games and may enjoy computers.

Spatial

Children with Spatial intelligence tend to be good at images and pictures. They may enjoy drawing pictures, doing mazes or puzzles, and building things with blocks or Legos®. They may be interested in machines and will likely have a good sense of where things are and where they belong.

Musical

A Musical intelligence is evident in children who hum or sing a great deal. These children may enjoy musical instruments and listening to records, and they easily remember songs or nursery rhymes. They may also be good at discriminating various sounds in the environment.

Bodily-Kinesthetic

Bodily-Kinesthetic intelligence is characterized by children who are good at sports and movement activities. They will demonstrate good gross and fine motor skills and enjoy activities such as swimming or competitive sports.

Interpersonal

Children who demonstrate an Interpersonal intelligence tend to have lots of friends and are easy to get along with. These may be the children who settle conflicts between other children and who greatly enjoy group games. They seem to have an awareness of the feelings of other people. An educational focus for these children would be on helping them understand other people.

Intrapersonal

Intrapersonal intelligence is seen in children who have a strong sense of independence or a strong will. They tend to do more things alone rather than playing in a group. They may have a strong sense of self-confidence. An educational focus for these children would be on helping them understand themselves.

Naturalist

This intelligence refers to children who have a strong interest in nature or animals. These children will prefer to play outdoors and enjoy playing with rocks, sticks, water, sand, animals, snow, or leaves.

Directed Play

Included in Appendix A is information on play materials and games associated with the multiple intelligences, sample lesson plans showing how individual activities can be taught in various ways, and words of the alphabet associated with multiple intelligences.

Ecological Theory and Play

The "ecological" theory of learning and development focuses on stimuli in our environment that determine or influence our behavior. The theory rests on the work of Bronfenbrenner (1977), who proposed four nested levels of the environment: the microsystem (the immediate environment a person is in at the moment), the mesosystem (a collection of all the microsystems), the exosystem (including factors such as TV or other media), and the macrosystem (societal values, laws, and regulations). Each of the four levels of the environment is separate and distinct from the others but at the same time interrelated.

The microsystem refers to the immediate setting or environment within which a person is interacting and it is the system most relevant to Directed Play. A microsystem can be a classroom, bedroom, or playground sandbox. Within a given microsystem, individuals are influenced by whatever materials or people are in that specific setting at that time. The materials or people within a microsystem can be manipulated to influence or promote certain behaviors.

It is useful to examine how the four different levels of the environment influence the behavior of children. Young children are obviously influenced by such things as the types of toys available or what they have seen on TV. However, when ecological theory is applied to the play of young children, a more specific focus is needed. Our work with children has shown us that there are four environmental variables that can influence the play of children. They are People, Places, Things, and Time (Rettig, 1998). Each variable will be described below.

People

People refers to who is present during play. As an ecological factor, people may include adults or other children. The number of adults or children present and their level of involvement greatly influences play behaviors. Differences in the age, gender, or race of peers may also bear on the play behaviors of children.

The Child

Ecological "people" considerations need to include an examination of the characteristics of individual children. Children can differ in many obvious ways, such as age or gender. However, the income or education level of a child's family, the values of the family, the type or severity of a disability, or even what part of the country a family lives in can influence a child's play. For example, Smilansky (1968) indicated that children from low-income homes engaged in less sociodramatic play than children raised in middle-class homes. One of the primary reasons for this finding was that children in the low-income homes had fewer toys and fewer opportunities to play with new toys than did their middle-class counterparts. Because of this lack of exposure, these children needed time to explore and manipulate the toys before they could engage in higher-order forms of play.

There is no doubt that young children with disabilities have certain characteristics that can influence their play skills. Due to the nature of their disabilities, children with mental retardation, visual or hearing impairments, or physical disabilities affect play settings differently from their nondisabled peers. For example, a child with a pronounced physical impairment may look, move, or act differently from other children. These differences might adversely affect the extent to which other children seek out this child for play. Strain (1985) found that key determiners in the acceptance of other children were attractiveness, athletic ability, and limited disruptiveness.

It is essential that we consider individual differences in children and determine how these differences might affect play with toys or peers. Observing the play, language, and social skills of children is an important first step. Such observations yield important information on strengths and deficits in play behavior. For some children, it may be necessary to teach them how to play with certain toys or how to smile and greet another child.

Peers

Peer factors that influence the play of young children include age, gender, race, or number of peers available. In addition, how well children know each other or the presence of children with disabilities can also influence play, at least initially. Young children are aware of differences in other children. We need to help children understand that these differences are a natural part of life.

In the last 20 years typically-developing children have been used as peer models to promote the social integration of young children with disabilities. Using peers as models is known as a peer-mediated or peer-initiated approach. One of the lessons learned from the study of social integration is that children will not seek out children with disabilities to play with unless there are specific interventions in place. Simply placing children with and without disabilities in the same classroom is not enough. We must make sure that they interact, and play is an easy way to promote this.

When left to their own devices, children will seek out children similar to themselves for play. This means that we must plan to help children play with the children that they might not ordinarily play with. Typically-developing children will need to be taught about children with disabilities and will need to be taught to involve these children as playmates.

Adults

The number of adults present in a play setting and their level of involvement are other important ecological factors to consider. Johnson, Christie, and Yawkey (1987) identified four levels of adult involvement in play. These four levels involve a gradual increase in adult involvement in play and are dependent upon a child's needs. The four levels of adult involvement are:

Parallel Play—occurs when an adult is close to the child and plays with the same materials as the child; however, there is little adult interaction with the child, and no attempts are made to direct the child's play.

Coplaying—occurs when an adult participates in an ongoing play activity with a child, but the child still directs the play activity. The adult participates by responding to questions or subtly introducing new elements into the play episode.

Play Tutoring—occurs when an adult assumes more direct control over a play episode by initiating new play activities or by directly teaching new play behavior to a child.

Spokesperson for Reality—occurs when an adult is not directly involved in a child's play but encourages them to make a connection between their play and the real world by asking questions or identifying what is real and what is not.

Adult involvement is an important component of the Directed Play approach. In most activities, adults will assume a coplaying or play-tutoring role. It is important that adults:

1. Identify the target skills for children

2. Set up the environment with appropriate props and materials

3. Help children to know their roles in the play episode

4. Provide direction as necessary to help children work through the play activity

5. Assume a role in the play of the children

6. Ask questions that relate to the play theme, not questions that require right or wrong answers from children

The level of adult involvement should be reduced gradually until children can enjoy the play episode without any direct adult involvement. It is important for adults to be close enough to see and hear easily what children are doing but not so close that they interfere with play. Before entering a play setting, adults should always take a moment to observe what children are doing and try to involve themselves naturally into the play episode.

Place

Place refers to the "where," or physical setting, for play. It is important to consider factors such as the amount of space available, how that space is arranged, and whether play takes place inside or outside. According to Smith and Connolly (1980), children should each have a minimum of 25 square feet for a play area. This amount of space helps prevent the negative effects of overcrowding. While it is not likely that the amount of space will be increased in our classrooms, it is possible to reduce the number of children in a play area at one time, and this is the primary reason why Directed Play limits the number of children in a playgroup.

It is important to consider how a classroom is arranged. Related learning centers should be next to each other. For instance, a dramatic play area and a block area should be next to each other because they both tend to be loud areas. Quiet areas, such as a reading area, should be across the room. Fine motor, easels, and manipulatives can be in the same area as snack time because a tile floor is needed for easy cleanup.

Shelves or partitions help break up play areas. The shelves or partitions should be high enough that children cannot see over them but low enough that adults can. Wall-to-wall carpeting can eliminate some unwanted sounds. Also, be alert to background noises, such as music, which may be distracting to some children.

Time

A less well-known environmental variable is time. Directed Play makes use of Extended Time. The amount of time available for play and the use of play themes extended over several days or weeks are an important part of this approach. Extended Time helps children to achieve higher-order levels of play, and there are indications that children will engage in more complex and mature forms of play when given longer play periods (Christie, Johnson, & Peckover, 1988; Tegano & Burdette, 1991). For example, if we only provide a 20-minute free play period for children, they will just be getting started in play when we direct them to stop. The children may have just built their block tower, or set up their "farm," when they are asked to move to another activity. With a 40-minute play period, children will have an adequate amount of time to expand and elaborate on their play theme.

An older, but related study, shows how time can influence child behavior. Krantz and Risley (1972) reported on two groups of children engaged in a story-reading task. One group went to the reading task immediately after a physical activity. The visual attention of this group of children, measured in the first 15 minutes of the story-reading activity, was 63 percent. The second group of children was provided with a brief rest time after the physical activity and before the story reading. Their attention measured in the first 15 minutes was 86 percent. Providing a brief rest or transition time between activities served to increase the children's measurable attention to a story by 23 percent.

Children need an adequate amount of time for play. They need time to set up the play episode and time to get involved in elaborate pretend. By increasing the time available, we can assist them in reaching higher-order forms of play. This is also an important consideration in observing and assessing play skills.

Things

Toys and playthings can influence play behavior. The types of toys available, the number of toys available, and the cultural significance of the toys can all influence play. Questions have been raised regarding the nature of toys and playthings currently found in our society and what these playthings may be teaching children. Violent video games and computer programs are an obvious example. But toys and playthings can convey values to children in less direct ways. For instance, are Barbie® dolls suggesting to children that young women should be thin and blond? What does this mean to children who may have physical impairments or who otherwise do not fit this conception?

The number or availability of toys may be an important ecological variable affecting the play behaviors of children. Brown (1996) found that the behaviors of young children were influenced by two different toy conditions: a limited toy condition and a plentiful toy condition. This study involved two children and one or two paintbrushes. Children in the one paintbrush condition engaged in more resource and exchange behaviors in an effort to get the paintbrush. When two paintbrushes were available, children engaged in more social and paint task behaviors. In the limited toy condition, children engaged in more conflict behavior than in the plentiful toy condition.

In a study by Rettig (1995), children with and without disabilities were brought to a play area in dyads and exposed to three different toy conditions: full toys, partial toys, and no toys. Each of nine dyads was exposed to the three toy conditions in a counterbalanced order. An analysis of more than 460 five-minute observation sessions showed that there was a steady increase in the percentage of time engaged in positive social interactions from the full toy to the partial toy to the no toys conditions. Conversely, there was a steady decrease in the amount of time spent in solitary play. For example, the children engaged in solitary play 35 percent of the time in the full toy condition, 25 percent of the time in the partial toy condition, and only 9 percent of the time in the no toy condition. At the same time, interactions among children went from 54 percent of the time in the full toy condition to 65 percent in the partial toy condition to 75 percent in the no toy condition. And when toys were present, children spent approximately 80 percent of their time involved with toys but nearly 75 percent of their time playing with one another when no toys were present.

Directed Play puts a great deal of emphasis on the playthings available for children because materials guide play. It is well known that if we give children constructive play materials they will work at creating something, and if we give them dramatic play materials we will enhance and increase the likelihood of sociodramatic play. Giving children social toys increases their levels of socialization. Other considerations regarding the importance and use of toys are discussed in the next chapter.

Directed Play activities have a foundation in both ecological theory and the various intelligences. Setting up play environments for children requires educators to consider the influence of people, places, things, and time. Furthermore, we must consider how activities can be taught in different ways to appeal to the interests and learning strengths of children.

Toys and Play Materials

Play among children has always involved the use of toys and other playthings. Examined from a cultural and ecological perspective, toys provide an insight into the norms and values of a society. The toys that children play with reflect the place and era in which they live. Children growing up around bodies of water may play more with toy boats than children raised in landlocked areas. And toys involving "spacemen" did not become common until the 1950s and 1960s, when space exploration was in the public eye. Many toys children play with today are based on characters in TV shows or movies.

Because toys and playthings have such an important role in determining and influencing the play of young children, adults need to make sure that available toys are appropriate and reflect cultural diversity. Staff should evaluate the toys to make sure that there are a variety of them and that they cross different developmental domains. Toys should also be examined for accessibility and cultural bias. Some Native American families, for example, may consider certain toys or pictures to be bad luck or evil.

A good way to ensure that there is an adequate number and variety of toys available is to group toys by developmental domain. **Table 2.1** has a general listing of toys and playthings classified by developmental domain. Some toys and materials cross more than one domain. These are items that should be easy to find.

Prop Boxes

A practical suggestion for increasing and organizing playthings is the use of prop boxes (Boutte, Van Scoy, & Hendley 1996; Myhre, 1993). A prop box is a collection of similar play materials that can be used to organize related materials and promote thematic play. For example, a prop box could be developed around a music theme by containing a variety of musical instruments. Materials for prop boxes can be compiled from thrift stores, garage sales, families of children in the school, or made by children and families. Materials can be stored in prop boxes for easy organization and can be shared between classrooms. Be sure to label the boxes by theme. To increase novelty, put prop boxes away for a month and then bring the materials out. The children will be excited to see the things again. A number of ideas for the development of prop boxes are listed in **Table 2.2**.

Table 2.1

Toys and Developmental Domains

Language

Books on topics that relate to themes, such as safety, occupations, emotions, families, animals, counting, or disabilities; cars and trucks; toy money; cash registers; picture menus; kitchen and house items; social interaction toys, such as commercially available farm, garage, or airport toys with people; calendar; memory games; picture-matching cards; alphabet and number cards; story-sequencing cards; puppets; toy telephones

Cognitive

Nesting cups; puzzles of various sizes and difficulties and with different themes, such as body parts, occupations, and animals; records, tapes, or CDs of music that supports themes (e.g., body parts); one-inch colored blocks; assorted toy foods, animals, vehicles, people, buildings, and books; alphabet and number cards; color and shape materials; water toys, including buckets, cups, boats, and paintbrushes; sand toys, such as buckets, scoops, spoons, and dump trucks

Social

Teddy bears and other stuffed animals (promotes security); doctor's kit (promotes empathy); various card and board games; keys; purses; helmets; dolls; toy foods; dress-up clothing from different cultures; furniture; pots and pans; child-sized silverware and plates; books on going to the doctor, dentist, moving, or divorce; musical instruments and toys; Nerf® balls; pictures of emotional expressions (happy, sad, surprised, angry, disgusted, interested, scared)

Self-Help

Assorted clothing, lacing, zipping, and button boards; various dolls with clothes; books on toileting; child-sized blankets and pillows; plates, silverware, and cooking utensils; brushes, shoes, and play jewelry

Fine Motor

Paper, crayons, markers, puzzles, beads, and lacing materials; Duplos®, Legos®; chalk, scissors, glue sticks, play-dough or clay, easel paints, and finger paints; latches, knobs, zippers, buttons, and pipe cleaners; wikki stix, small blocks, and parquetry; adapted scissors; water toys; sand toys; pop beads; lacing materials; peg boards; tongs; tweezers; clothespins

Gross Motor

Balls of assorted sizes; beanbags; tricycles; small wooden ladder; paint easels and paint; child-sized steps; beach balls; indoor and outdoor climbing equipment; blocks (wood, cardboard, Duplos®); balance beam, crawl tunnel, scooter board, and Hula Hoops®; wooden boat; volleyball net, goals, bases, plastic balls, and bowling materials; rolling mats; child-sized brooms

Table 2.2

Examples of Prop Boxes

Post Office—envelopes, stamps, small mailboxes, toy zip code book, paper, pencils

Restaurant—picture menus, child-sized cooking utensils, silverware, plates, cups, cash registers, toy money

Seasons—winter: mittens, gloves, boots, heavy coats, stocking caps, earmuffs, toy sleds, snowman puzzles; summer: shorts, suntan lotion, sunglasses, swim fins, sandals, beach balls.

Grocery Store—sacks or bags, cash register, toy money, purses, assorted empty boxes, canned goods, shopping carts

Pet Store—various stuffed animals, toy money, cash registers, toy foods, and water bowls

Doctor's Office—toy medical kits with various medical instruments, cloth "bandages," telephone

Transportation—toy cars, trucks, airplanes, boats, motorcycles, bicycles, roads, signs, bridges

Shoes—moccasins, wooden shoes, slippers, boots, tennis shoes, and sandals.

Special Needs—sign language cards, crutches, glasses, or Braille cards

Camping—tents, sleeping bags, cooking utensils, flashlight, toy fishing poles and fish

Sensory Items—various items chosen for differences in touch, smell, sound, or taste. For example, sandpaper (scratchy, rough); cotton balls (soft, light); perfume; pinecone (prickly, rough); assorted spices (smell); cactus (sharp); flowers (texture and smell); silk, velvet, or fur (soft, smooth); horn or bells that make different sounds; shaving cream

Dressing—winter, spring, summer, and fall clothing and accessories; zippers, snaps, and lace boards; shoes to tie

Arts and Crafts—foil, crepe, construction paper, tissue, magazines, fabric scraps, fur, feathers, yarn, wood scraps, string, straws, pipe cleaners, buttons, beads, markers, Popsicle® sticks, glue, nontoxic paints, macaroni, tongue depressors, paper, tape

Nature—acorns, beans, leaves, shells, pinecones, fur, sand, small plastic flowerpots, artificial flowers, toy animals or insects

Hats—baseball caps, football or fire helmets, rain hats, men's and women's dress hats, stocking caps, clown hats, top hats, visors

General Considerations for the Selection of Toys

Toys are an integral part of Directed Play. Toys must be chosen and used carefully to ensure that children are safe and are progressing toward targeted objectives. A number of factors must be considered in selecting toys and playthings.

1. ***There should be an adequate number and variety of toys for each child.***

   Too few toys may lead to disagreements and negative behavior. Each child participating in an activity needs to have materials for play. If four children are playing in a firefighter theme each child must have a fire helmet and related materials. Consider also what skill a toy or plaything is teaching.

2. ***Classrooms should have a variety of toys that address each of the six developmental domains.***

   Early childhood educators would do well to examine the number and variety of toys in their classrooms to ensure that there are adequate toys across all developmental domains. It is possible, for example, that a classroom could have a large number of gross motor play materials but almost none that promote social skills. Depending on how they are used, some toys will cross more than one domain. Toys and playthings can also be categorized by which multiple intelligences they address (see Appendix A).

3. ***Novelty is important.***

   When children are presented with a new toy they need time to explore and manipulate it before higher-order forms of play can occur. Novelty in toys and playthings pique children's interest. Children naturally add novelty to their play by combining unrelated play materials. We should not discourage this. One way to promote novelty is to put some toys or playthings away for a while and then get them out again some weeks later.

4. ***The degree of realism.***

   Realistic toys are essential for children who have not yet reached consistent levels of symbolic or pretend play. As children become more skilled at pretend play, there is less need for realistic-looking toys. For example, cardboard boxes can be excellent playthings for children who engage in symbolic or pretend play. The box can become anything in the child's imagination. However, cardboard boxes are less suited for children who don't yet engage consistently in symbolic play.

5. ***Toys and playthings should be examined for structure and degree of participation.***

   This involves examining what the child does and what the toy does. Some playthings, such as a jack-in-the-box, are limited in what they do and thus limit a child's play. Other materials, such as sand or blocks, are open-ended and can be used in many ways. Consider the child's abilities and limitations. Make use of items such as beach balls, which are very light and are very responsive to even a slight kick or push.

Directed Play

6. *Are toys social or isolate?*

Social toys are those that produce more social interactions among children. Isolate toys produce more solitary play. Adults trying to increase socialization among children should provide social toys. If it is necessary for children to work quietly for a while then provide isolate play materials. This is also an important consideration in assessing children. If children are given isolate play materials, they will likely engage in solitary play. To examine social interactions among children it is necessary to give them social toys.

Social Toys: cars and trucks, dolls, blocks, balls, dress-up clothes	**Isolate Toys:** books, play-dough, crayons and paper, puzzles

7. *For some children, particularly those with visual or physical disabilities, toys can be adapted so that they can be used independently.*

Adaptations can involve the use of magnets, Velcro®, string, or dowel rods. For instance, magnets can be attached to a toy so that it will stick to a metal tray and attaching string to a crayon would make it easier to retrieve if dropped. In addition, it is important that toys be easy for children to reach and play with independently. Toys should be on low shelves with pictures showing where different toys are to be placed.

8. *Toys must be safe and clean.*

Use caution when selecting toys that may pose a choking hazard with very young children (e.g., marbles, "pop" beads). Toys and playthings should be examined frequently to be sure that there are no loose parts, sharp edges, etc. In addition, toys need to be cleaned frequently to reduce the occurrence of illnesses. Some cloth toys can go through a washing machine; some plastic toys can be washed in a dishwasher.

9. *Toys must be developmentally appropriate for children.*

The chronological and developmental age of the child needs to be considered when choosing a toy. Children who have not yet reached a level of consistent symbolic, or pretend, play will need realistic-looking toys. As children get older, the need for realistic toys diminishes. Commercially developed toys usually indicate an age range for the toy; use this as a guide.

10. *Readily accessible and inexpensive playthings.*

"Toys" are usually defined as miniature replicas of real things, but "playthings" is a much broader term. Many playthings are just as good as, if not better than, commercially available toys. For example, rocks and leaves can teach children about color, size, shape, and weight. Children can jump into a pile of leaves and throw rocks into water. Cardboard boxes can be excellent playthings for children. They are inexpensive and can be used in many different ways. Many activities in Directed Play make use of cardboard boxes. Other cardboard playthings can include empty toilet paper rolls turned into binoculars, paper towel rolls used as telescopes, or long wrapping paper rolls used as oars for a boat.

Many hours of play can be spent with cardboard boxes, empty plastic kitchen containers, and pots and pans. Empty plastic containers of different sizes and colors, such as butter tubs, can be used in a variety of activities. Such materials are inexpensive yet provide positive play experiences for children of any age. Such materials can be used for functional play, matching activities, and pretend play, and can cross the motor and language domains. Such materials are usually unstructured, so younger children, or children who prefer more highly structured materials, may have a difficult time initially with such materials.

Commercially Available Toys and Games

Commercially available toys and games can be very useful in guiding the play of children. These materials need to be chosen carefully to ensure that they are safe and developmentally appropriate. Commercially available toys can include fire stations, garages, assorted cars and trucks, assorted people and dolls that reflect cultural diversity, animals (farm and wild), airports, trains, Duplos®, Legos®, wooden blocks, bowling sets, castles (e.g., Little Tikes®), and board games such as Candy Land®.

Toy Adaptations

The nature and extent of a child's disability may make it difficult or impossible for them to use toys independently. In such cases, it will be necessary to adapt or modify toys. Musselwhite (1986), in her book on adaptive play and children with special needs, describes strategies to adapt toys for children with varied disabilities. These include stabilizing or enlarging playthings, reducing required responses, removing distracting stimuli, or adding and enhancing cues.

Efforts to enhance or modify toys do not need to be expensive or time-consuming. Velcro®, magnets, cardboard, C-clamps, string, or dowel rods can all be used to easily adapt play materials. Attaching magnets to a toy will help it stick to a metal tray, such as a cookie sheet. Attaching string to a toy will allow a child to retrieve it easily if it falls off a table or lap tray. Dowel rods can be placed as boundaries or attached to small, drilled holes in puzzle pieces to make them easier to pick up. A bell can enhance the auditory stimulation a toy makes when moved or shaken.

It is advisable to consider the specific nature of a child's disability when adapting toys. Children with visual impairments, for example, should have toys selected and adapted based on tactile qualities. For children with physical impairments, the positioning or stability of the toys is an important concern. For children with mental retardation, reducing the amount of distracting stimuli may be an important component. Throughout the Directed Play curriculum, suggestions are given for adaptations and modifications of the toys and how they can be used with children.

With any toy modification, be sure that the adaptation is safe. Younger children, for example, might be tempted to put small magnets in their mouths.

> ### Table 2.3

Suggestions for Toy Adaptations and Modifications

- Glue textures or Braille dots to keys on toys/computer

- Use a foam hair curler around a wand for grasp

- Adapt a standard puzzle by drilling small holes and putting in small dowel rods for grasping

- Put Lego® tables at wheelchair height

- Add Velcro® to standard wooden blocks to increase stability

- Make use of remote control toys attached to adaptive switches

- Put Velcro® around a crayon and have the child wear a mitten

- Put sand in a small sandbox that can be placed on a table

- Put a bell inside a tennis ball to increase stimulation

- Attach a board to the back of the seat on a tricycle to increase stability

- Have play materials on low shelves so that children can access them independently

- Put older computers on the floor for easy access by children

Sources of Assistance

Toy-Lending Libraries

Toy libraries are a service that provides parents and professionals with stimulating toys and an opportunity for shared play. In the beginning, toy libraries were established to provide specialized toys that were not readily available or expensive toys needed by children with special needs. Though the specific focus of toy libraries may differ from community to community and country to country, the primary emphasis has been on play as a means of development. Toy libraries help children and parents gain access to a wide variety of toys and playthings and can assist parents with professional advice about play. Toy-lending libraries are found worldwide.

In 1984, the USA Toy Library Association was founded with the goal of promoting the public value of play, creating toy libraries, and serving as a resource for parents and professionals. The USA Toy Library Association publishes a quarterly newsletter, *Child's Play*, and has also published a booklet on how to start up and manage a toy library, which includes sections on staffing, funding, insurance, and cataloging.

USA Toy Library Association
Wilmette, IL
(874) 920-9030
http://usatla.deltacollege.org/

Lekotek

Lekotek is a family resource center serving primarily children with special needs. First established in Sweden, Lekoteks now exist worldwide. Lekoteks have an extensive library of toys, adaptive equipment, and books. In the 1990s, Lekotek extended its services to include children who are born with the HIV virus or were exposed to drugs in utero, as well as teenage mothers and children at risk from environmental factors.

Lekotek attempts to meet the special needs of young children with disabilities and their families by providing adapted toys and family support. Lekoteks are staffed by trained professionals and may be associated with some type of diagnostic or habilitation center. Lektoek leaders are knowledgeable about commercial and educational toys and have experience in adapting toys for use by young children with disabilities. Lekotek staff can model play strategies for parents or teachers by making use of their large collection of unique and conventional toys.

National Lekotek Center
Evanston Civic Center
2100 Ridge Ave.
Evanston, IL 60201
800-366-PLAY
http://www.lekotek.org/

Other Web Sites

Several web sites are available that can help staff or parents select good, safe toys. These include the Consumer Product Safety Commission (www.cpsc.gov/), the National Safe Kids Campaign (www.safekids.org/), the Toy Industry Association (www.toy-tma.com/), and the National Association of State Public Interest Research Groups (www.toysafety.net/).

Play and Children With Disabilities

It is well accepted that young children with disabilities display differences and deficits in play behaviors compared to typically-developing children. What is not as well-known is how specific exceptionalities affect the play of these children. When working with children with various disabilities, it is important to know how a specific disability will affect a child's play.

This chapter has information on the effects of different disabilities on the play of young children. For each exceptionality, information is presented on its general characteristics and specific play behaviors and deficits. The play characteristics and intervention strategies presented in this section have been summarized from a large number of literature sources and our own professional experiences.

Common Deficits

An examination of the play behaviors of children with disabilities reveals two common themes. First, the delays these children experience in play are linked to delays in the various developmental domains (motor, language, social, and cognitive). Since play is dependent on socialization, movement, and communication, delays in these domains will affect how well children are able to play. Teaching skills within these developmental domains will improve the quality and quantity of a child's play.

A second common difficulty shared by children in these disability categories is a delay in the development of symbolic play. Symbolic play, or pretend or "make-believe" play, is dependent on cognitive, language, and social skill development. Because these children can be delayed in one or all of these developmental domains, they tend to develop symbolic play behaviors at a later age than typically-developing children. This delay in symbolic play makes it difficult for these children to interact with typically-developing children and requires intervention to help promote this important skill. Strategies for helping to improve symbolic play can include making use of structured and realistic play materials, teaching the child a sense of self, and role playing or modeling symbolic play for the child to imitate.

General Intervention Considerations

There are some general considerations to keep in mind for play interventions across the disability categories. First, focus on teaching skills within the developmental domains. Teaching children language, social, and motor skills will promote more age-appropriate play behaviors. Second, follow a sequence of teaching children a sense of self, followed by play with toys, play with adults, and finally play with peers. In order to play with peers successfully, children must first be given an understanding of who they are and have experience with various types of toys, as well as an opportunity to play with adults who can provide consistent and supportive play experiences. Third, be alert to the influence of environmental (ecological) variables that can influence or affect play. These variables include people, places, things, and time. Children with disabilities usually need structured play settings and realistic play materials.

Children With Mental Retardation

General Considerations

There are many causes of mental retardation (MR), including conditions such as Down's syndrome, Fragile X, and fetal alcohol syndrome and other prenatal substance exposure. Though children with specific forms of MR can have individual differences in development, they usually share certain characteristics. Children with mental retardation typically show deficits in language acquisition and use, sustained and selective attention, motivation, and adaptive behaviors (i.e., grooming, self-care, or social skills). The learning and behavior problems demonstrated by these children also depend on the severity of the mental retardation (mild, moderate, or severe). Most children with MR are classified as mildly retarded and can be very successful in inclusion programs. It is important to consider the developmental and not chronological age of the children when looking at their learning and behavior. Children with mild MR will exhibit play behaviors and characteristics that are comparable to typically-developing children of a younger age. As the degree of severity becomes more pronounced, the children with MR will show greater play deficits, and the need for specific intervention increases.

Be sure to provide age-appropriate toys for these children, based, again, on the child's developmental age rather than chronological age. Children with MR often tend to engage in solitary-functional play with toys, so assist them in using these toys in constructive or dramatic ways. Toys should be chosen that have a good cause and effect (for example, toy telephones that talk when their buttons are pushed). Mirrors can be a good way to help promote a sense of self. Adults should assume a play tutor role to directly teach the children how to play with different toys. Be sure the toys used are realistic.

Provide a lot of social interaction modeling for these children to imitate. They will need a lot of repetition to learn these skills. Limit group activities to two to three children at first. To promote group interaction, use simple, direct sentences, such as "Put the horse in the barn like Susie." Provide opportunities for these children to share, and reward them when they do share. Giving two children items that they need to combine may prompt this. For example, one child has a horse and another the water so they will need to combine these to give the horse a drink. Give them roles to play in sociodramatic play activities and assist them in knowing what to say and what to do. Let them stay in the same role for several days.

Table 3.1

Children With Mental Retardation

Common Play Characteristics or Deficits

- Engages in more solitary/functional play.
- Exploratory behaviors are more erratic.
- Engages in less group play and less dramatic play.
- Spends more time playing alone.
- Less variety in pretend play themes.
- Less able to integrate pretend play with social interactions.
- Will share toys less often.
- More likely to make disruptive initiations.
- Will not smile at others as often as typically-developing children.
- May not transition easily and will show signs of stubbornness.
- Will combine unrelated toys together less often.
- Less variety of toys used in play.
- More dependent on structured play materials.
- Tends to prefer more structured play areas.
- Will engage in stereotyped behaviors in the absence of play materials.

Intervention Strategies

- Gradually incorporate pretend play themes into social interactions with other children.
- Teach appropriate ways of initiating interactions with other children.
- Teach appropriate ways of responding to the initiations of other children.
- Model play with toys and peers for children to imitate.
- Reinforce appropriate play behaviors using tangible and nontangible rewards.
- Work to enhance language and communication through modeling and imitation.
- Provide more structured and realistic toys and gradually introduce nonrealistic toys as children develop symbolic play skills.
- Adapt toys to elicit more visual, auditory, or tactile stimuli (i.e., putting a bell inside a tennis ball).
- Provide developmentally appropriate toys and play materials. Consider the developmental age of the child instead of his or her chronological age.

---

27   Chapter 3

Children With Autism

General Considerations

General characteristics common to young children with autism include deficits in language acquisition and use, deficits in social and emotional development, and an insistence on routine or "sameness." The children may respond negatively to cuddling or touching, fail to make eye contact and connect with caregivers, display unusual repetitive body movements like rocking or flapping their hands, or fail to exhibit the creative play behavior of peers the same age. These deficits combined do much to explain why these young children can show the most pronounced play deficits of any exceptionality. Alternative forms of communication are often needed with children whose autism is more severe. These children need a consistent environment, routine, picture schedules, and frequent reinforcement.

Children with autism may need considerable instruction in how to play with toys and peers. Adults should assume a play tutor role, as well as a spokesperson for reality role (see Chapter 1). Provide single, direct instructions in how to play with toys. Demonstrate and have them model play with different toys. They may cling to a certain plaything, so use redirection and verbal and physical prompts to get them involved in something different. Use their ritualistic nature to your advantage by always letting them know what you're going to do and by establishing routines. Provide pictures of objects or settings to go along with the play. Teach them to look at other children with direct statements, such as "Look at Jimmy." Use dolls to promote a sense of self by having them bathe and dress the dolls and point to different body parts. Also put a lot of emphasis on emotions and facial expressions. The emotion activities in the Personal-Social section will help with this.

Be a spokesperson for reality by redirecting them away from self-stimulation. If they try to bring toys into a play area that don't "fit" the play, make direct statements, such as "Horses don't belong in the doctor's office." Use short, direct sentences with these children. State directives in positive terms rather then negative terms. Tell them what you want them to do, rather than what you don't want them to do.

Praise children with autism and provide tangible rewards for appropriate play. Tangible rewards might be poker chips. Give them poker chips for a specific behavior such as an appropriate social interaction or use of words. For every five poker chips they can have a bite of a favorite food.

It may be helpful to pair these children with slightly older peers who have well-developed language and social skills. Reward peers for initiating social interactions and for being persistent in seeking these children out for play.

Directed Play

Table 3.2

Children With Autism

Common Play Characteristics or Deficits

- Will display play deficits in both the use of toys and play with peers.

- May show some of the greatest deficits in play skills of all exceptionalities.

- Will engage in limited social interactions with peers.

- Will engage in less creative forms of play.

- Will engage in more repetition of manual manipulations with play materials or other objects.

- Will be less likely to attribute animate characteristics to dolls and other playthings.

- Engages in less symbolic play.

- May not understand that other people have thoughts and feelings or that other people have different beliefs and thoughts. This is referred to as Theory of Mind (Waterhouse & Fein, 1997).

Intervention Strategies

- Model the use of toys for children to imitate.

- Work to enhance a sense of self through the use of photographs, facial expression, and emotion pictures; role playing; identifying body parts; and play with dolls.

- Gradually introduce play with peers.

- Work to enhance communication through pictures or sign language and have children imitate words and phrases.

- Provide structured, realistic play materials.

- Reward appropriate play behaviors with tangible and nontangible rewards.

- Continue interventions for an extended period of time.

- Pictures of events of play; scripts of what to say during play.

- Provide a predictable schedule.

Children With Asperger Syndrome or Pervasive Developmental Disorders

General Considerations

Asperger syndrome is a developmental disability in which a child's language and cognitive skills are normal but they will show problems with motor development and delays in social and emotional development. Children with Asperger syndrome will have difficulty with social communication, and, even when language production seems normal, the appropriate use of language in social contexts and for social purposes is often "out of sync." They can be very rigid, obsess on a topic or interest, have restricted or repetitive patterns of behavior, and can have difficulty with changes in routine.

Pervasive developmental disorder (PDD) is a severe pervasive condition that begins in early childhood. It is characterized by abnormal social behaviors, including unusual mannerisms and delays in speech and language, and often includes stereotyped or preservative behaviors.

Children with Asperger syndrome and PDD need a lot of social dialogue. Help them to say certain things at certain times. For example, "Billy, look at your friend and say 'Can I play with you?'" During an activity such as doctor's office, show them pictures of a doctor's office for a visual reference. When you assign them roles in a dramatic play, let them stay in the same role for several days. Use direct, simple sentences when speaking to them.

Provide a lot of sensory stimulation as the child can tolerate it. Provide a variety of sensory items, such as sand, foam, and lotion. Reward their efforts to be involved in these activities.

Provide many realistic toys for them to play with. Give them pictures as a visual reference during play. For example, during a grocery store activity give them a picture list of items to help them know what to ask for. Reward their appropriate social initiations toward other children and help them with appropriate body contact with others.

Read through the information presented on symbolic play in the Personal-Social section. Activities such as "Who Am I?" and the emotion and facial expression activities will be good activities for this type of child.

Children With Attention Deficit and Attention Deficit Hyperactive Disorder

General Considerations

Attention deficit disorder (ADD) and attention deficit hyperactive disorder (ADHD) are two related, but distinct, disorders that are seen among young children. Inattention, impulsiveness, and hyperactivity can be common symptoms. Children will show symptoms of these conditions in school, home, and playground settings. However, the symptoms are not as pronounced when children are in structured settings with consistent adult attention.

These children will benefit from well-structured play areas and clearly defined rules. Novelty in toys will promote and sustain their attention, so vary the types of play materials available. These children can attend for extended periods of time when they are involved in something they are interested in.

Table 3.3

Children With Asperger Syndrome or PDD

Common Play Characteristics or Deficits

- Difficulty initiating peer interactions appropriately.
- Difficulty understanding body language and facial expressions.
- Difficulty with reciprocal interactions with other children.

Intervention Strategies

- Provide assistance with problem solving during peer interactions.
- Provide clear rules for play.
- Role playing to teach play routines and language.
- Set up opportunities to share with peers.
- Set up opportunities for noncompetitive games and movement.
- Set up opportunities for give and take in play activities.
- Provide a predictable schedule.

Table 3.4

Children With ADD/ADHD

Common Play Characteristics or Deficits

- Can be very talkative.
- Can display less-developed social skills.
- May have problems following rules.
- Can be impulsive and inattentive.
- May not stay "engaged" with toys for an extended period of time.

Intervention Strategies

- Use picture schedules.
- Prepare for transitions in advance.
- Have them repeat back directions.
- Reward appropriate play with toys and peers.
- Pictures of events in play.
- Scripts of what to say during play.
- Make use of novelty in toys and activities.

Chapter 3

Children With Developmental Delays or Learning Disabilities

General Considerations

It is sometimes difficult to identify young children with learning disabilities (LD) because LD is often considered to be a "school" disability. That is, this disorder is not usually identified until children begin elementary school. For example, definitions of learning disabilities include references to reading, writing, or math, which are not relevant to young children. However, young children who exhibit perceptual motor difficulties, high levels of impulsiveness, or distractibility may be showing signs of what later might be identified as LD. These children may also have difficulty with colors and shapes, number concepts, and learning left and right, but can also show play behaviors similar to that of typically-developing children.

Children with developmental delays (DD) are those who are delayed in development for their age but not so severely as to be identified as mentally retarded. These children may have "splinter skills," which means that they can do some things very well and struggle with other things.

Children with learning disabilities or developmental delays will benefit from an emphasis on language development. Help them to integrate language and toys into sociodramatic play themes. Help them to recognize social cues, such as facial expressions. Provide a lot of music and movement activities.

Children With Behavior and Emotional Disorders

General Considerations

It is also difficult to identify young children with behavior disorders (BD) or emotional disorders (ED) unless the behavior is very extreme. Children who are identified as BD or ED can fall into one of two broad classifications: (1) externalizers, children who

Table 3.5

Children With DD/LD

Common Play Characteristics or Deficits
- Perceptual motor difficulties; may seem uncoordinated or clumsy.
- Impulsive; can't wait for their turn.
- Difficulty with auditory memory.
- Problems learning left and right.

Intervention Strategies
- Have children repeat directions they have been given.
- Put an emphasis on language and early literacy.
- Make use of rhyming and music.

direct their behavior outward, or (2) internalizers, children who direct their behavior within themselves. Children who are externalizers usually are seen as aggressive or non-compliant, while children who are internalizers may display anxiety problems and be withdrawn. Aggressive, externalizer children are the easiest to identify because their problems "stand out." Children with anxiety disorders may be thought of as just shy and not receive the special services they need.

Abuse and neglect are sometimes also seen among these children and may be a primary cause of their emotional or behavior disorders. These children can come from homes that are dysfunctional or homes in which interpersonal relationships are inappropriate. We must constantly be alert to any signs of abuse and neglect and report any incidents to a supervisor immediately.

Children experiencing abuse or neglect need to be treated very carefully. Crittenden (1989) has written an excellent article on the problems these children can experience and how we should teach them. She notes, for example, that these children need a consistent, predictable environment. She also concludes that discipline and punishment must be used very carefully and that the specific methods will depend on the type and extent of a child's abuse or neglect.

Treatment for children with BD or ED may involve Play Therapy. This technique places an emphasis on child-initiated play. A play therapist takes a nondirective role in the play setting and waits for opportunities to talk to children about what they are doing or feeling. Adults carefully observe what children are doing and wait for opportunities to help children understand their behaviors and feelings.

Available materials should permit reality testing, encourage insight, and allow a child with BD to express needs symbolically. Play materials should be simple and durable, promote verbalizations, and be provided with a minimum of clutter. As a general rule, complex board games or constructive toys should be avoided. Suggested materials include: paper and crayons, small blocks, puppets, family dolls, cars, trucks, balls, and a doctor's kit. Baby bottles, dishes and child-sized cooking utensils, and even punching bags can also be made available. Such play materials represent familiar objects to the child and provide opportunities to express feelings such as aggression or dependence.

Interventions for children with BD/ED should focus on helping them establish and maintain appropriate social interactions with peers and adults. They will need help in learning social language cues, nonverbal communication, and appropriate body contact and touching.

To promote these things, you should provide many opportunities for cooperative interactions. For example, at snack time give each child items that all will need. One child can have five straws, another five crackers, and another five napkins. Each must share and cooperate with the others. When playing house or some other sociodramatic play activity, they should be prompted to go along with the ideas of other children and not try to control every aspect of the play.

These children have a need to be accepted and to belong. The "I Am Special" activity in the Personal-Social section can assist with this. It may also be necessary to help foster feelings of empathy. Doctor's office activities may be helpful in promoting this.

33 Chapter 3

Table 3.6

Children With BD/ED

Common Play Characteristics or Deficits

Externalizing Problems:

- Often aggressive and rejected by peers.

- May distort or misunderstand social cues.

- Behaviors may be influenced by context; children who are externalizers will display less on-task behavior and more aggression in free play than in structured setting and more negative interactions on a playground.

- May be less likely to pick up on metacommunication signals (nonverbal communication, such as facial expressions).

- Less likely to differentiate rough and tumble play from aggression.

- Rejected children will display more aggressive behaviors, will try to exert control during interactions, and will be more disagreeable than typically-developing peers.

Internalizing Problems:

- Children experiencing neglect may be passive and less talkative, but have fewer incidents of antisocial behavior.

- May be ignored by other children more often.

- More likely to initiate sharing through requests than through offers.

- Opposing the play of others may be more common than aggression or taking without asking.

Intervention Strategies

- Provide structured play environments rather than unstructured ones.

- Establish three or four rules and consistently enforce them.

- Redirect children as needed when they first start to display inappropriate behaviors.

- Reward appropriate play with toys or peers.

- Make use of Play Therapy techniques that involve watching children as they play with puppets, toy telephones, or drawing materials. Use their play to promote communication and discussion of feelings and emotions.

- Reduce violent or aggressive theme play by the use of prompts or contingent time out.

- Teach and reward appropriate social skills such as sharing, turn-taking, and smiling.

- Identify important metacommunication signals, such as facial expressions, tone or volume of speech, and shape/movement of the hands.

- Use prompts and praise to elicit appropriate targeted behaviors.

- Avoid punishments if possible.

- Group children with younger playmates.

- Extend interventions into the home as much as possible.

- Provide a predictable schedule.

Children With Language or Hearing Impairments

General Considerations

Language disorders are one of the most common reasons why young children receive special services. There is a wide range of language and/or speech disorders, including articulation and fluency disorders. These children will show delays in the acquisition and use of speech and language.

Hearing impairments are also included in this category because the types of difficulties experienced by these children are similar to those with speech/language problems. One of the biggest barriers faced by children with hearing impairments is communicating with other children and adults. Teaching children sign language is an important method of communication, and even children as young as 18 months can learn some simple signs. Efforts should be made to teach sign language to all children.

Due to their language difficulties, these children may spend more time playing alone. Set up interventions to promote social initiations and teach appropriate responses to other children. Use direct, simple sentences to help them know what to say. Encourage other children to seek these children out as playmates. Reward other children for their persistence.

For children with hearing impairments select toys with good visual and tactile qualities. Help them to incorporate language and toys into sociodramatic play themes.

Table 3.7

Children With Language or Hearing Disorders

Common Play Characteristics or Deficits

- Will display the same developmental sequence in play development during the sensorimotor period (birth to two years of age) as typically-developing children.

- May approach other children less often.

- Many spend more time playing alone.

- Will find it difficult to engage in cooperative play with other children because of speech/language barriers.

- Language disorders linked to deficits in symbolic play.

Intervention Strategies

- Provide specific speech/language therapy as needed.

- Teach words and concepts related to play themes.

- Model appropriate language for children to imitate. Be a good language model.

- Teach appropriate ways to initiate and respond to others.

- Teach sign language to everyone.

Children With Physical or Health Impairments

General Considerations

There are a wide variety of physical and health impairments that can affect children. Physical disabilities can include cerebral palsy (CP), spina bifida, or muscular dystrophy. These conditions affect a child's ability to control voluntary motor movements. The physical limitations imposed by these conditions often require children to use leg braces, wheelchairs, or walkers. Proper holding and positioning is very important for these children. Consult physical or occupational therapists if you have questions. Don't make a child with a physical impairment stay in the same position for an extended period of time.

Moving around is difficult and challenging for children with physical impairments. Intelligence is not affected by these conditions, though children will have had fewer opportunities to "act" on things in their environment. Augmentative communication systems may be needed for children who have trouble speaking. Children should be encouraged to be independent in all activities.

This category of exceptionality can also include severe health problems, such as juvenile rheumatoid arthritis, cystic fibrosis, diabetes, or epilepsy. These conditions may make it difficult for a child to perform certain tasks and may cause them to tire easily. They may also be on medications that can affect their behavior or alertness.

Children with physical disabilities can be assisted in playing independently by adapting toys to suit their impairment. Efforts to enhance or modify toys do not need to be expensive or time-consuming. Make use of Velcro®, magnets, cardboard, C-clamps, string, or dowel rods. Magnets attached to play materials will help them stick to a metal tray, such as a cookie sheet. Attaching string to a play material allows a child to retrieve it easily if it falls off a table or lap tray. Dowel rods can be placed as boundaries or attached to small, drilled holes in puzzle pieces so that they can be picked up easily. A bell can be attached to a play material to enhance the auditory stimulation the toy might provide when moved or shaken. State technology support projects (see Appendix B) or Lekoteks (see Chapter 2) can provide information on different types of adaptive computer equipment or ways in which children can use battery-powered toys.

Children With Visual Impairments

General Considerations

Children with visual impairments are those whose visual difficulties are so severe that special materials or supports are needed. Children in this classification can be blind or have visual limitations with some remaining sight. Intelligence is not affected by severe visual impairments, though these children will have had fewer exploratory experiences than typically-developing children.

Directed Play

Table 3.8

Children With Physical or Health Impairments

Common Play Characteristics or Deficits

- Deficits in play are due to a reduced ability to move about the environment.
- Can show social interaction skills beyond those of other disabilities.
- Can tire easily.
- Speech may be affected because of problems with voluntary motor movements.

Intervention Strategies

- Occupational Therapists and Physical Therapists can promote proper movement and positioning and encourage appropriate use of play materials.
- Sensory integration, perceptual motor skills, and movement patterns all need to be addressed.
- Must be provided with opportunities to engage in typical play with outdoor equipment, such as swings, slides, and merry-go-rounds.
- Make use of Velcro®, magnets, tape, string, or dowel rods to provide support or stability to toys and playthings.
- Make use of new technologies such as communication boards or single switches for use with computers or tape recorders.
- Encourage and reward social interactions by and with other children.
- Children need to be repositioned frequently. Make use of standing tables, prone boards, and adapted chairs. Make sure their feet are supported when sitting in a chair.

Children with visual impairments need help in learning about the world around them. Provide them with realistic toys and objects that have good tactile and auditory qualities. The "Nuts and Bolts," "Lock It Up," and "Miniature House" activities are well suited for these children. Be prepared to describe everything around them and talk to them frequently about how things sound or feel. Put an emphasis on developing their sense of self, as this is an important prerequisite for the development of pretend play.

Encourage play with other children by first having them play with only one other child. Then gradually increase the number of children in the group. Be aware of the effects of large groups on children with visual impairments. The unpredictable movements of other children can be disturbing.

Table 3.9

Children With Visual Impairments

Common Play Characteristics or Deficits

- May spend more time playing alone.
- May spend more time interacting with adults.
- Will engage in less functional toy use.
- Will ask more and different kinds of questions.
- Deficits in symbolic play are linked to delays in knowledge of sense of self and delays in the use of personal pronouns.
- Can be easily intimidated or distracted by the unpredictable movements of peers.

Intervention Strategies

- Must be provided with opportunities to engage in typical play with outdoor equipment, such as swings and slides. Provide as much support and guidance as necessary.
- Increase knowledge of sense of self through the use of personal pronouns, identification of body parts, and play with dolls.
- Select toys for tactile and texture qualities.
- Make use of real-world objects in play. Note how things connect, operate, or are related to other things.
- Discourage "blindisms" (i.e., rocking, stereotypical behaviors).
- Talk to the children frequently about objects, sounds, and textures. Be prepared for a lot of questions.
- Modify the environment in terms of light, distance, and contrast (white on black).
- Make use of new technologies such as talking computer programs.

Directed Play   38

Observation and Assessment of Play

Observing young children at play is an important way to understand their development (Fewell & Glick, 1993). It can be easy and inexpensive, yet it allows educators to gain information about children that would be difficult to assess in more traditional ways.

Work in the area of play observation has focused on two approaches: *play assessment* and *play-based assessment*. The distinction between play assessment and play-based assessment is an important one. In play assessment, specific play skills, such as solitary, functional, or cooperative play are identified. Play-based assessment, on the other hand, focuses on developmental domains, such as social skills or language. It uses play observation as a way to gain information about a child's development.

This chapter will focus on the observation and assessment of play. A rationale for play assessment will be presented, along with a foundation and history of these efforts. Information will also be given on how to conduct play observations, and several play assessment instruments will be discussed. We have also included a simple data collection form that can be used for many of the Directed Play activities.

Rationale for Play Observation and Assessment

There are two reasons why play observation and assessment should be used. First, observing children in play provides a natural context for assessing different developmental domains. When children play they use language, social, and motor skills in "natural" ways. Assessing how children talk and interact in play may be preferable to more structured and artificial assessment settings. Second, observing children in play takes advantage of arena assessment procedures, in which several professionals observe and assess children at once. In arena assessment, one staff member can engage a child in play while others observe and assess different areas of development. Arena assessment can save time and provides opportunities for staff discussion of a child's behavior as it occurs.

A Foundation for Social and Cognitive Play Observations

Three significant works have contributed to and helped to define current play assessment instruments. As shown in **Table 4.1**, Parten, Piaget, and Smilansky each developed a system to assess the social and/or cognitive play of children. Parten categories

Table 4.1

A Foundation for Play Observations: Types of Play Observed

Parten (1932):

Unoccupied, Onlooker, Solitary, Parallel, Associative, and Cooperative.

Piaget (1962):

Practice play, Symbolic play, Games with Rules.

Smilansky (1968):

Functional play, Constructive play, Dramatic play, and Games with Rules.

focus more on social types of play, whereas Piaget and Smilansky focused more on cognitive levels of play. Many of the play assessment instruments developed over the years have been based on the types of play identified by these authors.

Some researchers have developed play scales that combine the social categories of Parten (1932) with the cognitive categories of Smilanksy (1968). When the Parten and Smilansky categories are combined, for example, the result is a grid of 12 specific play behaviors. Each of the four Smilansky cognitive play categories (functional, constructive, dramatic, and games with rules) is combined with solitary, parallel, and group play. Hence, categories such as solitary-functional, parallel-constructive, or group-dramatic are created. For example, a child who is playing alone using building blocks would be demonstrating solitary-constructive play. A child who is one of three children playing "doctor" in a dramatic play area would be displaying group-dramatic play. The combination of these two broad categories of play has also assisted researchers in better understanding the importance of solitary play (Johnson, Christie & Yawkey, 1987).

Setting Up the Environment for Observing and Assessing Play

Many environmental variables need to be considered when observing children's play. As described in Chapter One, these variables include setting, peers, toys, and time.

Setting

The space and structure of the play setting should be examined for its influence. For example, there are indications that a limited play space with many children may result in more negative or aggressive types of behaviors among children (Smith & Connolly, 1980). Smith and Connolly suggest that 25 square feet per child is an appropriately sized play space. Conversely, a large play area, such as an outdoor playground, will likely result in a higher frequency of gross motor and rough-and-tumble play, like running and chasing.

Peers

A second factor to be considered when observing play involves the quantity and type of children available. The number of other children, how familiar they are with one another, gender, age, and developmental level of peers can all influence social interactions. Having other children available as potential playmates is important. It would be impossible to assess a child's level of social interactions if no other children were present to play with.

Toys

Toys are a third variable that must be considered when observing play. Some toys are more social in nature and produce a greater frequency of social interactions among children (Beckman & Kohl, 1984; Rettig, Kallam, & McCarthy, 1993). Social types of toys can include cars and trucks, dolls, balls, and dress-up clothes. Isolate toys are generally thought of as toys that children play with individually, such as crayons, play-dough, and puzzles. Wolery and Bailey (1989) suggest that if the purpose of an observation is to assess a child's social interactions, social toys must be provided.

Certain toys lead to certain types of play. Blocks and paints will produce more constructive play, and dress-up clothes or kitchen items will produce more dramatic play. In addition, the number of toys available may also influence interactions. Rubin and Howe (1985) suggest that fewer toys result in more social interactions. Conversely, more toys contribute to a larger occurrence of isolate play.

Time

Another guideline for observing play includes the need for repeated observations of a child's play behavior (Wolery & Bailey, 1989). This means that children must be observed over a period of days to accurately determine their play skills. A "one time" observation of a child at play will not be representative of the child's overall play behavior. Plan on conducting at least five to six observations over several days during free play.

Conducting Observations

It takes both training and experience for a person to be able to observe and record the play behaviors of children objectively and accurately. A knowledge of normal growth and development, types of play, and familiarity with the children observed are all important. Following certain guidelines will help to ensure that play observations yield important information.

Establish the Purpose for the Play Observations

The purpose for conducting the play observations should be clear to all involved in conducting the observations. Play observations can be conducted to look at specific skills, such as a child's involvement with toys, or to look at a child's developmental domains, such as language or social skills. A checklist of behaviors to be observed can be created to make the observations easy to record.

Conduct Enough Observations

Observers should plan on conducting play observations over at least six or seven sessions to be sure that they are getting a true indication of the child's behavior. Doll and Elliott (1994) suggest that at least five 10-minute observations conducted over several weeks are necessary to adequately assess a child's social behavior. They found that three-quarters of the behaviors observed could be predicted reliably with five observations. In addition, it may be necessary to observe children in both indoor and outdoor settings to get a better indication of their sociodramatic play skills (Johnson, Christie & Yawkey, 1987).

Observers Should Not Be Obvious

It is important that observers not inadvertently influence play by their presence in a play area. Observers need to position themselves close enough to the target child to hear and see the child's behaviors but not so close that it interferes with the observation. There can be problems observing children if they are familiar with the adult; the target child may try to interact with the observer during the observation. Observers generally should redirect the child back to the play area with only minimal interaction.

Data Collection Should Be Easy ~form

Data on children's play can be collected in a variety of ways. The more complex the observation system the more information can be collected. However, complexity can make it difficult to obtain reliable data. Less complex observations systems are easier to use but may generate less information. Compromise between the complexity of the observation system and the ease with which data can be collected is needed.

When conducting observations using time-sample or interval-sample techniques, a method that works very well is to use a clipboard with a data sheet and stopwatch attached. The stopwatch should be positioned at the top center of the clipboard where it is easily seen. It should be an analog, not digital, stopwatch, so that the observer can easily see the seconds pass. Using this method, it is easy for the observer to watch a child and keep an eye on the stopwatch for the time intervals.

Other techniques involve the use of auditory prompts via a tape recorder or other device. Using this technique, a tone is heard that provides a signal for the observer to either observe or record a child's behavior.

Definitions Should Be Established for Observed Behaviors

Before observations are conducted, each observer should have training in what behaviors are being observed. It is necessary that definitions for each type of play be established and that each observer know these definitions. For example, what is solitary play and how is this different from parallel play? Or, what behaviors make up social play and how is this different from isolate play?

Directed Play

Table 4.2 shows the definitions of behaviors on an observation form used to assess play with toys and social interactions (Rettig, 1995). Such definitions are necessary to ensure that every observer is looking for the same type of behavior.

This observation form (**Figure 4.1**) was developed for a project conducted by the authors that examined the effects of different quantities of toys on the social interactions of young children. Children were observed for five minutes, with observers alternating observing and recording every 10 seconds.

Even when definitions are established, the nature of play among children is not always clear-cut. Children will frequently display a behavior that is not defined and that can leave observers confused over what to record. In such occurrences it is helpful for observers to make note of these behaviors. Later, all observers can discuss them and reach a consensus on how a behavior will be recorded in the future.

Data Collected Should Be Accurate and Reliable - *Compare observations*

One of the first lessons individuals learn when they begin play observations is that two or more people do not always see behaviors in the same way. It is therefore important that observers practice and make use of interobserver agreements. Interobserver agree-

---

Table 4.2

Definitions for Categories of Play Behaviors

Solitary Play
Child is playing with a toy and not engaged with another child. This also includes parallel play, with no social interaction.

Onlooker/No Play
Child is watching another child or is not involved in any type of play.

Initiation but No Response
Child tries to initiate an interaction with another child, but the second child does not respond.

Positive Interactions With Toys
Child engages in positive interactions (smiling, talking, laughing, sharing, etc.) while involved with the play materials.

Negative Interactions With Toys
Child engages in negative interactions (hitting, yelling, pushing, etc.) while involved with the play materials.

Positive Interactions With No Toys
Child engages in positive interactions with another child that do not involve toys or playthings.

Negative Interactions With No Toys
Child engages in negative interactions with another child that do not involve toys or playthings.

Teacher Interactions
Child interacts with the adult observer; action initiated by either the child or adult.

ments are usually obtained by having two or more observers simultaneously but independently observe and record a child's behavior. After the observations are conducted, observers compare their findings. Interobserver reliability is often computed by taking the number of agreements divided by the number of disagreements and multiplying by 100. In the beginning of an observation, interobserver agreements will often be only 30 to 40 percent. But over time and with practice this number will increase. In order to collect reliable data, interobserver agreements should be 90 percent or greater and should be calculated often over the course of data collection.

An example of how observers can see behaviors differently occurred one summer among three graduate students observing a child play on a playground. The students were using an observation system that included Parten's (1932) categories of no play, solitary, parallel, onlooker, and cooperative play. Each of the three observers was watching a young child with a hearing impairment. During one of the 15-second observation intervals, the child was sitting on a tricycle watching a man mow the grass outside of the playground. Although definitions for each category of play had been developed and reviewed, each of the three observers recorded the child's behavior differently. One observer recorded it as solitary play because the child was sitting on the tricycle. A second observer recorded it as onlooker play because the child was watching the man mow the grass, and the third observer recorded the behavior as no play because the child wasn't doing anything. In this particular example none of the three observers was wrong—they just interpreted the child's behavior differently.

Make Use of Videotape Recordings

Video cameras are an excellent tool for play observations. Although the presence of a video camera may initially disrupt a play setting, over a period of time, children will not notice the camera or alter their behaviors because of it. The cameras should not be placed in a highly visible location. A corner of the classroom may be a good location, as it can keep the video camera out of traffic areas.

Videotape recordings of children's play can have several advantages. First, these recordings are an excellent way to assist in training observers and can help even experienced observers improve their observation skills. Observers can replay a videotape recording several times and look for different behaviors or variables that are influencing play. When firsthand observations are being conducted, and the attention of the observer is focused on a target child, it is generally difficult to observe other behaviors or activities in the classroom or play setting. What were other children doing? What were adults doing? How was language used? Who interacted with whom? Videotape recordings have the advantage of allowing observers to watch repeatedly a particular play setting and may provide important information that was not observed firsthand. Videotape recordings also serve as a good pretest-posttest measure of a child's play behaviors. Videotape recordings of play behaviors at the beginning of the year and at the end of the year can provide evidence of child progress.

Directed *Play*

Investigate the Use of New Technologies

New technology that can greatly assist in the collection of data in play observations is becoming increasingly available to educators. This new technology basically involves the use of handheld or other portable computers to assist in the collection and analysis of observational data (Repp, Karsh, Acker, Felce & Harman, 1989; Saudargas & Bunn, 1989). The Ecobehavioral Assessment Systems Software (EBASS) is an example of a software program that has been developed for standard classroom observations (Greenwood, Carta, Kamps, Terry, & Delquadri, 1994), and portable computers are available in notebook size, subnotebook size, and even palm size. Such portable computers could easily be used by an observer instead of the more traditional paper-pencil method. Software that makes statistical calculation and even graphing easy greatly assists in the collection and interpretation of the play observation data.

Example Observation Forms

Rather than relying on research-based play assessments it can be beneficial to develop your own play observation forms. These observation forms would have the advantage of being directly focused on your setting and could be adapted for individual children as needed.

We include here two examples of play observation forms that can be used or adapted for different settings and purposes. These forms were created using a spreadsheet program. The first is a simple example of a play observation form, and the second is a more sophisticated extension to the first form.

Both of these forms use a time sampling method of observation. A child is observed for a five-minute continuous time period, divided into 10-second intervals. An observer or observers will watch a child for 10 seconds, then use the next 10 seconds to record what was observed. For each minute, 30 seconds of data will be recorded.

Play Observation Form

The play observation form (**Figure 4.2**) includes categories for play area and types of play. This would be a good form to use for individuals learning to conduct play observations. The specific play areas found in your setting could easily be adapted or added to this form.

It is important that the setting and time period be recorded at the top of the form. This will help identify specific environmental factors that can assist in the analysis of the observation data. It is also important that several observations of the same child in the same setting and time period be made to identify trends or patterns in his or her play behavior. Depending on the child, it may be necessary to conduct at least five play observations over several days to get a good pattern. Once interventions are implemented, these forms can also be used to measure the impact of the intervention. Pre-intervention and post-intervention play observation forms should be saved for comparison.

The play area category should include a listing of all the play areas available to the child during the specified time period. An observer would watch a child for 10 seconds and then in the next 10-second interval record with an "X" which area the child was playing in. This is determined by noting the greatest amount of time a child was in an area. For example, if a child was in a block area for six seconds and then moved to the dramatic play area, the block area would be recorded, because it comprised the majority of the 10-second interval. The play area category can provide important information on a child's level of engagement or time on-task.

The type of play category is consistent with Parten's social play categories and includes columns for five types of play, as well as columns to mark if a child was involved with a teacher or if a child was in time out. Again, the column marked will be the one in which the child was involved for most of the 10-second interval. The type of play categories can provide good information on what a child is doing within a play area.

Figure 4.3 shows a completed five-minute play observation for Devon. Devon spent time in two play areas, dramatic play and books and music. He spent eight intervals, or 53 percent of his time, in dramatic play and 47 percent of his time in books/music. This suggests that Devon was engaged and on-task in each play area. Under the type of play categories he had 11 intervals of solitary play and four intervals of parallel play. Solitary play accounted for 73 percent of his play behaviors across the play areas. This suggests the need for intervention to get Devon more involved with peers.

Figure 4.4 shows a completed five-minute play observation for Kendall that is much different from Devon's. Kendall's play observation shows that she had little engagement in a specific play area and frequent occurrences of solitary and parallel play. It shows one interval of an interaction with a teacher and one interval in which she was in time out. If additional observation forms revealed a similar pattern, this would suggest that Kendall is in need of intervention to engage in more play within one play area and to engage in more cooperative play with her peers.

Another example of a play observation form developed for classroom use is shown in **Figures 4.5**, **4.6**, and **4.7**. This observation form can be used to gain information on the play and social interactions of both typically-developing children and children with disabilities. The form can easily be adapted for playground observations as well by substituting playground play areas for classroom play areas. In either case it is important that the specific play space is well defined so that there will not be confusion as to when a child is in one area or another. This form is an adaptation of a form developed by Dr. Nancy Peterson at the University of Kansas and used in research studies through the Early Childhood Research Institute (Peterson & Rettig, 1982).

The form has categories for the date, child's name, the setting in which the observations were performed, the name of one or two observers, and the count of all children and adults in the play area at the beginning and end of the play observation. Categories for more than one observer are important to determine interobserver reliability scores (see discussion on accurate data collection). The count of children and adults in the play area is important to determine who was available as a playmate. For example, when this form was used once it was found that at the beginning of the play period there were several typically-developing children available as playmates. However, by the end of the observation intervals many of these children were no longer in the play area.

The observation form is divided into three main categories: Play Area, Area Count, and Behaviors observed. The Play Area segment should contain a list of all the play areas available for children and provide information on a child's level of engagement, as well as play area preferences. In the example, the play areas include housekeeping, sand and water table, blocks, books, manipulatives, art, computer, and a miscellaneous category. The miscellaneous category is used if a child was not in one of the identified play areas, if, for instance, he or she was in transition, in time out, or in the bathroom. It is important to note that each of these play areas was well defined and distinct. For the blocks area, masking tape was placed on the floor so that staff could easily determine if a child is in or out of that area.

The Area Count category provides information on who was available to play within a distinct time period. The number of typically-developing children, the number of children with disabilities, and the number of adults present should each be recorded. This category does not focus on who a child was playing with, simply who was available to play during that time interval. This information would be useful in helping to determine how children group themselves.

The Behaviors category includes columns for play behaviors, adult interaction, and the initiation or response to social interactions. The play behavior categories include "unoccupied," which in this form includes "no play" and "onlooker play." The solitary play category includes "solitary" and "parallel play," as both do not involve social interactions with other children. The cooperative play category is used to indicate if children are interacting with other children in play.

The completion of this form requires an uninterrupted six-minute time period. This six-minute period is divided into 10-second intervals. An observer would observe for 10 seconds and record for 10 seconds and then repeat this procedure for the entire six minutes. For each one-minute time period, 30 seconds of data is obtained.

On each line of the data sheet an observer would put an 'X' under one of the play areas, record the number of other children and adults in the play area during that 10-second interval, put an 'X' under the appropriate play column, and note any adult interaction and any initiation or response to peers.

Figures 4.6 and **4.7** show completed data sheets. **Figure 4.6** shows data collected for Megan during a classroom observation that included two observers. The count of children and adults available during the beginning and end of the six-minute period is noted. It can be seen that for the first three minutes, Megan was engaged in the block area in solitary/parallel play. Although there was a typically-developing child and one to two children with disabilities in the play area, Megan did not interact with them. During the fourth minute Megan was not in a defined play area and was not engaged in play but was involved with an adult. A note could be made on the form to describe what happened during this interval. For the remainder of the time period Megan was involved in the manipulatives play area. Other children were also in this play area, but in only one instance did she initiate a social interaction. This data sheet shows that Megan did engage in two different play areas. Her play was primarily solitary/parallel and did not involve other children. If repeated observations revealed this same pattern, an intervention to help Megan increase her social interactions would be appropriate.

Figure 4.7 shows a completed play observation for Ryan. This observation was completed by two observers, who should compare their results to determine interobserver reliability. It is readily apparent that there was more variety in the play behaviors of Ryan than there was with Megan. An examination of the play area category shows that Ryan played in three different play areas during the six-minute observation. He also had one interval in the miscellaneous category that involved an adult interaction. Ryan's involvement in several play areas indicates that he did not have significant time on-task in any play area.

In most instances, other children were available as playmates and in six different intervals Ryan did engage in cooperative play with other children. There were also four intervals of positive social initiations or response. What is not indicated on this sheet is who specifically Ryan played with. This is important information that could provide an indication of play with a typically developing child or a child with a disability. A simple notation of who Ryan was playing with, such as their initials, could be added during the recording interval.

Data Collection Form

The data collection forms shown in **Figures 4.8** and **4.9** provide an easy way to keep track of child performance. **Figure 4.8** has room for up to 20 days worth of data, while **Figure 4.9** has room for up to 10 days. These forms, also referred to as 0–5 data collection forms, can be used for a wide variety of target objectives and activities. They can be used to record information on one child learning up to four different skills or used to record information on four different children within a group activity. The forms are easy to use and are self-graphing, and percentages are easily generated. Four out of five correct responses is 80 percent, three out of five is 60 percent, and two out of five is 40 percent.

To use these forms, list the target objective(s) on the left-hand side of the form. Room is provided for up to four objectives and relevant comments. The date is recorded in the space above the numbers. For each day record the number of correct and incorrect responses children make. Record correct responses with an "O" and incorrect responses with an "X," or use a notation system that works best for you. After all five opportunities, you can mark a square around the number of correct responses for that day. The "0" within the vertical numbers is only used to indicate no correct responses that day. Later, the squares can be linked together to provide an easy visual display of progress.

The forms ensure that each child is presented with at least five opportunities to perform a skill each day. The data on child performance can be collected in one sitting or recorded from opportunities throughout the day. Although you may present more than five opportunities for a child to respond each day, only record the first five on this form. This form can also be modified for 10 response opportunities instead of just five. This might be appropriate for children with disabilities who need much more practice at individual skills.

Figures 4.10, **4.11**, and **4.12** are examples of how this type of form can be used to keep track of child performance in Directed Play activities. **Figure 4.10** shows the data collection form being used for one child, Katie, who is working on verbally identifying four colors. The form allows staff to easily determine when a certain color has been mastered and which ones need more work and shows that Katie mastered verbal identification of red after 12 sessions, blue after 16 sessions, and green after nine sessions. She also identified yellow after 20 sessions, and her work on this color demonstrates some of the "bounce" in performance that can sometimes be seen in children's progress.

Figure 4.11 shows the form being used in a small group activity involving four different children. Two of the children are working on following one-step commands, one child is working on following two-step commands, and one child is working on following three-step commands. The data sheet reveals that Mallory can successfully and consistently follow a one-step direction after eight sessions and is ready for a different objective. The data for Kara shows that after 10 sessions she is not making progress in following two-step commands. Her objective needs to be revised. The data for Desmond shows that after 18 sessions he has followed a one-step command with 80 percent accuracy for three consecutive days and achieved 80 percent or better in eight out of nine of the previous sessions. This indicates that he is ready to move on to a different target objective. The data for Kasey indicates that she has made steady progress toward meeting her target objective of following three-step commands.

In **Figure 4.12** the 0–5 data sheet is being used for two children, each working on two different objectives. The first child, Kate, is working on target objectives of identifying two objects and saying the letter "A" when shown. She has mastered the "how many" objective after nine sessions and completed the identification of the letter "A" after 13 sessions. Kara's objectives are to count to five and to say the letters of the alphabet in rote fashion. The data reveal that Kara is having difficulty counting to five without prompts. After 20 sessions she is still only completing this task correctly 50 to 60 percent of the time. However, she is showing some improvement that justifies continuing this activity. In reciting the letters of the alphabet Kara demonstrates a similar pattern. There is slow progress in this task, and it would be useful to have a data sheet that included all the letters of the alphabet. This would provide more information on which letters Kara was missing consistently.

Observation Instruments for Specific Exceptionalities or Specific Types of Play

A number of play observation instruments have been developed for children who have specific exceptionalities. Four are discussed below.

Schneekloth (1989) describes a Play Object Complexity Scale (POCS) that could be used to evaluate a play environment. This rating scale was designed to assess the complexity of equipment in a play area. A series of 13 items is divided into three main categories: physical properties, space organizers, and moveable parts. Colors, surfaces, edges, and access points are some of the specific items assessed. According to Schneekloth, the more complex the equipment the more complex the observed play behaviors. The POCS provides a way to assess the play environment and to determine the complexity of the play equipment.

An instrument to assess playfulness with young children identified as gifted was used by Barnett and Fiscella (1985). The 33 items in the scale were divided into five behavior categories: physical spontaneity, manifest joy, sense of humor, social spontaneity, and cognitive spontaneity. Using a five-point Likert scale, teachers responded to each item for children whom they were familiar with. Though not an observation system, this scale does yield information on the quality and quantity of children's play.

Foreman (1982) described a notation system used in a study to examine the block play of young children. The coding system consisted of 38 shorthand symbols, such as up, down, stack, bridge, or row, that could be combined to record a complete series of actions. Such a notation system is useful for teachers trying to assess the block play of young children with disabilities.

The Mayes Hyperactivity Observation System (MHOS) (Mayes, 1991) was designed to evaluate hyperactivity in standardized free play conditions. The MHOS involves observing a child for a 10-minute interval with a set of seven commercially available, standardized toys. Locomotion, adaptive play, sensory inspection, and nonadaptive play are some of the categories of behavior that can be recorded. This observation instrument can yield information on attention deficit, impulsivity, and inappropriate play.

Observing children at play can provide important information on their language and social skills, as well as their progress in obtaining developmental milestones. It is important for observers to set up the environment carefully to ensure that observations are accurate and reliable. The physical setting, the number and types of toys available, and the number of peers available can all influence play observations. Several observation forms are provided in this chapter to guide play observations and to aid in collecting data on child performance.

Sample Observation Form

Name: _____ Condition: _____ Observer: _____ Date: _____

	Solitary	Onlooker No Interaction	Initiation No Response	Positive Interact With No Toys	Negative Interact With No Toys	Positive Interact With Toys	Negative Interact With Toys	Teacher Interaction
1								
2								
3								
4								
5								

© 2003 by Sopris West Educational Services. Permission is granted to the purchaser to photocopy this page. Sopris West (800) 547-6747 - product 161DP

Play Observation Form

Target Child: _____ Date: _____

Observer: _____ Setting/Time: _____

	PLAY AREA								TYPES OF PLAY						
	Manipulatives	Dramatic Play	Books/Music	Computer	Art	Blocks	Miscellaneous	No Play	Onlooker	Solitary	Parallel	Cooperative	Teacher	Time Out
1														
2														
3														
4														
5														

© 2003 by Sopris West Educational Services. Permission is granted to the purchaser to photocopy this page. Sopris West (800) 547-6747 - product 161DP

Play Observation Form

Target Child: __Devon__   Date: __11-1-01__

Observer: __MR__   Setting/Time: __Free Play 9:00 a.m.__

	\#\#PLAY AREA\#\#							\#\#TYPES OF PLAY\#\#						
	Manipulatives	Dramatic Play	Books/Music	Computer	Art	Blocks	Miscellaneous	No Play	Onlooker	Solitary	Parallel	Cooperative	Teacher	Time Out
1		X									X			
		X									X			
		X								X				
2		X								X				
		X								X				
		X								X				
3		X									X			
		X									X			
			X							X				
4			X							X				
			X							X				
			X							X				
5			X							X				
			X							X				
			X							X				

53% dramatic play area

$\frac{11}{15}$ = 73% solitary play

© 2003 by Sopris West Educational Services. Permission is granted to the purchaser to photocopy this page. Sopris West (800) 547-6747 - product 161DP

Play Observation Form

Target Child: __Kendall__   Date: __11-1-01__

Observer: __MR__   Setting/Time: __Free Play 9:15 a.m.__

	PLAY AREA							TYPES OF PLAY						
	Manipulatives	Dramatic Play	Books/Music	Computer	Art	Blocks	Miscellaneous	No Play	Onlooker	Solitary	Parallel	Cooperative	Teacher	Time Out
1	X										X			
	X										X			
							X	X						
2						X						X		
						X						X		
							X	X						
3	X									X				
	X									X				
	X									X				
4	X									X				
		X									X			
		X									X			
5		X									X			
							X						X	
							X							X

$\frac{4}{15}$ = 26% solitary $\frac{5}{15}$ = 33% parallel

Observation Form for Play and Social Interaction

Date: _____

Target Child: _____ 1st Observer: _____

Setting: _____ 2nd Observer: _____

Group Count: **Beginning**   **End**
                    Nonhandicapped _____   Nonhandicapped _____
                    Disabilities _____   Disabilities _____
                    Adults _____   Adults _____

	Play Area								Area Count			Behaviors							
	Housekeeping	Sand and water	Blocks	Quiet/books	Manipulatives	Art	Computer	Miscellaneous	Nonhandicapped	Disabilities	Adults	Unoccupied (Play)	Solitary (Play)	Coop. (Play)	Adult Interaction	Positive (Init.)	Negative (Init.)	Appropriate (Response)	Inappropriate (Response)	No (Response)
1																				
2																				
3																				
4																				
5																				
6																				

© 2003 by Sopris West Educational Services. Permission is granted to the purchaser to photocopy this page. Sopris West (800) 547-6747 - product 161DP

Observation Form for Play and Social Interaction

Date: 4-24-01

Target Child: Megan   1st Observer: Jones

Setting: classroom   2nd Observer: Smith

Group Count:

Beginning
- Nonhandicapped 2
- Disabilities 4
- Adults 2

End
- Nonhandicapped 1
- Disabilities 4
- Adults 2

	Play Area							Area Count			Behaviors							
	Housekeeping	Sand and water	Blocks	Quiet/books	Manipulatives	Art	Computer	Miscellaneous	Nonhandicapped	Disabilities	Adults	Unoccupied	Solitary (Play)	Coop.	Adult Interaction	Positive (Init.)	Negative	Appropriate (Response)	Inappropriate	No
1			X						1	1	0		X							
			X						1	1	0		X							
			X						1	1	0		X							
2			X						1	1	0		X							
			X						1	2	1		X							
			X						1	2	1		X							
3			X						1	2	0		X							
			X						1	2	1		X							
			X						1	2	1		X							
4								X	0	0	1	X			X					
								X	0	0	1	X			X					
					X				1	3	1	X								
5					X				1	3	1		X							
					X				1	3	1		X							
					X				1	3	1		X					X		
6					X				1	3	1		X							
					X				1	2	0		X							
					X				1	2	0		X							

Observation Form for Play and Social Interaction

Date: 4-24-01

Target Child: Ryan   1st Observer: Wilson

Setting: classroom   2nd Observer: Smith

Group Count:

Beginning
- Nonhandicapped 2
- Disabilities 4
- Adults 2

End
- Nonhandicapped 2
- Disabilities 4
- Adults 1

	Play Area: Housekeeping	Sand and water	Blocks	Quiet/books	Manipulatives	Art	Computer	Miscellaneous	Area Count: Nonhandicapped	Disabilities	Adults	Behaviors - Play: Unoccupied	Solitary	Coop.	Adult Interaction	Init. Positive	Negative	Response Appropriate	Inappropriate	No
1	X								O	2	1		X							
	X								O	2	1		X							
		X							O	2	1		X							
2		X							1	3	0			X		X				
		X							1	3	1		X					X		
								X	0	0	1	X			X					
3					X				1	1	0		X							
					X				1	1	0		X							
					X				1	1	0			X		X				
4					X				1	1	0			X		X				
	X								1	2	0		X							
	X								1	2	0		X							
5	X								1	2	0		X							
	X								1	2	0			X						
	X								1	2	0			X						
6				X					0	0	0	X								
				X					0	0	0		X							
				X					0	0	1		X		X					

Figure 4.8

Data Collection Form

Child's Name: ______________________________ Date: ____________________

Target Objectives	Dates																			
	5	5	5	5	5	5	5	5	5	5	5	5	5	5	5	5	5	5	5	5
	4	4	4	4	4	4	4	4	4	4	4	4	4	4	4	4	4	4	4	4
	3	3	3	3	3	3	3	3	3	3	3	3	3	3	3	3	3	3	3	3
	2	2	2	2	2	2	2	2	2	2	2	2	2	2	2	2	2	2	2	2
	1	1	1	1	1	1	1	1	1	1	1	1	1	1	1	1	1	1	1	1
	0	0	0	0	0	0	0	0	0	0	0	0	0	0	0	0	0	0	0	0
	5	5	5	5	5	5	5	5	5	5	5	5	5	5	5	5	5	5	5	5
	4	4	4	4	4	4	4	4	4	4	4	4	4	4	4	4	4	4	4	4
	3	3	3	3	3	3	3	3	3	3	3	3	3	3	3	3	3	3	3	3
	2	2	2	2	2	2	2	2	2	2	2	2	2	2	2	2	2	2	2	2
	1	1	1	1	1	1	1	1	1	1	1	1	1	1	1	1	1	1	1	1
	0	0	0	0	0	0	0	0	0	0	0	0	0	0	0	0	0	0	0	0
	5	5	5	5	5	5	5	5	5	5	5	5	5	5	5	5	5	5	5	5
	4	4	4	4	4	4	4	4	4	4	4	4	4	4	4	4	4	4	4	4
	3	3	3	3	3	3	3	3	3	3	3	3	3	3	3	3	3	3	3	3
	2	2	2	2	2	2	2	2	2	2	2	2	2	2	2	2	2	2	2	2
	1	1	1	1	1	1	1	1	1	1	1	1	1	1	1	1	1	1	1	1
	0	0	0	0	0	0	0	0	0	0	0	0	0	0	0	0	0	0	0	0
	5	5	5	5	5	5	5	5	5	5	5	5	5	5	5	5	5	5	5	5
	4	4	4	4	4	4	4	4	4	4	4	4	4	4	4	4	4	4	4	4
	3	3	3	3	3	3	3	3	3	3	3	3	3	3	3	3	3	3	3	3
	2	2	2	2	2	2	2	2	2	2	2	2	2	2	2	2	2	2	2	2
	1	1	1	1	1	1	1	1	1	1	1	1	1	1	1	1	1	1	1	1
	0	0	0	0	0	0	0	0	0	0	0	0	0	0	0	0	0	0	0	0

O = correct X = incorrect

© 2003 by Sopris West Educational Services. Permission is granted to the purchaser to photocopy this page. Sopris West (800) 547-6747 - product 161DP

Data Collection Form

Child's Name: _____   Date: _____

Target Objectives	Dates									
	5	5	5	5	5	5	5	5	5	5
	4	4	4	4	4	4	4	4	4	4
	3	3	3	3	3	3	3	3	3	3
	2	2	2	2	2	2	2	2	2	2
	1	1	1	1	1	1	1	1	1	1
	0	0	0	0	0	0	0	0	0	0
	5	5	5	5	5	5	5	5	5	5
	4	4	4	4	4	4	4	4	4	4
	3	3	3	3	3	3	3	3	3	3
	2	2	2	2	2	2	2	2	2	2
	1	1	1	1	1	1	1	1	1	1
	0	0	0	0	0	0	0	0	0	0
	5	5	5	5	5	5	5	5	5	5
	4	4	4	4	4	4	4	4	4	4
	3	3	3	3	3	3	3	3	3	3
	2	2	2	2	2	2	2	2	2	2
	1	1	1	1	1	1	1	1	1	1
	0	0	0	0	0	0	0	0	0	0
	5	5	5	5	5	5	5	5	5	5
	4	4	4	4	4	4	4	4	4	4
	3	3	3	3	3	3	3	3	3	3
	2	2	2	2	2	2	2	2	2	2
	1	1	1	1	1	1	1	1	1	1
	0	0	0	0	0	0	0	0	0	0

O = correct   X = incorrect   ☐ = _____

© 2003 by Sopris West Educational Services. Permission is granted to the purchaser to photocopy this page. Sopris West (800) 547-6747 - product 161DP

Data Collection Form

Child's Name: __Katie__   Date: __Language Group__

Target Objectives	Dates

(Data chart with Target Objectives: Red ("will say red when asked 'what color?'"), Blue, Green, Yellow across dates 11-5 through 12-6, with O = correct and X = incorrect markings)

O = correct   X = incorrect

Data Collection Form

Child's Name: _____ Date: _____ Small Group Cognitive

O = correct   X = incorrect   □ = total correct per day

© 2003 by Sopris West Educational Services. Permission is granted to the purchaser to photocopy this page. Sopris West (800) 547-6747 - product 161DP

Data Collection Form

Child's Name: _____   Date: _____ Cognitive/language

Target Objectives	Dates

Kate — How many "2"

Kate — Says letter "A" when shown

Kara — Counts to "5" without prompts

Kara — Says letters of alphabet rote

O = correct   X = incorrect

© 2003 by Sopris West Educational Services. Permission is granted to the purchaser to photocopy this page. Sopris West (800) 547-6747 - product 161DP

Directed Play

Strategies for Successful Classroom Management

Lose Yourself in the Play

Directed Play activities should be fun. The easiest way to maintain good classroom management is for children to be active and having fun. The more fun you have, the more fun they will have. Engage in parallel play with the children. Follow their leads in play, but gently guide or "direct" them to higher forms of learning by making comments about things or by making suggestions of what to do or say. The more you can lose yourself in their play, the more fun it will be for everyone and the easier it will be to manage behaviors.

Rules

Rules are to a classroom what laws are to a society. They let us know what is acceptable and what is not acceptable. It is essential that you establish a few classroom rules. For most settings four or five rules should be sufficient. Rules should be reviewed frequently and explained so that children understand them. It may be necessary to develop or revise rules periodically.

Rules should be stated in positive terms, "do" statements as opposed to "don't" statements. For example, "Keep hands and feet to yourself" or "Raise your hand to ask a question." This helps to establish positive expectations for children.

Rules should be enforced consistently for everyone. If there are too many rules it is difficult to enforce them consistently. Try to develop natural consequences for rule violations, but recognize that young children are still learning social and language skills.

Respect and Dignity

It is very important that children be treated with respect and dignity. This respect is reflected in how we treat them and how we talk to them. When you must discipline children be firm but not mean. Be consistent across both behaviors and children and always talk to them in a calm manner. It is also helpful to use a system such as "1, 2, 3." On "1" you redirect the behavior; on "2" you redirect and remind them of consequences; on "3" you impose the consequence. This gives children warning and time to control their own behavior. Tell children you will only ask them three times to do something. If they have not complied by the third time, physically assist them in doing what was asked. In addition, be sure to attend to the children when they are behaving appropriately and call attention to their positive behaviors.

Being respectful also means that we are aware of children's emotions. What may seem unimportant to us may be very important to a young child. Furthermore, children may have a very good reason for feeling as they do. We need to help children understand their feelings and learn how to act when they feel a certain way.

Motivation

Motivation and curiosity are usually the same things in children. However, some children will lack motivation in at least one activity. The play-based nature of the Directed Play curriculum addresses this. Play-based activities should be fun, so try to make a game out these activities. Motivation can also be enhanced by focusing on things the children enjoy, providing external rewards, or providing an appropriate level of challenge. Children enjoy a challenge, but it needs to be something that is not too difficult for them to achieve.

Work to Enhance Self-Esteem

If children feel good about themselves they are more likely to behave appropriately. Techniques to increase self-esteem can include helping children identify their uniqueness, creating an "I Can" list, and providing opportunities for children to be successful. The "I Can" list is an ongoing list of things that children have learned how to do.

Rewards and Praise

Rewarding children is the easy way to promote positive, prosocial behaviors. Rewarding children should always involve praising them. Young children enjoy pleasing adults; so let children know when they have done something positive. This will encourage them to do it again.

It may be necessary to set up a reward system. Be very specific about what behavior(s) will be rewarded. When children engage in the targeted behavior they should be rewarded immediately and consistently. This reward may involve something tangible, such as stickers, as well as praise. Always tell children why they are being rewarded.

As the targeted behaviors become better established, you won't need to reward the children as often. Gradually reduce the tangible rewards they receive, but always continue praising them.

Directed Play

Transitions

Because transitions in early childhood programs are often unstructured, these time periods are associated with behavior problems. Several strategies can be used to help children transition between activities or areas smoothly. First, have a set routine so that children know what is expected. Teach children how to line up and move slowly from one area to another. Encourage them to be at least an arm's length away from the child in front of them. Second, have a designated signal that informs students that an activity is coming to an end and that they need to get ready to move. This will allow children time to complete a task and put materials away. Third, have children do something while transitioning. For example, give them a command that they are to walk and sound like a duck, or that they should walk like an elephant. Fourth, don't make children wait too long. The longer children have to wait, the more likely it is that they will engage in inappropriate behaviors. Fifth, make use of picture schedules that children can use to move pictures of activities from one area to another.

Redirection

Redirecting children can be an easy and effective way to reduce the occurrence of inappropriate or negative behaviors. Redirection is simply telling the child to do something else that is more appropriate. In many instances the redirection may provide a child with an alternative way to engage in the same behavior. For example, one way to handle children who bite is to give them something appropriate to bite. If a child has a tendency to bite others, give him or her something to chew on, such as a plastic straw, gum, or even a chew toy. This will satisfy the child's need to bite without harming anyone else.

Redirection is also consistent with an important concept related to punishment. This concept states that we should not take a behavior away without replacing it with something else. This means that when we tell a child to stop what they are doing, we should give them something appropriate to do instead. Telling children to "stop" may inhibit a behavior for a moment, but giving them another option teaches them to engage in a more appropriate behavior.

Look for the Reasons for Misbehavior

If children are misbehaving, be sure to look for ecological or environmental reasons as a possible cause. These might include overcrowding, inappropriate expectations for behavior, inconsistent messages from adults, not enough toys, or sensory problems, such as hearing loss. Changing the environment may eliminate the misbehavior. Be observant of what happens before and after an inappropriate behavior. Inappropriate behaviors are likely caused by something that happens to the child, so it is important to know what that is.

Controlled Choices

Give children controlled choices. This means that you provide two options or choices that they choose from, for example, apple or grape juice, coming to the table or going to time out, walking nicely in line or staying in the room. Giving children choices treats them with respect and gives them a sense of ownership regarding what happens to them.

Time Out

Time out is a punishment procedure used to decrease the occurrence of unwanted behaviors and should not be used more than is absolutely necessary. Time out is a fairly well-known procedure used in many home and school settings. However, caution needs to be exercised to ensure that time out procedures are used appropriately and effectively. Punishment can lead to many unwanted negative side effects and should only be done if other methods have proven ineffective.

Time out involves removing children temporarily from whatever they are doing. The assumption is that what they are doing is what they enjoy and that removing them will reduce the unwanted behaviors. If children seem to enjoy going to time out, there is a possibility that they don't like what they are doing at the time.

It should be made quite clear to children what behaviors warrant time out. It is also essential that there be an established location where time out will occur. This setting should be in an out of the way location, away from traffic areas, but one where the child can easily be seen. Children should never be locked in a dark room or away from where they can be seen.

The length of time a child spends in time out should be relatively brief. For many children, 15–30 seconds is enough to let them know that a certain behavior will not be accepted. Under no circumstances should a child be placed in time out for an extended period of time. In some instances it may be necessary to have a child in time out for up to two to three minutes if they are upset and need to calm down.

For children who are sent to time out frequently, look for various ecological or environmental variables that may be the cause. Overcrowding, for example, can lead to inappropriate behaviors, so it may be necessary to reduce the number of children in a given area at one time.

It may also be desirable to have a quiet location where children can go to calm down and refocus when they are not being punished.

Directed Play

Be Aware of Cultural Differences

We are a multicultural society. Our country is made up of peoples from many different cultures. Children from one culture can act or behave differently from children in another culture. Take time to learn about the cultures of children in your setting and what is expected or not expected of them. For example, in some cultures direct eye contact is seen as an indication of attention or respect. In other cultures it is not. In some cultures it is acceptable to touch a child's head or hair; in others it is not. Peoples of different cultures may have different values or ideas about time, humor, manners, or even cheating in games. Any or all of these could be seen as misbehavior to an uninformed adult. It is important that we recognize individual differences among children and help them to learn that these differences are not bad.

Conflict Resolution

Conflicts are a part of life and can be a tool to help children learn about interpersonal relations. Conflicts among children can occur for any number of reasons: deficits in peer interaction skills, not perceiving social situations correctly, overcrowding, or disputes over possessions. One of the most common sources of conflict among young children centers on toy possession. We can minimize these sorts of conflicts by having an ample amount of play materials available for children.

The social interaction and conflict resolution skills of children increase with age. Younger children, ages 1–2 years, will engage in more overt physical behavior during conflicts, while older children, ages 4–5 years, engage in more verbal justification and mutual agreement. Several studies have shown that the majority of conflicts among children involve possession of a toy, are brief in duration (15 seconds or less), occur during ongoing play, and end with one child's withdrawal. The more intense the conflict the longer it is likely to last, and, when conflicts are more intense, they are more likely followed by negative interactions.

When conflicts do occur, give children a chance to deal with them without adult intervention. However, if children are unable to resolve the conflict, or if physical aggression is present, adults must intervene. Teach children conflict resolution skills, such as using "I" messages when talking, not interrupting when someone else is talking, no name calling, and the importance of compromise. Children must learn these important skills and must be rewarded when the skills are demonstrated.

67   Chapter 5

Personal/Social Skills Activities

Body Parts	70
Self-Help Skills	79
Emotions and Individual Differences	92
Home and Family	106
Sociodramatic Play	113
Cooperative Play	121
Disability Awareness	125
Buddies	131

Body Parts

 ## Mirror, Mirror

Target Objective
Recognition and naming of body parts

Developmental Domains
Cognitive, Self-Help, Language, Social

Multiple Intelligences
Intrapersonal, Linguistic, Interpersonal, Bodily, Musical

Materials
One large mirror or smaller mirrors for each child.

Preparation/Set-Up
Large mirror in horizontal position.

Procedures

1. With children in a small group, have each child stand and look into a large mirror. Arrange positions so that all children can see one another.

2. Have each child point to body parts as you name them.

3. Children can take turns saying a body part for the other children to point to.

4. Bring the children back together as a group. Everyone sings "I Have Two Eyes" and performs the actions mentioned in the song.

Adaptations for Children With Disabilities

Monitor a child's progress by keeping data on each body part named. A data sheet with the names of common body parts can be checked with a plus or minus for correct or incorrect responses. Provide adult assistance as needed. Children can also identify body parts on a doll or an adult in a one-to-one situation. Increase the number of body parts named as children get older.

I Have Two Eyes

I have two eyes to see with,

I have two feet to run.

I have two hands to wave with,

and nose I have but one.

I have two ears to hear with,

and tongue to say, "Good-day."

And two red cheeks for you to kiss,

and now I'll run away.

2. Body Part Game

Target Objective
Recognition and naming of body parts

Developmental Domains
Cognitive, Language, Self-Help, Social

Multiple Intelligences
Intrapersonal, Linguistic, Bodily, Interpersonal, Musical

Materials
None.

Preparation/Set-Up
Large motor area.

Procedures

1. Tell a small group of children that today they are going to play a game about body parts.
2. Have children choose a partner.
3. One child points to a body part on self, and the other child has to name it.
4. Children should take turns pointing and naming. Encourage children to point to different body parts by saying things such as, "Use your right hand to touch your left ear."
5. Conclude the activity by singing and performing actions to " My Hands."

Adaptations for Children With Disabilities

Have a list of names of body parts, and mark with a plus or minus sign which ones a child identifies correctly or incorrectly. Ask each body part at least five times. A data collection sheet is provided in Chapter Four. Start with face and add other body parts as child shows mastery. Provide adult assistance as needed.

My Hands

My hands say thank you

With a clap, clap, clap.

My feet say thank you

With a tap, tap, tap.

Clap, clap, clap,

Tap, tap, tap.

3 Animal Body Parts

Target Objective
Identification of body parts on animals

Developmental Domains
Language, Cognitive, Gross Motor

Multiple Intelligences
Naturalist, Linguistic, Bodily, Musical

Materials
Pictures and toys of 8–10 different animals and pictures of animal footprints.

Preparation/Set-Up
Have pictures available.

Procedures

1. Show the pictures and animal toys to the children and tell them that they are going to say the names of the different body parts on the animals.

2. With children in a small group, say the body parts on each of the animals.

3. Have the children identify and name the body parts on each animal. The children should be familiar with the animals.

4. Note that some animals have some body parts that others do not (e.g., dogs don't have horns, snakes don't have legs).

5. Next, have the children imitate how certain animals move. Include wings, tails, and whiskers.

6. Show the children pictures of footprints of different animals and compare these to the feet of the children.

7. Ask and discuss with the children what they have learned about body parts and footprints of animals.

8. Conclude the activity by singing and moving to "Jump or Jiggle."

Adaptations for Children With Disabilities

Make a list of the names of the body parts and identify which ones the child correctly identifies and names. Children can match pairs of animal footprints.

Jump or Jiggle

Frogs jump. Caterpillars hump.

Worms wiggle. Bugs jiggle.

Rabbits hop. Horses clop.

Snakes slide. Seagulls glide.

Mice creep. Deer leap.

Puppies bounce. Kittens pounce.

Lions stalk, but I can walk.

4 Matching Faces

Target Objective
Matching body parts, socialization, names of children, recognition of differences

Developmental Domains
Cognitive, Language, Social

Multiple Intelligences
Linguistic, Interpersonal, Intrapersonal

Materials
Two photographs of each child's face.

Preparation/Set-Up
Have pictures available.

Procedures

1. Gather children in a group and tell them that they are going to play a matching game. Show the group the photographs individually and have them say the name of each child shown in the picture.

2. Put all of the photographs in a container and mix them up. Have children take turns pulling one of the pictures out of the container. Each child tells the name of the child in the picture.

3. Have the children select a second picture from the container and name who is in the picture.

4. Go around the circle of children and ask each child to hold up a picture and identify who it is. Ask who has the matching picture. The second child holds up the matching picture, and then both children move to put their pictures next to each other in the center of the circle.

5. Continue this process until all pictures have been matched and gathered into the center of the circle.

6. Have older children match a picture with the written name of each child.

Adaptations for Children With Disabilities

Point out similarities and differences in the faces. Note hair color or length, shape of the faces, etc. Provide extra practice for those who need it.

73 Chapter 6

Body Parts and Multiple Intelligence Activities

Intrapersonal — Children name own body parts while looking in a mirror.

Interpersonal — Children name body parts on a partner with or without a mirror; children trace around the body of another child lying on a large piece of paper or a sidewalk with chalk.

Naturalist — Children name body parts on a variety of animals. Talk about how they are alike and different by comparing two or three animals.

Logical — Children count how many eyes, legs, fingers, and toes on self, other children, or animals.

Spatial — Children draw picture of self, using marker, crayon, or paint on construction paper.

Linguistic — Children tell five things about themselves (hair color, boy/girl, etc.) or name as many body parts as they can. Children play "Simon Says," taking turns saying and moving body parts.

Bodily — Children name and move different body parts with eyes closed.

Musical — Children participate in singing and moving to "Head, Shoulders, Knees, and Toes," "Hokey Pokey," "Where is Thumbkin."

Directed Play

5 Body Part Movement

Target Objective Recognition of body parts, following directions	**Materials** Music (optional), music cards depicting song.
Developmental Domains Gross Motor, Language, Cognitive	**Preparation/Set-Up** Large group or motor area.
Multiple Intelligences Musical, Bodily, Linguistic, Intrapersonal	

Procedures

1. Organize children in a group and tell them that they are going to move and sing to music.

2. In a large or small group, have children move, dance, and sing.

3. Movements and songs can include "Hokey Pokey," or "Head, Shoulders, Knees, and Toes."

4. Let different children take turns leading the group movements.

5. Repeat two or three times.

Adaptations for Children With Disabilities

Watch the children and note which children do and do not move a body part correctly when named. Provide physical assistance as needed. Have peers model movements. Slow the music down if needed or sing the song if the music is too distracting.

75   Chapter 6

6 Constructing a Person

Target Objective
Identification/naming of body parts, increase fine motor skills, cutting, gluing, drawing.

Developmental Domains
Self-Help, Fine Motor, Cognitive, Language

Multiple Intelligences
Intrapersonal, Linguistic, Spatial

Materials
Construction paper, glue sticks, blank paper, markers or crayons, scissors.

Preparation/Set-Up
Precut or outlined shapes—circle for head, oval for body, narrow straight rectangles for arms and legs, shorter ones for hands and feet. Have a model made to show children.

Procedures

1. Give a small group of children seated at a table the precut shapes or have them cut out the predrawn shapes.

2. Tell children that they are going to make a person out of the shapes.

3. Have children practice constructing the person first, and then let them construct the person by gluing the shapes onto a blank paper.

4. Point out the names of the body parts children are gluing and be sure they get the pieces in the correct locations.

5. Use markers or crayons for facial features and hair or other details, such as the patterns on clothes.

6. Encourage the children to tell the location of different parts (e.g., head on top, feet on bottom).

7. Have the children answer questions about the location of body parts, such as "Where is the arm?"

8. Lastly, gather the children in a small group and let them show one another their pictures.

Adaptations for Children With Disabilities

Some children will benefit from having part of the person constructed or preglued. Children should have an example to copy. Some children will need several repetitions of this activity to master these concepts and skills. Give the children extended time to complete this activity. See the Fine Motor chapter for other construction activities.

7   Camera and Camcorder Fun

Target Objective
Recognition of individual differences, cause and effect, recognition of objects and events, sequence of events

Developmental Domains
Social, Language, and Cognitive

Multiple Intelligences
Linguistic, Intrapersonal, Interpersonal

Materials
Instant or digital cameras, film, camcorder, blank videotapes, VCR, TV. It is important to have cameras that produce pictures immediately. There will be an expense for cameras, film, and film developing. However, not every picture children take needs to be developed. Advantages of the new digital cameras are that they allow you to see a picture before it is developed or printed. There will be an initial cost for camcorders. But once purchased the cost of operating them is not that significant. Blank videotapes are relatively inexpensive, and it is possible to use tapes over again. It may also be possible to borrow these materials from student families.

Preparation/Set-Up
Make sure film is in camera or tape is in camcorder and that they are ready to operate. Cameras should have an automatic focus.

Procedures

1. This is an activity that will need to be carefully supervised. If only one camera or camcorder is available, children will need to share it.

2. Talk to children about what they are going to take pictures of before they start. You may want to give some prior practice by showing an event or "scene." The more familiar children are with an activity the more natural the interactions will be.

3. Begin by having children take pictures of other children, either individually or in groups. This can spark some nice discussion among children. Children can make some funny poses or wear funny clothes.

4. For camcorder recording, children might videotape other children playing in one of the thematic areas. The tape can be played and children can discuss what everyone was doing.

5. Children can be videotaped playing in the dramatic play area. Afterwards, they can watch themselves playing. This can increase the quality of dramatic play.

77   Chapter 6

Cameras and Multiple Intelligences

Intrapersonal   Pictures are taken of the children playing in different activities or dressed in clothes of different seasons.

Interpersonal   Children take pictures of other children or family members.

Logical   Pictures can be taken of quantitative, directional, or positional concepts—empty/full, first/last, on/under.

Spatial   Children take pictures from different angles, for example, standing, lying down, standing sideways, upside down, or standing on a chair.

Musical   Children take pictures of children singing, dancing, or playing instruments.

Naturalist   Children take pictures of trees, changes in seasons, planting flowers, or children swimming outside.

Bodily   Children take action verb pictures—running, eating, jumping, climbing, throwing, catching.

Linguistic   Children make books out of their pictures using words and sentences. Two books can be created, one that focuses on the child and a second that focuses on others. One book can contain pictures of the child and narrative, such as "This is Tommy. He is four years old." Another book can contain pictures of friends and family, school, or pets, and sentences can be used to describe these things.

Adaptations for Children With Disabilities

Pictures and photos are a necessity for young children with language delays. Children with physical impairments will need assistance with stability. A tripod can be helpful for all children. Pictures of children or their creations can serve as important material for portfolios. Children exhibiting behavior problems can be videotaped (with parental permission) while engaging in inappropriate behaviors. The child and an adult can later watch the videotape together and discuss what is happening.

Self-Help Skills

Dressing and Clothes Fastening

Dressing and clothes fastening are skills children usually learn naturally. As their motor and cognitive skills improve, young children gradually achieve independence in these skills. Young children with disabilities, however, will often require more time and assistance. Young children with mental retardation and those with physical and visual impairments will experience the greatest difficulties.

To help young children with disabilities learn dressing and clothes fastening skills you will need to set up opportunities for them to practice. This is necessary, because the everyday environment does not give children enough opportunities to practice these skills. For example, a child learning to take off his or her shirt may only have one or two chances a day to perform this task. At this rate it would take a very long time for young children with disabilities to master this simple task. Don't be afraid to repeat these activities. Young children with disabilities need this additional practice.

Clothes fastening is the part of dressing that involves zippers, snaps, buttons, buckles, lacing, and tying. Clothes fastening requires a good pincer grasp, coordination, and, often, the use of both hands. Provide children with play materials, such as dolls, oversized clothes, or button and zipper boards that will allow them to practice these skills. Giving children larger buttons may help them to perform and practice this skill before they move on to smaller buttons.

Dress-Up Play

Target Objective
Dressing, fastening skills (buttons, zippers, snaps, buckles), clothes on and off, front/back, inside/outside

Developmental Domains
Fine Motor, Language, Social, Self-Help

Multiple Intelligences
Bodily, Linguistic, Intrapersonal

Materials
A variety of clothing, including oversized shirts, shoes, large buttons, front zippers, shoes with laces, snapping vests, belts with buckles, full-sized mirrors.

Preparation/Set-Up
Clothes available in a dramatic play area.

Procedures

1. Organize a group of two to four children in the dramatic play area and tell them that they are going to practice putting on and taking off clothes.

2. Let each child practice putting on and taking off clothes that have snaps, zippers, and buttons.

3. Make sure children look at themselves in a mirror while wearing different clothes. Make statements about the color or style of the clothes.

4. Vary the clothes that are available.

Adaptations for Children With Disabilities

Keep track of which children have difficulty with this activity and give them extra practice. Watch to see if children have trouble with dressing or with fasteners or both. Buttons, zippers, and snaps all require a good pincer grasp. It may be helpful to provide larger buttons or snaps that can be easier to fasten.

9   What You Wear—What's Different?

Target Objectives
Recognition and discrimination of objects, problem solving, same and different

Developmental Domains
Self-Help, Cognitive, Language, Fine Motor

Multiple Intelligences
Linguistic, Interpersonal, Intrapersonal

Materials
Different pieces of clothing.

Preparation/Set-Up
None.

Procedures

1. Tell a small group of children that they are going to play a guessing game about what's different.

2. Have the children take turns standing in front of the group and saying, "Look at me."

3. The group makes observations about the clothing a child is wearing.

4. The performing child then moves behind a partition or screen and changes something about what they are wearing (e.g., change shirt or shoe, put on hat).

5. The child comes back and stands in front of the group and says, "What's different?"

6. The group takes turns naming what is different in complete sentences (e.g., "Your shirt is different" or "You are wearing a hat").

Directed Play   **80**

7. Let each child have a turn changing something.

8. Begin with obvious changes, then move to more subtle changes, such as jewelry or an untied shoe.

9. Ask the children to recall the changes in clothing for different children.

Adaptations for Children With Disabilities

Make use of obvious changes in clothing. Use brightly colored clothing or clothing that makes sound. Make sure all children are identifying and then naming what is different. It may be necessary to break children into two groups, one group of older, more developmentally advanced children, and another of younger children.

10   Buddy Dress-Up

Target Objectives
Increase self-help skills, dressing, fastening, socialization, cooperation, sequence of events

Developmental Domains
Self-Help, Social, Language, Fine Motor, Cognitive

Multiple Intelligences
Bodily, Interpersonal, Linguistic, Intrapersonal

Materials
Slightly oversized clothes, large mirror.

Preparation/Set-Up
Enough clothes for each group of children, including boots, coats, shirts, or hats.

Procedures

1. Have a group of four to six children select partners.

2. Tell them that they are going to work together to dress each other.

3. The children take turns dressing and undressing each other by placing the oversized clothing over their own clothes, except for shoes and socks.

4. Each child should have the opportunity to button, zip, snap, buckle, or tie fasteners.

5. Bring the group together again and ask the children to talk about what was easy or hard about this activity.

6. This activity can be done during different seasons and should be repeated throughout the year.

Adaptations for Children With Disabilities

Provide adapted Velcro® closures, physical assistance, and large buttons with wide holes. Watch how children are putting on clothes and provide verbal and physical prompts as necessary. Use the mirror(s) to help children see skills being performed to increase imitation.

Shoe Game

Target Objectives
Identification and recognition of objects, self-help, matching same and different, on and off, left and right.

Developmental Domains
Self-Help, Cognitive, Language

Multiple Intelligences
Bodily, Intrapersonal, Musical, Logical, Linguistic

Materials
Children's shoes.

Preparation/Set-Up
Make note of the shoes children are wearing.

Procedures

1. Have children sit in a circle. Tell them that they are going to take off their shoes, put them in a pile, and then have to find their shoe in the pile.

2. Direct each child take off either their right shoe or left shoe; assist as necessary.

3. Collect the shoes from each child and place them in a pile in the middle of the circle.

4. Call children by name, one at a time, and have them pick out their shoe from the pile and put it on.

5. Once all the children have picked out their shoes, repeat the activity with the other foot.

6. In another activity, have a child find and give back all of the other children's shoes. Give each child an opportunity.

Tying My Shoes

I know how to tie my shoe,

I take the loop and poke it through.

It's very hard to make it stay,

Because my thumb gets in the way.

7. For more challenging activities, include other shoes in the pile (e.g., slippers, adult shoes, or boots), have children take off both shoes, or have children tie their shoes. With older children, practice the concept of left and right by having them take off and put on the left or right shoe by request.

8. Conclude the activity by singing, "Tying My Shoes" while miming actions.

Adaptations for Children With Disabilities

Provide assistance in getting shoes on and off as needed. Point out characteristics of the shoes, such as size, color, or design. Watch all children and note which ones have trouble with this task. Give these children extra practice. This activity can also be played with mittens and gloves in the winter.

Hair Care, Brushing Teeth, and Bathing

Hair Care

Target Objectives
Increase self-help, grooming, identification, and use of objects

Developmental Domains
Self-Help, Language, and Social

Multiple Intelligences
Intrapersonal, Linguistic, Interpersonal, Bodily, Musical

Materials
Dolls with hair, wigs, and various hair items, including combs, brushes, clips, curlers, mirrors. One comb or brush for each child.

Preparation/Set-Up
Make sure that combs/brushes are clean and that children only use their own.

Procedures

1. With children in a small group, show and discuss the hair care items. Let children hold and manipulate them.

2. Using dolls with various kinds of hair or wigs, have children practice combing and brushing the hair.

3. Children can also experiment with putting curlers, clips, or ponytails in the hair.

4. Point out how different people have different colors, lengths, and styles of hair.

5. Using their own combs or brushes, have children stand in front of the mirror and comb their own hair or the hair of a peer.

6. Have the children sing "Brush Your Hair Everyday" while miming actions.

Adaptations for Children With Disabilities

Make sure children know the names of the items and what they are used for. Encourage children to use a gentle touch when combing or brushing. Repeat the activity throughout the year.

Brush Your Hair Everyday

Brush your hair everyday,

Give your hair a treat.

Part it, braid it, brush it back,

But always keep in neat.

Brush it once, brush it twice,

Keep it nice and clean.

Brush and brush the tangles out,

And see the lovely sheen.

---

13 Brushing Teeth

Target Objectives
Learn how to brush teeth

Developmental Domains
Self-Help, Social

Multiple Intelligences
Linguistic, Intrapersonal, Interpersonal, Musical, Bodily

Materials
Toothbrush for each child, toothpaste, mirror, water, towels.

Preparation/Set-Up
This activity is best done individually or in pairs after a meal or snack.

Procedures

1. Tell children they are going to practice brushing their teeth.

2. Make sure each child has his or her toothbrush and toothpaste.

3. Assist children as needed.

4. After all children have brushed, bring the group together and sing, "This is the Way We Brush Our Teeth," "My Toothbrush," and "Brushing Teeth" while miming movements.

Adaptations for Children With Disabilities

Children with disabilities are going to need extra time and individual practice in this task. Work with them one-on-one. Use task analysis, a listing of all the steps necessary to complete a task. Look at the sequence and observe where a child is having the most difficulty, then provide extra practice in those specific skills.

Directed Play

My Toothbrush

I have a little toothbrush,

I hold it very tight.

I brush my teeth each morning

And then again at night.

Brushing Teeth

Up and down and round and round

I brush my teeth to keep them sound

To keep them sound and clean and white

I brush them morning, noon, and night.

14 Happy Teeth Picture

Target Objectives
Understand importance of healthy teeth, increase fine motor skills, cutting and gluing.

Developmental Domains
Fine Motor, Self-Help

Multiple Intelligences
Bodily, Spatial, Intrapersonal, Musical

Materials
White paper, scissors, glue, washable markers or crayons.

Preparation/Set-Up
Heads can be drawn in advance or completed with the group. The "teeth" can be precut for younger children.

Procedures

1. Tell children that they are going to make a face with a mouth and teeth.

2. Provide predrawn heads with large open mouths.

3. Children cut small white pieces of paper from one-inch strips for teeth.

4. Children glue the teeth into two rows—upper and lower. Have children count the number of teeth in their mouth.

5. Children finish by drawing eyes, nose, and hair.

6. Place completed faces on a bulletin board.

7. Conclude by reciting "I Brush My Teeth" while miming movements.

I Brush My Teeth

I brush my teeth, I brush my teeth,

Morning, noon, and night.

I brush them, floss them, rinse them clean,

I keep them nice and white.

I brush them once, I brush them twice,

I brush them till they shine.

I always brush them up and down,

These precious teeth of mine.

Adaptations for Children With Disabilities

Provide assistance with cutting and pasting as needed. Adaptive scissors may be easier for some children. See the "Happy Teeth Mural" in the Fine Motor chapter for an additional activity.

15 Washing Babies

Target Objectives
Increase self-help skills, social skills, caring for another, safety and gentle touch

Developmental Domains
Self-Help, Social, Language, Cognitive

Multiple Intelligences
Bodily, Interpersonal, Musical, Linguistic, Intrapersonal

Materials
Multicultural plastic dolls that can get wet, three to four small tubs of soapy water, towels, soap, hairbrushes, washcloths.

Preparation/Set-Up
Fill the small tubs with water and arrange them in a circle on the floor or on the table. Have soap, towels, and dolls available. Conduct this activity on a tile floor or use a plastic mat.

Procedures

1. Bring a small group of children to the water tubs and explain that they are going to give the babies a bath.

2. Give each child a doll; have them undress and bathe the doll.

3. Point out the proper way to hold the baby to prevent the doll's head from going underwater.

4. Identify and name on the doll the body parts the children are washing.

5. Be sure the children wash the head, feet, and hands.

6. Have the children dry off the dolls. Again point out how to hold the "babies."

7. Have the children dress the dolls when finished.

8. Discuss care of others, gentle touch, trust, and responsibility.

> ### Baby's Bath
>
> Baby's ready for his bath.
>
> Here's the baby's tub,
>
> Here's the baby's washcloth.
>
> See how he can rub.
>
> Here's the baby's cake of soap,
>
> And here's the towel to dry;
>
> And here's the baby's cradle
>
> Rock-a-bye-bye.

Directed Play

9. Conclude the activity by singing "Baby's Bath" while miming movements.

10. An alternative song is "After a Bath." Use a towel as a prop.

Adaptations for Children With Disabilities

Assist children in holding the babies as needed. Be sure to describe all the body parts to a child with visual impairments. Provide a chair or support as needed for children to participate. Keep data on body parts. Ask children to point to or name different body parts and record correct and incorrect answers using the 0–5 data sheet.

After a Bath

After my bath, I try, try, try

To wipe myself till I'm dry, dry, dry.

Hands to wipe, and fingers and toes

And two wet legs and a shiny nose.

Just think how much less time I'd take,

If I were a dog, and I could shake, shake, shake.

Cooking and Eating

Snack time is a great opportunity for cooking experiences and sensory stimulation. Recipes can be selected that follow a certain theme or promote an awareness of cultural diversity. For example, to promote facial understanding and colors, the children can make jack-o-lanterns using orange-frosted circle cookies with chocolate chips for the face. There are many easy foods to cook, including eggs, popcorn, biscuits, toast, puffed rice treats, celery with peanut butter and raisins, and pudding.

Cooking gives children experience in cause and effect relationships, measuring, taking turns, following directions, sequencing events, language use, and cooperating. Foods, with their different smells, textures, and tastes, are an excellent way to promote sensory skills.

Snack time is also an excellent opportunity to help children learn to eat independently, socialize with other children and adults, and practice eye-hand coordination. Have a routine for snack time. Include getting to the table, getting served, eating, asking to be excused, and cleaning up.

Snack foods need to be chosen with thought and care. Avoid foods that are high in sugar or fats. Be alert to any food allergies the children may have. Determine what foods are best for certain children depending on their health and developmental needs. Provide adequate amounts of each food and don't rush children to eat. Try to choose foods that are nutritious and easy to manage, such as peeled fruit, cheese slices, or dry cereal.

Children with orthopedic handicaps may do better at pouring and cutting if they are standing. Standing boards can give them security while standing and free their hands for other things. Give children additional practice pouring at a sand or water table.

A variety of adaptive spoons, cups, bowls, and plates are commercially available and help to increase independence. Simple adaptations, such as Velcro® or suction cups on the bottom of a bowl or plate, also increase stability.

Feeding Problems

Children may exhibit problems with eating for physical or behavior reasons. Physical problems can include poor lip closure, excessive drooling, tongue thrust, poor chewing ability, or high muscle tone. These problems may require consultation with a speech pathologist or occupational or physical therapist. Behavioral problems can include: refusal to eat certain foods, narrow range of food preferences, refusal to eat solid foods, refusal to eat at the specified time, or dawdling. Listed here are some general ideas to support positive eating habits:

- Be sure children are seated with feet supported. Food should be at the level of a child's stomach.

- Do not make comments about how much food is eaten.

- Do not threaten a child for refusing to eat.

- Do not force-feed children who are not eating.

- Use child-sized portions or about 1 tbsp. of food for each year of age.

- Use unbreakable, child-sized utensils.

- Use and vary attractive food shapes and colors.

- Encourage children to try at least one bite of a new food.

- Encourage children to participate in preparing the food.

- Allow choices of foods within the same category, e.g., greens beans instead of peas.

- Have children alternate bites between preferred and less preferred foods.

- Praise the children for positive eating behaviors.

- Provide finger foods or other foods that can be easily manipulated to help children feel successful in self-feeding.

Eating and Multiple Intelligences

Cooking and snack time experiences can easily incorporate the multiple intelligences. Examples of activities for different intelligences include:

Intrapersonal Children identify and name foods that they like to eat.

Interpersonal Children bring different fruits to class that are combined to make a fruit salad. Make a list of foods that everyone likes. Children work in pairs to make a Buddy Sandwich (see page 91).

Logical Children follow directions to make something (e.g., macaroni and cheese). Children count the number of seeds in a piece of fruit. Children make frozen juicicles to address concepts of time and cold. Foods can be organized by color, type, texture, smell, or size. Discuss and demonstrate how some foods can be converted into other foods (e.g., apples make applesauce, peanuts make peanut butter). Children count how many straws or napkins are needed. Sing "Five Little Cookies."

Five Little Cookies

Five little cookies with frosting galore,

Mother ate the white one, then there were four.

Four little cookies, two and two, you see

Father ate the green one, then there were three.

Three little cookies, but before I knew,

Sister ate the yellow one, then there were two.

Two little cookies, oh, what fun,

Brother ate the brown one, then there was one.

One little cookie, watch me run,

I ate the red one, then there were none.

Linguistic Snack time can also be used to promote concepts of color, taste, texture, or categories. For example, the following foods correspond to certain colors:
- Red—strawberry, Bing cherries, cranberry juice, red apples
- Yellow—lemonade, banana, scrambled eggs, pineapple juice
- Purple—grape juice, plums, grape jelly

- Brown—chocolate pudding, brown bread, peanut butter, peanut butter cookies
- Orange—carrots, oranges, cheese
- Green—lettuce, pickles, limes

Spatial Children cut sandwich pieces into different shapes. Children identify the shapes of foods—long, short, round, small, curvy, straight.

Bodily Color pictures of fruits or vegetables. Provide tasks that involve pouring, cutting, spreading, or peeling. Have children practice pouring sand, rice, or water into cups at a water or sand table. Peel fruits (bananas are easy to start with; oranges and tangerines can also be used).

Musical Children pass a food (e.g., a potato) around a circle to music. When the music stops, the child holding the food must name it. Pair singing with movement.

Sing "Open, Shut Them" before snack.

Sing "I'm a Little Teapot."

Sing "Two Little Apples."

Sing "I Eat My Peas With Honey."

Two Little Apples

Away up high in the apple tree,

Two little apples
looked down at me.

So I shook that tree
as hard as I could,

Down came the apples,

Mm, they were good.

I Eat My Peas With Honey

I eat my peas with honey,

I've done it all my life.

I know it may seem funny,

But it keeps them on my knife.

Naturalist Set up a garden and grow simple fruits or vegetables. Plant seeds in the classroom. Children take the husks off corncobs. Discuss what foods come from what animals (e.g., eggs, milk, bacon). Discuss what foods come from plants (e.g., peas, green beans, carrots, potatoes). Show how foods can be eaten raw or cooked and how colors and taste may be different. Make a snowman out of marshmallows. Discuss what animals eat and what keeps plants alive.

16 Buddy Sandwich

Target Objectives
Increase self-help, social, cooperation, half, whole, turn-taking, sharing, sequencing

Developmental Domains
Fine Motor, Self-Help, Social, Language

Multiple Intelligences
Interpersonal, Spatial, Bodily, Intrapersonal

Materials
Bread, peanut butter, jelly, two dull knives.

Preparation/Set-Up
Table or countertop.

Procedures

1. Have children wash hands and tell them that they are going to work together to make a sandwich.

2. Have children select a partner and then make a sandwich together. One child puts the peanut butter on one piece of bread and the other child puts jelly on another piece of bread.

3. Have them put the sandwich together and assist them in cutting the sandwich in half as you point out the concepts of whole and half.

4. Talk with the children about how the foods look and smell.

5. Provide assistance as needed for younger children.

6. Each child gets half of the sandwich to eat.

Adaptations for Children With Disabilities

Physically assist children as necessary. Knifes with bigger grips or blades that are wider can help. Give children time to perform this task independently. Watch children to see where they have difficulty with this task.

Emotions and Individual Differences

The development of the sense of self is an important prerequisite for symbolic play. Children must have an understanding of who they are before they can pretend to be someone or something else. An awareness of feelings, and that other people have thoughts and feelings, is an important accomplishment for children. It is this awareness that children with autism, deafness, or mental retardation may not have developed yet.

17 Who Am I?

Target Objectives
Increase sense of self; recognize other people and their feelings

Developmental Domains
Cognitive, Social, Language

Multiple Intelligences
Intrapersonal, Interpersonal, Linguistic, Musical, Bodily

Materials
Mirrors and pictures of individual children and other people, including family, teachers, and students. Take pictures of children using instant cameras or digital cameras so that children can see the picture of themselves as soon as possible.

Preparation/Set-Up
All materials available in a small group area.

Procedures

1. Have children look at themselves in mirror and compare photographs of themselves and other children making different faces. Have them identify themselves by name.
2. Encourage use of personal pronouns such as "I," "me," and "mine."
3. Talk to children about different facial expressions and what they mean.
4. Sing "Me in the Mirror" while miming actions.

> **Me in the Mirror**
> I look in the mirror,
> And what do I see?
> I see myself there,
> Looking at me.
> Do I have a happy smile?
> Or am I sad today?
> No matter how I'm feeling,
> I'm terrific anyway.

Adaptations for Children With Disabilities

Children with developmental delays will need a lot of practice on these concepts. Children with autism or a hearing impairment may need a considerable amount of time in this activity. Show children pictures of themselves and help them to make statements of who it is (e.g., "That is me" or "I am smiling"). The use of personal pronouns is an important step toward symbolic play skills.

Directed Play

18 Feeling Faces

Target Objectives
Recognize facial body parts, recognize simple emotions on faces

Developmental Domains
Personal/Social, Language, Self-Help

Multiple Intelligences
Intrapersonal, Interpersonal, Linguistic, Musical, Bodily

Materials
Four-foot-long rectangular mirror, pictures of the children and/or familiar adults smiling and frowning.

Preparation/Set-Up
Arrange children in a small group so that everyone can look in a mirror. Have pictures available.

Procedures

1. With children in a small group, have each child stand in front of the mirror.
2. Have them point to and name eyes, ears, nose, mouth, eyebrows, and cheeks.
3. Make sure each child has a turn identifying for the group.
4. Have the children practice smiling and frowning in front of the mirror.
5. Have the children identify or name the feeling on one another's faces, as well as their own.
6. Point out how the mouth is shaped differently when we smile and when we frown.
7. Children can look in the mirror individually or as a group.
8. Have children say or sing, "We smile when we are happy, we frown when we are sad."
9. Conclude by singing "Feelings" while miming movements.

Feelings

Sometimes on my face you'll see

How I feel inside of me.

A smile means I'm happy, a frown means sad,

And when I grit my teeth, I'm mad.

When I'm proud I beam and glow,

But when I'm shy, my head hangs low.

Adaptations for Children With Disabilities

Use a checklist with columns marked happy and sad. Each time a child is asked to identify the emotion, mark on the checklist if they were correct or incorrect. You can also use the 0–5 data sheet to record the recognition or identification of different emotional expressions. Do this each day the activity is presented. Model facial expressions for them to imitate. Work individually with children as needed.

19   Make Me Laugh

(This game comes from Canada and uses the Inuit word for silence, *muk*.)

Target Objectives Emotional expressions, problem solving, concept of silence or quiet, laughing	**Materials** None. **Preparation/Set-Up** None.
Developmental Domains Social and Emotional, Language	
Multiple Intelligences Linguistic, Bodily, Intrapersonal, Interpersonal	

Procedures

1. Tell children that they are going to play a game that comes from Canada and that the game involves making people laugh.

2. Have all children sit in a circle. Ask for a volunteer and have the child move to the center of the circle.

3. Children in the circle say "*muk*" and then must remain silent and with a straight face.

4. The child in the middle of the circle is to try and make a child in the circle laugh by using only gestures or facial expressions.

5. Give different children an opportunity to sit in the middle of the circle and try to "break the *muk*."

Adaptations for Children With Disabilities

Give children suggestions for what they can do to try and make the others laugh. Model or imitate actions that get emotional reactions. Pair with pictures of funny things or events.

Directed *Play*

20 Happy Face Collage

Target Objectives
Identify body parts, cutting or tearing, emotions

Developmental Domains
Fine Motor, Personal/Social, Language

Multiple Intelligences
Spatial, Intrapersonal, Interpersonal, Musical, Bodily

Materials
Magazines and catalogs, scissors, glue sticks, paper.

Preparation/Set-Up
Children sitting at a table. Pictures can be pretorn from the magazines or precut for younger children.

Procedures

1. Arrange children in a group and tell them they are going to make pictures of happy faces using pictures in magazines.

2. Have them tear or cut pictures out of magazines of people with happy faces.

3. Glue or tape the pictures to create a happy face collage.

4. Once all children are finished, let each child show his or her collage to the other children. Note similarities and differences.

5. Conclude the activity by singing "Looking Glass" while miming actions. (Song can be adapted to include sad or angry.)

Adaptations for Children With Disabilities

Provide physical assistance with tearing or cutting pictures from magazines. Have pictures present and ready to glue. Adaptive scissors can be helpful. Draw circles or lines around faces on the magazine page. This allows for easier cutting around the heads. See the Murals section in Chapter Eight for a related activity.

Looking Glass

I looked in my looking glass.

What kind of face did I see?

I saw a happy face looking at me.

I guess I'm happy today.

21 Emotions in Action

Target Objectives
Emotions—happy, sad, afraid, surprised

Developmental Domains
Cognitive, Language, Social

Multiple Intelligences
Intrapersonal, Linguistic, Interpersonal

Materials
Pictures or drawings of facial expressions, large mirror.

Preparation/Set-Up
Prepared head and faces with Velcro˚.

Procedures

1. With children seated in a semicircle around you, show them pictures of facial emotions, including happy, sad, afraid, and surprised.

2. Be sure the pictures differ only by facial expression.

3. Name each picture and have children repeat after you.

4. Ask the children to name or identify what kinds of things make them happy, sad, scared, or surprised.

5. Children should try and demonstrate these feelings with face and body. Have children make these different facial expressions and actions while looking in a mirror or with a partner in a group.

6. Discuss physical responses, for example, heart racing when scared, crying when sad.

Adaptations for Children With Disabilities

Have a data sheet ready that lists each of the four emotional expressions. Each time a child is asked to identify or name the emotion, put a circle or "X" on the data sheet to record correct or incorrect responses. Provide extra time and practice on the expressions they have trouble with. This is an important activity for children with autism or Asperger syndrome. If children are sitting on the floor, make sure that no one is "W sitting." "W sitting" is when they sit with their legs behind them and to the side. Children who do this tend to do it too much, which may result in damage to hips and knees.

Directed Play

22 Making Faces

Target Objectives
Recognition of facial body parts, personal/social, fine motor skills

Developmental Domains
Cognitive, Social, Language, Self-Help

Multiple Intelligences
Spatial, Bodily, Logical, Linguistic

Materials
Assorted, precut, laminated eyes, nose, mouths, hair, ears, faces with Velcro® attached to the back.

Preparation/Set-Up
All materials readily available.

Procedures

1. Tell children seated in a small group on the floor or at a table that they are going to make different faces.

2. Give each child a precut blank "face" with Velcro® placed so that children can put on eyes, nose, mouth, ears, and hair.

3. All facial parts should be laminated so they can be used over again.

4. Have assorted precut facial body parts that children can attach to their "face."

5. Facial body parts include: blue, brown, and green eyes; two to three different shapes of noses; happy, sad, surprised, mad mouths; two to three different sizes of ears; and black, brown, red, and blond hair and hair pieces of different lengths and styles.

6. Each facial piece should have Velcro® attached to the back.

7. Let the children experiment in creating different faces. Encourage them to tell about the "people" they are creating.

8. To promote cultural awareness, have "faces" that are different shapes and colors.

9. This activity can also be adapted to include body parts instead of faces. Using the same procedures, children can mix and match different arms, legs, hands, feet, or heads.

10. Using a digital camera, the children take pictures of their newly created faces.

Adaptations for Children With Disabilities

Identify and repeat the names of facial body parts as children place them on the faces (e.g., "Those eyes are green eyes" or "That's long brown hair"). Give children an adequate amount of time to practice and explore different combinations. Keep track of names of body parts and colors and have children repeat the names of those they do not know.

23 Emotion Sort and Move

Target Objectives
Emotional expressions, categories, personal/social, moving to music, cooperation

Developmental Domains
Cognitive, Language, Social, Fine Motor

Multiple Intelligences
Logical, Musical, Interpersonal

Materials
Assorted pictures of faces with distinct emotional expressions. Be sure that the pictures differ only by facial expression.

Preparation/Set-Up
Pictures or drawings of emotions, mirror (optional).

Procedures

1. Tell children seated in a small group that you are going to talk about what we look like when we feel different emotions. Model different facial expressions for children to imitate.

2. Have children put pictures or drawings of faces into categories of happy, sad, surprised, and scared.

3. Follow the activity by singing, "If You're Happy and You Know It" while miming actions. Lyrics can be adapted for "sad."

4. Children can sit or stand in a circle to sing.

Adaptations for Children With Disabilities

Keep data on each child's ability to sort the pictures correctly. Make note of any emotion that gives them difficulty. Have children look in a mirror while they make different facial expressions. This is an important activity for children with autism or Asperger syndrome.

Why Are Bad Words Bad?

Target Objectives
Increase social awareness, meaning of words

Developmental Domains
Cognitive, Social, Language

Multiple Intelligences
Linguistic, Interpersonal, Intrapersonal

Materials
Children's book, *Elbert's Bad Word*.

Preparation/Set-Up
None.

Procedures

1. Arrange children in a small semicircle.

2. Tell the children that you are going to talk about bad words and explain that bad words are any word that makes someone feel bad.

3. Ask children to tell you any "bad words" that they know. This can include words such as "dummy," "shut up," "stupid," as well as profanity.

4. Be nonjudgmental when children say these words. Remember that children do not fully understand the meaning of these words. They have only heard these words and know that they cause a reaction by the listener.

5. For each of the words, tell them if it is a "bad" word or not. Again, tell the children that bad words make someone feel bad.

6. Read the children's book, *Elbert's Bad Word*, and discuss it. This book focuses on a boy who says a bad word.

Adaptations for Children With Disabilities

Some children will only use profanity when they are being punished or are angry. Give these children other words to say instead. Substitute words might include "darn it," "shucks," "golly gee," or "thunderbolt." Tell children in a matter-of-fact voice that "it is a bad word and I don't like bad words. Please do not use that word around me." You may need to focus on one or two words at first for some children. Children may choose their own substitute words, as long as they are not using them in a hurtful way.

25   **Bad Words Gone Forever**

Target Objectives
Story recall, bad word concept, decrease use of bad words

Developmental Domains
Language, Cognitive, Social

Multiple Intelligences
Linguistic, Intrapersonal, Interpersonal

Materials
Elbert's Bad Word book, drawing paper, washable markers or crayons.

Preparation/Set-Up
Have materials readily available.

Procedures

1. Gather in a small group and reread *Elbert's Bad Word*. Encourage children to recall facts before the story is read, then again after it is read.

2. Identify and name bad words they know. Then, substitute a word such as "darn" that would not make someone feel bad.

3. Move to the floor with drawing materials.

4. Give each child a paper and markers and have them identify and draw (scribble) a bad word, like in the book. Encourage them to describe what it looks or might feel like.

5. When done, the children wad up the papers and throw them away, thus getting rid of the bad word forever.

Adaptations for Children With Disabilities

Provide assistance as needed.

Directed Play

26 Girls and Boys

Target Objectives
Recognition of individual differences, following directions

Developmental Domains
Cognitive, Social, Language, Fine Motor

Multiple Intelligences
Linguistic, Intrapersonal, Interpersonal

Materials
None.

Preparation/Set-Up
Large open area.

Procedures

1. Tell children in a large group that they are going to play a game of girls and boys.

2. Divide the children into two groups, boys and girls, by first asking all the girls and then the boys to stand and move to one side of the room.

3. Take a moment to note individual differences between boys and girls, such as clothing or hairstyle or length.

4. Give simple one-step directions to each group, such as "Boys jump" or "Girls dance."

5. Make sure children in each group are doing what was directed and redirect if necessary.

6. Gradually increase the number of directions given to each group.

Adaptations for Children With Disabilities

In an informal manner, ask a child to point to all the boys and then all the girls. Provide assistance and correction as needed. Assist the child in identifying himself or herself as a boy or girl and pair the name with the sign for boy or girl. Differences based on gender are among the first that children are aware of, usually by age two. Awareness of racial or ethnic differences can occur by age three and differences based on disability by age four.

27 Same and Different People

Target Objectives
Knowledge of self, individual differences, self-esteem, understanding of groups.

Developmental Domains
Social, Cognitive, Language

Multiple Intelligences
Linguistic, Intrapersonal, Interpersonal

Materials
None.

Preparation/Set-Up
Children arranged in a large group.

Procedures

1. Tell children that you are going to play a game about how we are the same and different. The teacher will sort the children into groups. The children are to follow the directions by moving into an appropriate group.

2. Identify ways in which we can be the same and different. Start with something simple such as boys and girls. Have all the boys stand up and group together, then have all the girls stand up and group together. Have the children all sit back down in the group.

3. Continue the game by grouping in other same and different ways. These might include color or length of hair, skin color, color or type of clothing or types of shoes worn that day, who wears glasses and who does not, who has brothers and sisters and who does not, who lives in a house and who lives in an apartment, and who rides a bus and who does not.

4. Throughout this activity, be nonjudgmental. It is important to show children that the differences between us are not bad.

Adaptations for Children With Disabilities

Provide extra practice as needed on same and different concepts. Give children with visual impairments plenty of time to touch and explore faces. Help children to understand that differences are not bad.

Directed Play

28 Guess Who It Is

Target Objectives
Increase awareness of individual differences, discrimination abilities, recognition of people and things, disability awareness

Developmental Domains
Language, Social, Fine Motor

Multiple Intelligences
Intrapersonal, Interpersonal, Bodily, Spatial, Linguistic, Musical

Materials
Blindfold (optional).

Preparation/Set-Up
Large, open motor area, blindfold available.

Procedures

1. Arrange the children in a small group and tell them they are going to play a game of guessing who someone is without seeing him or her.

2. The children will take turns guessing who is standing beside them by just using touch.

3. Have one child volunteer to stand in the center of the group and shut their eyes or wear a blindfold.

4. Silently choose another child to stand beside the blindfolded child.

5. Help the child with the blindfold gently touch the other child and try to guess who it is.

6. Have children note such things as hair length or how tall another child is.

7. Repeat with other children until all children have participated. Follow up by discussing what the experience felt like.

8. Conclude the activity by singing "Eyes to See With" while miming actions.

Eyes to See With

Eyes to see with,

Ears to hear with,

Nose to smell with,

Teeth to chew.

Feet to run with,

Hands to work with,

I'm a lucky child,

Aren't you?

Adaptations for Children With Disabilities

Keep track of which children have the most difficulty with this task and give them extra opportunities to practice the skill. Pair children with an adult or familiar peer first before an unknown peer.

29 I Am Special

Target Objectives
Knowledge of self, family, individual differences, self-esteem

Developmental Domains
Social, Cognitive, Language

Multiple Intelligences
Linguistic, Intrapersonal, Interpersonal

Materials
Poster board, glue or tape.

Preparation/Set-Up
Children bring pictures of themselves to school.

Procedures

1. Have children bring pictures of themselves to school. Pictures should include both current pictures and pictures of the child at younger ages.

2. Create an "I am Special" board by gluing or taping the pictures to the poster board. Write the child's name on the board in large letters.

3. Show and discuss each "I am Special" board with the group. Hang it up to display.

Adaptations for Children With Disabilities

Keep data on how many things children say about themselves. Have children create an "I can" list of all the things they can do or things they can do now that they could not do when they were younger. When children are looking at pictures, help them to identify body parts, color of clothing, or other items. Identify other people in the pictures and what their relationship is to the child.

Directed Play

30 Drawing Self

Target Objectives
Recognize and draw body parts, recognition of self, understanding of individual differences

Developmental Domains
Fine Motor, Personal/Social, Language

Multiple Intelligences
Spatial, Linguistic, Interpersonal, Intrapersonal, Musical, Bodily

Materials
Drawing materials, construction paper or large bolt paper, crayons, chalk.

Preparation/Set-Up
Have drawing materials available.

Procedures

1. Tell children that they are going to draw a picture of themselves.
2. Give the children the drawing materials and let them begin.
3. Assist children as necessary in knowing what to draw (e.g., how many ears, eyes, and where they go).
4. As an alternative, children can take turns tracing one another with chalk while lying on paper or on the sidewalk.
5. Have the children draw in the details of the face and body.
6. When completed, let each child show his or her picture to the other children.
7. With children still arranged in a small group, sing and move to "I Clap My Hands."

I Clap My Hands

I clap my hands,
I touch my feet,
I jump up from the ground.
I clap my hands,
I touch my feet,
And turn myself around.
I clap my hands,
I touch my feet,
I sit myself back down.
I clap my hands,
I touch my feet,
I do not make a sound.

Adaptations for Children With Disabilities

Be sure to talk and describe what children are doing and identify all body parts and materials. Note how many body parts children draw and which ones have been left out. Provide extra time and practice to review the body parts. Use hand-over-hand assistance as needed. Younger children should only draw faces. Five-year-olds should be able to draw people with head, four limbs, and several facial body parts.

Home and Family

31. Family Pictures

> **Target Objectives**
> Recognition of people in pictures, differences in families, name family roles
>
> **Developmental Domains**
> Cognitive, Social, Language
>
> **Multiple Intelligences**
> Linguistic, Intrapersonal, Interpersonal, Musical
>
> **Materials**
> Have children bring pictures of family members.
>
> **Preparation/Set-Up**
> Pictures available.

Procedures

1. Tell children that you are going to talk about families.

2. Have children take turns showing pictures of their family to the other children and naming family members in the pictures using complete sentences. Then, have them name their relationship to that person.

3. Point out similarities and differences in families—brothers, sisters, grandparents, stepparents, aunts, uncles, mother, and father.

4. Conclude by singing and moving to "All Kinds of Families."

Adaptations for Children With Disabilities

Help children name family members in pictures and encourage them to use complete sentences. Keep data on how often children correctly name each family member. Provide extra practice naming those family members not named correctly. Model and imitate naming the pictures, the relationship of the person, or the event in the pictures.

All Kinds of Families

There are all kinds of families that I see,

Some are two and some are three.

Some are eight and some are four,

And some are more and more and more.

Directed Play

32. Drawing My Family

Target Objectives
Recognition and understanding of family members, understanding roles in a family, increase fine motor skills

Developmental Domains
Social, Fine Motor, Language, Cognitive

Multiple Intelligences
Spatial, Bodily, Interpersonal, Linguistic, Musical

Materials
Blank paper; crayons, markers, or paints.

Preparation/Set-Up
Drawing materials available.

Procedures

1. Give children drawing materials and tell them that they are going to draw a picture of their family.

2. Children draw pictures of their family. Encourage them to talk about the family members they are drawing and tell the names and relationships.

3. Label and display the pictures in the room.

4. Children can use paints instead of markers or crayons.

5. Let the children show and discuss their pictures with other children.

6. Conclude by singing "Some Families" while miming actions.

Adaptations for Children With Disabilities

Make sure children draw all members of their family. Point out size comparisons between adults and children. Encourage children to draw as many body parts as they can. Tape the paper to the table to assist children with physical disabilities.

Some Families

Some families are big,

Some families are small,

Some families are short,

Some families are tall.

Some families live close,

Some live far away.

But they all love each other,

In their own special way.

33 Rooms of the House

Target Objectives
Identify, name, and sort household rooms and objects; draw a picture of home.

Developmental Domains
Language, Cognitive, Social, Fine Motor

Multiple Intelligences
Linguistic, Logical, Spatial, Interpersonal

Materials
Pictures of homes showing various rooms in a house, paper and crayons or washable markers.

Preparation/Set-Up
Have materials readily available.

Procedures

1. With children seated on the floor around you, show pictures of different rooms in a house.

2. Name the rooms (kitchen, bedroom, bathroom, living room).

3. Talk about what people usually do in certain rooms (e.g., dining room for eating, bedroom for sleeping).

4. Identify and name specific objects found in each room (furniture, utensils) and tell what these things do.

5. Have the children discuss their homes and what kinds of furniture can be found in different rooms.

6. Finish by having children draw their own homes.

Adaptations for Children With Disabilities

Be sure children speak clearly and in complete sentences. Be nonjudgmental about what children say about their homes. Pair speech with signing for children who need it. Start with simple pictures for younger children and include pictures of items such as bathtubs, beds, and televisions.

Directed Play

34 Furniture Sorting

Target Objectives
Identification and use of objects, categories

Developmental Domains
Cognitive, Language

Multiple Intelligences
Linguistic, Interpersonal, Bodily

Materials
A wide variety of toy furniture, blocks, doll-house, and toy people.

Preparation/Set-Up
Toy furniture available, set up "rooms" out of blocks or use a commercial dollhouse.

Procedures

1. Have a small group of children sit on the floor. Tell them that they are to look at different pieces of furniture then put them in the rooms of the house in which they belong.

2. The children name, sort, and play with assorted toy furniture and items.

3. Point out what is similar and different about pieces of furniture, such as size, color, or function.

4. Next, have the children sort the items by room.

5. Toy people can be added to furniture.

6. Some children will associate some pieces of furniture with certain rooms more than others.

Adaptations for Children With Disabilities

Keep data on recognition of and use of objects for individual children using the 0–5 data sheet with all furniture names listed. Use familiar furniture such as bed, chair, or table with young children.

35 House Play

Target Objectives
Identification and use of objects, pretend play, personal/social

Developmental Domains
Cognitive, Language, Social

Multiple Intelligences
Linguistic, Interpersonal, Bodily

Materials
House props, chairs, bedding, kitchen items, cardboard box (optional).

Preparation/Set-Up
Two or three children in a dramatic play area.

Procedures

1. Have a small group of children play "house" using furniture in the classroom and other materials, such as dishes, blankets, or a cardboard box painted to look like a TV or cut so that a child could get inside and pretend to be on TV.

2. Help children assume different roles in a family (i.e., mommy, daddy, baby).

3. Try to have enough space to make at least two rooms in a house and have adequate props for each room (e.g., kitchen items in the kitchen, pillows and blankets in the bedroom).

4. Encourage children to act out typical daily activities such as cooking, cleaning, or caring for children.

5. Make statements to guide the play rather than asking questions.

Adaptations for Children With Disabilities

Some children with speech difficulties may be hard to understand when speaking. Adults should serve as translators to help other children know what is being said. Adults should assume a role as a family member in the play. Encourage imitation in chores and role-playing. Provide a script to be played often for any student with significant communication or behavior needs.

Directed Play

36 House Collage

Target Objectives
Identification and use of objects, increase cutting and tearing skills, cultural diversity

Developmental Domains
Personal/Social, Fine Motor, Language

Multiple Intelligences
Linguistic, Bodily, Interpersonal, Spatial

Materials
Magazines, glue sticks, construction paper, scissors.

Preparation/Set-Up
Some pictures can be precut for younger children.

Procedures

1. Have a small group of children sit at a table. Tell them they are going to cut out pictures to make a house collage.

2. Using magazines, have children cut or tear out pictures of rooms in a variety of homes.

3. Glue pictures to construction paper to make a house.

4. Provide pictures of people, especially children, to cut out. These pictures can also be taken from clothing or department store circulars and catalogs. Pictures should reflect a variety of ages, gender, and races for children to choose from to help promote self-awareness and cultural diversity.

5. Have children glue the pictures of people to their home.

6. Children can make a variety of homes with different people living in them.

7. Let children show their pictures to other children.

Adaptations for Children With Disabilities

Provide physical assistance as needed. Tape the construction paper to the table to increase stability. Have some pictures precut or have circles around the items to be cut. Make sure the page is torn from the magazine before trying to cut out an item. See the Fine Motor chapter for other construction activities.

37 Miniature House

Target Objectives
Awareness of body in space, spatial and positional concepts, cooperation, construction

Developmental Domains
Gross and Fine Motor, Cognitive, Language

Multiple Intelligences
Bodily, Spatial, Logical, Linguistic, Musical

Materials
A miniature house made from a cardboard box or a commercially available toy house, Legos®.

Preparation/Set-Up
Cardboard "house" should be precut and painted. Have Lego® or Duplo® blocks ready to use.

Procedures

1. Arrange children in two groups of three. Tell them they are going to build houses.

2. Using a large, oven-sized cardboard box or commercially available toy house, "miniaturize" the house environment.

3. Show the children how the walls, ceiling, and floors connect.

4. Let the children run their hands along the walls to feel the connections and the openings of the windows and doors.

5. Identify and name concepts such as corner, sides, top and bottom, floor and ceiling.

6. This is an important spatial activity for children with visual impairments or motor planning needs.

7. Follow this activity by using Legos® to build a house with walls, floors, ceilings, doors, and windows. Use Legos® rather than wooden blocks because they lock together.

8. Conclude the activity by singing "My House" while miming actions.

> ### My House
>
> I'm going to build a little house
>
> With windows big and bright
>
> With chimney tall and curling smoke
>
> Drifting out of sight.
>
> In winter when the snowflakes fall,
>
> Or when I hear a storm,
> (cup hands over ears)
>
> I'll go sit in my little house
>
> Where I'll be safe and warm.
> (arms across chest)

Directed Play   112

Adaptations for Children With Disabilities

Give children time to explore and manipulate the "room" and the blocks. Rather than asking, "What is this?" say "door" or "window" while pointing to it and something about its size or shape. Have children imitate what is being modeled to them. This is an extremely important activity for children with severe visual impairments. It allows them to begin to develop an awareness of their surroundings.

Sociodramatic Play

The development of symbolic ("pretend") play is linked to several areas of development including language and social/emotional skills. Hence, both language and social/emotional development need to be considered when trying to promote symbolic play. Included here are suggestions on how to promote symbolic play.

Sense of Self

One of the first things that can be done to help promote the development of pretend play is to help children develop a sense of self, that is, to help children see themselves as separate individuals. Erikson (1963) referred to this as "autonomy," and it is an extremely important social/emotional and developmental milestone. Children cannot pretend to be something or someone else if they do not first have a sense of self.

The "negativeness" often associated with the behavior of children around two years of age, characterized by a child constantly saying "no," is actually a very important accomplishment. Although this age can be a trying time for parents and caregivers, it is important that children begin to see themselves as individuals and demonstrate autonomy.

At around 18 months of age, children will begin to refer to themselves as individuals by saying "I," "me," or "mine." When they use these personal pronouns they are demonstrating that they have developed a sense of self. The development of a sense of self is an important prerequisite for the development of pretend play abilities.

Ways to Promote a Sense of Self

One of the ways parents and caregivers can promote a sense of self in a child is to make use of dolls. Dolls should be selected that are as similar as possible in appearance to the child. Having children identify body parts on dolls and then on themselves is a way to promote an awareness of self. Children can also be encouraged to wash or bathe and then dress the dolls.

A second way to promote a sense of self is to encourage children to refer to themselves while talking. For example, instead of a young child saying, "Want milk," a parent can prompt the child to say, "I want milk." The use of personal pronouns such as "me" or "mine" can also be modeled by parents or caregivers while talking. The use of personal pronouns is an important indicator that children do see themselves as unique individuals.

A third way to promote a sense of self is to have children look at themselves in a mirror. Parents or teachers can ask the child to identify body parts or even the emotions associated with certain facial expressions while looking in a mirror. It should be recognized, however, that individuals from certain ethnic or religious backgrounds might not want their children to look in a mirror.

Understanding Symbols

Another important way to promote the development of symbolic play skills is to help children develop a sense of symbols and what they represent. To do this, children should first be presented with real objects. Once they can identify real objects, parents and caregivers can expose them to play materials or pictures that represent these real objects. By matching the real object with a pretend object, we are helping the child develop a mental symbol of that object. Matching objects with symbols is important for symbolic play as well as for augmentative communication. For a child to make use of augmentative communication systems, they must be able to understand different symbols and how they are a part of communication.

Toys and Play Materials

There are two considerations regarding toys and playthings in symbolic play: how realistic toys are and their degree of structure. The level of symbolic play observed in children is influenced by these factors. For children who have not yet developed symbolic play skills, there is a greater need for toys that are very realistic in appearance. Children who do not have symbolic play skills will find it difficult to play in symbolic ways with toys that are not realistic in appearance. The ability to play with less realistic objects increases with age. It has been noted that when a group of two-year-olds was provided with two toy props, one realistic and one not, only the realistic object was used. When both of the toy props were unrealistic, the children could not perform the play behavior (Mann, 1984).

As a child's pretend play abilities increase, toys that are less realistic can gradually be introduced. Many realistic toys are available for children, including cars and trucks, baby blankets and pillows, garage and farm toys, toy telephones, and dolls. Gradually, parents and teachers can introduce less realistic or structured play materials. At the same time they can demonstrate or model novel uses for these play materials or combine toys in new and different ways.

The degree of structure of toys also must be considered. Highly structured toys, such as dolls or tea sets, tend to produce more dramatic play with younger children than less structured toys such as blocks or boxes (Rubin & Howe, 1985). Initially, young children will need structured toys to begin to learn how to play in symbolic ways. As their symbolic play skills develop, teachers or parents can gradually introduce less structured play materials.

Directed Play

It should not be assumed from the above discussion that a great deal of money is needed for realistic or structured toys. Rather, teachers or parents should be aware of what toys children are playing with and how structured or realistic those toys are. It may be possible, for example, to draw pictures on a cardboard box to increase the degree of realism for a child.

Role Playing

Another strategy to help promote pretend play among children is role playing. Teachers, parents, or older siblings can involve a young child in role-play activities, such as fire station or doctor's office. Children need a good model to imitate. It is important to have a more "sophisticated play partner" in helping younger children develop symbolic play skills (Gowen, 1995). The active involvement of caregivers can increase both the duration and maturity of the pretend play observed in children.

A way to use role playing to promote pretend play is to assign each person a role to play. Young children will need assistance in understanding their role. They will need instruction on what to say and what to do, and this can be modeled for the child. Caregivers can also imitate and extend what the child is doing, such as picking up and pretending to drink from a cup after a child picks up a cup. Parents or teachers can make comments or suggestions about what the child is doing. They should ask open-ended questions ("What things can we make to eat?") instead of simple yes/no questions ("Do you want to cook some food?").

Symbolic play themes involving role playing can also be developed following field trips to places such as the grocery store or a construction site (see the Thematic chapter for examples). Toys and play materials similar to those seen on the field trip can be provided so that children have an opportunity to model what they have seen. Parents, teachers, or older siblings can take a role in this play to help direct the younger children.

38 Grocery Store

(This can be an elaborate activity if set up to its fullest extent. It should be repeated several times with children assuming different roles.)

Target Objectives
Identification and use of objects, community awareness, socialization, sustained cooperative play with peers

Developmental Domains
Cognitive, Social, Language, Fine Motor, Gross Motor

Multiple Intelligences
Linguistic, Interpersonal, Logical, Bodily

Materials
Assorted food/drink containers, cash register, play money with purse or wallet, grocery cart or basket, sacks, smock or apron for checker/stocker, premade grocery list or laminated pictures of objects paired with words.

Preparation/Set-Up
Prepare the area for the grocery store. This play area should be set up for at least a week. Various empty food containers, boxes, etc. should be collected and displayed on shelves in an "aisle." Use objects children are familiar with and provide scripts if needed.

Procedures

1. One child will be the checkout clerk in charge of the cash register, another child will "stock the shelves," and two other children can be customers.

2. Take time to talk to each child about his or her role. Provide scripts and practice as needed.

3. The "customers" should talk with the adult about what kinds of foods to buy for meals, and a shopping list can be created from the laminated pictures.

4. The children will "go shopping," pay for the foods, sack the foods, and take them home.

5. The child stocking the shelves should have enough supplies to restock after the children shop.

6. Children take turns in each of the roles as they become more familiar with the activity.

7. Teachers should assign roles initially, and then have children take turns in each role.

8. This activity works best with four children in a group.

Directed *Play* 116

Adaptations for Children With Disabilities

Assist children in knowing what to do and say through modeling and scripted dialogue. Let children play the same role several times. Be sure children speak clearly and in complete sentences. Velcro® can be placed on the back of the laminated pictures and on a piece of cardboard so that children can create their shopping list. An adult should assume a role in the play and model actions or words that children can imitate.

39 Shoe Store

Target Objectives
Increase community awareness, self-help skills, sustained cooperative play and dressing skills, use of language

Developmental Domains
Social, Self-Help, Language, Cognitive

Multiple Intelligences
Interpersonal, Linguistic, Bodily, Intrapersonal, Logical

Materials
Various shoes and shoeboxes, chairs, money, cash register, and telephone. Something to measure foot size would also be an excellent addition. It may be possible to get old shoes from families.

Preparation/Set-Up
Have various types and sizes of shoes and shoeboxes available; some shoes can be placed in the shoeboxes. Arrange chairs like a shoe store. Numbers representing the cost of the shoes can be posted on the boxes. Use scripts if needed.

Procedures

1. With children in a small group, discuss briefly what a shoe store is and show pictures of a shoe store if available.

2. Divide the group into customers and shoe store staff and discuss what each is to do. If two adults are present have one adult with the staff and one with the customers. Provide a script if needed.

3. Have the "customers" try on different shoes with the assistance of the store "clerk." Make statements about the size, color, or style of the shoes.

4. When the customers have found the shoes they want they should pay for them.

5. Have children trade roles and repeat.

6. Repeat the play activity over the period of two weeks.

Adaptations for Children With Disabilities

Children with speech disorders may not speak clearly. Adults should be present to help "translate" if needed. This activity can be introduced and practiced with one or two children and the teacher prior to being done with the whole group. Encourage imitation of simple words and phrases and pair with sign language as needed. Let children try to resolve conflicts on their own before intervening.

40 Camp Out

Target Objectives
Recognition and use of objects, self-help, cooperative play

Developmental Domains
Social, Cognitive, Language, Fine Motor, Gross Motor

Multiple Intelligences
Linguistic, Interpersonal, Naturalist, Bodily, Musical

Materials
Assorted camping materials such as flashlights, blankets, blocks, backpacks, cups, frying pan, "fishing poles" (optional).

Preparation/Set-Up
Gather together materials. A real tent would be a nice addition, but putting a blanket over a table can easily substitute. Children will enjoy the privacy of the tent and may fight over who gets to be in the tent. Have one tent for every two children.

Procedures

1. Have children "hike" to their campsite, gather wood (blocks) for the fire, cook, and rest.

2. The children make up their campsite by setting up the tent, spreading out blankets or sleeping bags, and using blocks to make a campfire. Sit in a circle around the "campfire" and sing "Going on a Bear Hunt"[**Okay that lyrics are not provided?**] while miming actions.

3. Let children pretend to sleep, get up, and build a fire to cook.

4. Near the end of the activity children should gather together all materials and "hike" out.

5. As an added activity children can catch "fish" to cook.

6. For variation, children can hike outside to gather firewood (sticks) or set up real tents outdoors.

7. Let children collect rocks, sticks, and leaves.

8. While playing, point out concepts, such as same and different, colors and shapes, long and short, hard and soft.

9. Records or tapes of environmental or animal sounds can be played to add to the realism.

10. Reorganize the group of children and talk about going on a campout. As a related activity talk about what children should do if they get lost.

11. Repeat the play activity several times over a two-week period.

Adaptations for Children With Disabilities

Make statements to guide the play rather than asking questions. This activity will provide an opportunity for children to work on conflict resolution skills. In most conflicts, children will fight over possessions, so make sure there are enough props for all children. Prior training or practice may be needed for some children. Praise children for sharing and turn-taking. Provide scripts of what to say if needed.

Castle Play

Target Objectives
Pretend play, social interactions, sustained cooperative play

Developmental Domains
Language, Social, Cognitive, Fine Motor, Gross Motor

Multiple Intelligences
Linguistic, Interpersonal, Spatial, Bodily

Materials
A good castle with knights is available from Little Tikes® toys.

Preparation/Set-Up
Large motor area with toys accessible to children.

Procedures

1. This is a good activity for fantasy play. Have a group of two or three children play with the castle toys at the same time.

2. In a related activity, have children build a castle out of blocks. Set up roles and allow the children to pretend.

3. Use knight action figures and incorporate farm animals to extend the play.

Adaptations for Children With Disabilities

Adult assistance should be provided as needed. Adults should be present to encourage cooperative play rather than solitary or parallel play. Model appropriate actions and words for children to imitate.

42 Rocket Ship

Target Objectives
Pretend play, social interactions, sustained cooperative play

Developmental Domains
Cognitive, Language, Fine Motor, Social

Multiple Intelligences
Linguistic, Interpersonal, Spatial, Bodily

Materials
Larger cardboard boxes of different sizes, tape, paints (optional).

Preparation/Set-Up
Have three cardboard boxes ready to put together for a "rocket ship."

Procedures

1. Build a "rocket ship" out of three cardboard boxes.

2. Put a larger box on the bottom and a slightly smaller one on top.

3. Use tape to taper the top to look more like a point.

4. Have children paint or decorate their rocket ship. Cut holes in the side for view ports.

5. Have a rocket ship for every two children.

6. Encourage children to pretend that they have flown in and landed on a new planet or the moon.

Adaptations for Children With Disabilities

Provide adult assistance as necessary. Help children with what to do and say about "flying" a rocket ship. For children having difficulty engaging in cooperative play with others, reduce the number of children in the group or start by pairing children with only one other child. Provide scripts of what to say as needed. See the Murals section in Chapter Eight for a related activity.

Cooperative Play

 I Can't, but We Can

Target Objectives
Cooperation, socialization, problem solving

Developmental Domains
Gross Motor, Language, Social

Multiple Intelligences
Bodily, Interpersonal, Linguistic

Materials
Various and common materials.

Preparation/Set-Up
Large motor area with a soft surface. Be sure children have shoes on.

Procedures

1. Teaching children to cooperate is important in play and life. Simple activities can help to promote an "I Can't, but We Can" understanding.

2. Activities might include: using a plastic grocery sack with two handles to carry a heavy load like canned goods or sand, carrying sand or water in a large watering can or a five-gallon paint container, pushing a trike up an incline, pulling a heavy object with a rope, or having two children use straws to blow a beach ball across the room. Have a variety of materials brought from home or found in the classroom.

3. Have a child try to do the task alone. This should be set up so that it is difficult or nearly impossible for them to do it successfully.

4. Next pair them with a peer and explain how if they work together they can get the task done successfully.

5. Explain that by working together the children can do something that they cannot do alone.

6. Look for instances of children cooperating together in the classroom and praise the children.

Adaptations for Children With Disabilities

Pair children with supportive peers. Provide assistance as needed. Praise children for working together.

One Piece at a Time

Target Objectives
Cooperation, interdependence, turn-taking, problem solving, fine motor skills

Developmental Domains
Fine Motor, Language, Social

Multiple Intelligences
Linguistic, Interpersonal, Spatial, Bodily, Musical

Materials
Large 10–12 piece floor puzzle.

Preparation/Set-Up
Large open floor area.

Procedures

1. Arrange children in a small group. Tell them they are going to work to put a puzzle together.

2. Give each child one or two pieces of a 10–12 piece floor puzzle and make sure that each child knows that he or she has at least one piece of the puzzle.

3. Children hold their puzzle piece(s) and take turns finding where their piece of puzzle goes.

4. Children take turns until the puzzle is finished. Make statements to reward them for waiting their turn. Discuss what they needed to do to complete this task (e.g., waiting, taking turns, helping each other).

5. Repeat several times with children getting different puzzle pieces and give children turns to be the last one to put a piece in.

6. Conclude by singing and moving to "Being a Good Helper."

Adaptations for Children With Disabilities

Give children time to find where each piece goes. Encourage children to help one another but not to interfere. Make a solid-line outline of where the pieces go if needed. Some children will have a difficult time waiting for their turn. Praise them for waiting and taking turns. Pair children with patient peers or with an adult.

Being a Good Helper

Being a good helper

Is lots of fun to do.

It makes others happy

And makes me happy too.

When the job is finished,

My friends say "Thank you,"

And I say "You're welcome,

I'm glad I could help you."

Directed Play

Towers Together

> **Target Objectives**
> Cooperation, eye-hand coordination, pincer grasp, one-to-one correspondence, turn-taking, problem solving
>
> **Developmental Domains**
> Cognitive, Social, Fine Motor
>
> **Multiple Intelligences**
> Spatial, Interpersonal, Linguistic, Bodily
>
> **Materials**
> 10–12 wood or cardboard blocks per child depending on age.
>
> **Preparation/Set-Up**
> Floor or table depending on size of blocks.

Procedures

1. Tell a small group of children with assorted blocks that they are going to work together to build a tower as high as they can. Have children take turns placing their block on a "starter" block.

2. Have children take turns putting their block on top to make a tower. The purpose is to get the tower as tall as possible before it falls.

3. Repeat the activity three or four times and have different children start. An adult should take turns placing blocks as well for modeling and imitation.

4. As children are building their tower, point out concepts such as first, next, tall, and balance.

5. Follow up by having children build their own towers.

Adaptations for Children With Disabilities

Larger blocks will be easier to stack than smaller ones and should be available for younger children. Provide physical assistance as needed. Praise children who are waiting for their turn. Fewer children in a group will reduce the time children have to wait.

46 Buddy Drawing

Target Objectives
Increase socialization, fine motor skills, cooperation, problem solving, turn-taking

Developmental Domains
Fine Motor, Social, Language

Multiple Intelligences
Spatial, Linguistic, Interpersonal, Intrapersonal

Materials
Sheets of blank paper, crayons or washable markers.

Preparation/Set-Up
Have materials available; tape the paper to the table if necessary.

Procedures

1. Let children choose a partner and have them sit side by side. Tell them that they are to work together to draw a picture. Choose partners for the children if necessary due to age or ability.

2. Children draw a picture by taking turns. Each draws part of the picture using crayons or washable markers.

3. Younger children will need assistance in working together and problem solving.

4. It might be helpful to have them try and imitate or trace a picture, such as a house, rather than draw something from their own imagination.

Adaptations for Children With Disabilities

Children with visual impairments will need solid, thick, black boundaries, contrast, and larger size. Children with communication disorders may not talk while doing art and will need encouragement to talk about what they are drawing. Praise children for working together. Provide hand-over-hand assistance as needed. Watch for appropriate grasp and hand preference. Typical four-year-olds should be able to engage in cooperative play and to work together in a meaningful way. Assist with any peer conflicts.

Other examples of activities to promote socialization, turn-taking, and cooperative play include card games such as Old Maid, Go Fish, or Slap Jack, and board games such as Candy Land°, Lotto°, and Hungry Hungry Hippo°. Adults should assume a player's role in these games and provide guidance as needed.

Directed *Play*

Disability Awareness

If mainstreaming and inclusion efforts are going to be successful it is essential that typically-developing young children have some awareness of disabilities. Young children are aware of individual differences in other children and this awareness seems to follow a developmental trend. For example, most young children are aware of differences based on gender by age two, differences based on race by age three, and differences based on disability by age four.

Common disability awareness activities can include having children take turns being blindfolded and guided by another child around the room or having children take turns in a wheelchair or using crutches. Children can also be instructed to close their eyes and tell what they hear. Have children do this indoors and outdoors.

There are a number of sign language books, videos, and computer programs. Young children will enjoy learning something about sign language. There are also a number of children's books that can be used to help young children understand disabilities. For example, Woodbine House publishes books such as *Shelly, the Hyperactive Turtle*, *Lee, the Rabbit With Epilepsy*, and *Andy and His Yellow Frisbee*, a book that describes a boy with autism.

Eye Doctor, Glasses

Target Objectives
Disability awareness, community awareness, sustained cooperative play

Developmental Domains
Personal/Social, Language

Multiple Intelligences
Intrapersonal, Interpersonal, Linguistic

Materials
Various eyeglass frames, vision chart or pictures of familiar objects, chairs, and mirrors. A simple vision chart can be created on cardboard, using pictures or drawings of common objects, such as a birthday cake, a car, or a bird.

Preparation/Set-Up
Have materials available; tape the paper to the table if necessary. Arrange a chair for a child to sit in to get an "eye examination." Have various eyeglass frames arranged to resemble what would be found in a store for glasses.

Procedures

1. Set up an optometrist's office with a group of three children.

2. Have one child be the eye doctor, one the receptionist, and one the patient.

3. Have the receptionist greet the patient and then have the optometrist give the patient an eye examination by having the child look at a vision chart. Model appropriate language for the children to imitate.

4. Once done, have the patient try on different frames while looking in a mirror.

5. Have the children change roles and repeat. A fourth role of a parent can also be added.

6. While children are trying on frames, introduce some of the frames adapted to show examples of visual impairments. For example, have lenses restricted to a tunnel vision or use lenses that makes things look fuzzy.

7. Discuss with children that some people do not see well, that many people wear glasses, and that people who do not see find other ways to be independent.

Adaptations for Children With Disabilities

Physically assist children in putting glasses on. Some children will not like having the glasses on. Have frames that are firm but easy to move. Give children time to look through the lenses and to look at themselves in a mirror. Provide a picture sequence if needed.

48 Trust Walk

Target Objectives
Trust, cooperation, kindness, helping, safety

Developmental Domains
Cognitive, Language, Social

Multiple Intelligences
Logical, Spatial, Bodily, Linguistic, Intrapersonal, Interpersonal

Materials
Bandanna or scarf.

Preparation/Set-Up
Large motor area free of obstacles.

Procedures

1. In a small group of children, let children choose a partner. Tell them that they are going to work together. One child will have a blindfold and the other child will lead them around the room.

2. Let children decide who will go first. Tie the scarf or bandanna around the eyes of one of the children.

3. Have the other child guide the blindfolded child carefully around the room.

4. Stress to the children how important it is to be careful and watch them closely.

5. Have the children trade roles and repeat.

6. Follow up by asking children what it felt like not being able to see.

7. In a related, but more difficult, activity, have one child guide another around the room by only giving verbal directions. The child with the blindfold must listen and follow the directions of the speaker. This will require some knowledge of left and right. Children should use simple, one-step commands like "Take two steps forward."

Adaptations for Children With Disabilities

Provide physical assistance as necessary. Walk close to the children. Some children will not be comfortable with a blindfold, so allow them to complete the activity without the blindfold.

Hear Not

Target Objectives
Disability awareness, coping, problem solving

Developmental Domains
Language, Cognitive, Social

Multiple Intelligences
Linguistic

Materials
TV and video player, chairs or carpet squares.

Preparation/Set-Up
Large motor area with TV and VCR.

Procedures

1. This activity is designed to promote an awareness of deafness.

2. Have children watch a short familiar movie on the VCR.

3. Once completed, rewind it and have them watch it again with the sound turned off.

4. Ask the children if they still know what is going on and what is being said. Repeat with the sound turned on, then off again.

5. Watch another short movie that is unknown to the children.

6. Have them watch it again without the sound and have them discuss what is going on.

7. Encourage children to look at the mouth movements or body language of the actors or cartoon characters to help them determine what is said.

Adaptations for Children With Disabilities

Use this activity as an opportunity to discuss body language and metacommunication signals. Point out facial expressions or other visual cues that we use to help us understand other people. This is known as metacommunication and is an important interpersonal skill for children to learn. For example, a smiling face and open hands can indicate fun, rough-and-tumble play, whereas a frowning face and closed fists may indicate aggression. When watching something on TV, use the pause button to allow time to look at expressions or actions. Practice actions again.

50 Different Voices

Target Objectives
Recognition of speech sounds, types of voices, auditory processing and discrimination

Developmental Domains
Language, Social

Multiple Intelligences
Linguistic, Interpersonal, Intrapersonal

Materials
Tape recorder (optional).

Preparation/Set-Up
None.

Procedures

1. Have a small group of children take turns making different sounds with their mouths.

2. This is a good activity for children with speech disorders and to help other children understand differences in speech.

3. Let children experiment with different voices, like soft, loud, gruff, sweet, low, or high-pitched. Also, use silly words and sounds for fun.

4. As an adaptation, and if equipment is available, have children listen to different voices produced by augmentative communication devices or record the voices on a computer or tape recorder.

Adaptations for Children With Disabilities

If a child is using an electronic augmentative communication device it will produce speech that can sometimes be difficult to understand. Children will need exposure to this speech to better understand it. Words will be easier to understand than individual letters, and sentences will be easier to understand than words.

Directed Play   128

51 Sign Language

Target Objectives
Associate sign language and finger spelling with words and concepts, understand individual differences, increase socialization.

Developmental Domains
Cognitive, Language, Social, Fine Motor

Multiple Intelligences
Linguistic, Interpersonal, Intrapersonal, Bodily

Materials
Sign language books and picture cards. Sign language books can include *Signing Exact English* or *American Sign Language*.

Preparation/Set-Up
Have reference books available.

Procedures

1. Use reference books to teach some rudimentary sign language. Sign language is one of the major methods of instructing children who are deaf. For such children, sign language is an important functional skill.

2. All children would benefit from learning something about sign language. It is an important and easy way to increase the likelihood that children with and without hearing impairments will play together. Learning sign language is fun for children and can be helpful in communicating with many peers.

Adaptations for Children With Disabilities

Select familiar words or signs for children. Make the vocabulary functional. Practice using the sign to get a response such as "eat" and then give the child food. Pair speech with signs throughout the day.

52   Cognitive Mapping

Target Objectives
Increase sensitivity to blindness, awareness of body in space

Developmental Domains
Cognitive, Language, Fine Motor, Gross Motor

Multiple Intelligences
Spatial, Bodily, Linguistic, Musical

Materials
Blindfolds.

Preparation/Set-Up
Be sure the environment is free from dangerous objects, such as steps or items sticking out from shelves.

Procedures

1. Have children arranged in a small group.
2. Tell them they are to move around the room but will wear a blindfold.
3. Point out to children where things such as tables and chairs are located.
4. Have one or two children at a time put the blindfolds on. Children might also use hats or dark glasses.
5. With proper supervision, have them move about the classroom slowly.
6. Have them say and identify what they touch as they move around the room.
7. Have them count the number of steps they take from one place in the room to another.
8. Have them identify any sounds in the environment that help them to know where they are.
9. Let each child in the group have two or three turns.
10. Reorganize the group and discuss what it was like to move around without being able to see. Ask children what they had to do to remember where they were and what was around them.
11. Conclude by singing and moving to " I Have a Friend Who Cannot See."

I Have a Friend Who Cannot See

I have a friend

Who cannot see,

But can play the spoons

Upon his knee.

I have a friend

Who cannot walk

But can tell where you're from

By the way you talk.

Adaptations for Children With Disabilities

Provide assistance as necessary. Have children pull a toy or wagon around barriers rather than just walking around.

Buddies

The concept of a "buddy" is not new. For many years, summer camps, swimming pools, and schools have used this kind of system. It is a way to pair children for togetherness and safety. The word buddy is easily understood and is a friendly term that is easily accepted by children of all ages. Buddies are two or more children who work and play together. As applied here, it is similar in concept to peer tutoring.

A buddy is a same-aged or older peer who demonstrates empathy for others. This child is cooperative in nature and possesses good communication abilities. The buddy is a friend who helps others through the guidance and direction of an adult. It is likely that the buddy will be a same-sexed peer, but this is not required. What is important is that the buddy be willing and able to assist another child. Older buddies may be children with disabilities who can earn the opportunity to work and play with a younger student. For example, a fifth-grader with learning disabilities could earn the right to be a buddy for a kindergarten-age child by completing homework assignments. The older child would come to the kindergarten room once or twice a day to interact with the younger child. This system is good for both children. The younger child gets a friend and mentor. The older child is seen as competent and this helps to increase his or her self-esteem.

Any child who has difficulty completing routines or is getting into trouble within a group would be a candidate for a buddy. These children often require considerable adult attention, which may be minimized by having a buddy available to assist them. The buddy may help the child stay on-task, provide needed support, and teach in ways adults cannot.

Buddies can be used anywhere and everywhere. The original intent of our buddies was to aid the successful inclusion of children with special needs into the general education setting. However, it quickly grew into other ideas and programs because of its success. Examples of how buddies can be used include:

Lunch Buddies: Younger children with or without disabilities are paired with older children for lunch. After lunch they have an opportunity to work and play together. This can assist the younger children in learning appropriate social and self-help skills.

Classroom Buddies: An age-level peer is assigned and trained to assist another child who shows a need for support within the classroom.

Bus Buddies: An older peer is assigned to sit with a younger child on the bus. The older child likely will live in the same neighborhood as the younger child and can provide support and safety. A bus buddy may be the same child as the lunch buddy.

Playground Buddies: Peers are assigned and trained to play themes or games with identified younger peers who need support on the playground.

Chapter 7

Motor and Movement Activities

Motor and Movement	133
General Activities	136
Games With Rules	159
Yoga and the Young Child	170

Motor and Movement

Using and practicing gross motor skills are natural parts of play. Motor and movement activities can be conducted indoors or outdoors. Most outdoor play does involve motor and movement as children run, climb, ride tricycles, or play in sand. Motor activities usually require a great deal of space, so, if you cannot get outside, find a large room, gym, or hallway without a constant traffic flow. Ecological theory teaches us that children will naturally want to engage in large-muscle activities in large spaces. Children should be provided with considerable freedom in motor activities. However, more structured or Directed Play activities can be used to help children learn and practice specific skills. Motor activities are structured by the materials or equipment present, so use these materials to foster the skills you want to develop.

Motor and movement activities need to address body awareness, coordination, balance, endurance, flexibility, and strength. Activities should include no fewer than two of these areas; see **Table 7.1** for examples in each category. It is quite easy to combine motor skills in well-organized activities. However, children with motor difficulties may only be able to work on one skill in isolation at a time. While implementing motor activities throughout the day, keep in mind that they should be developmentally appropriate, motivating, and achievable for all children involved. Physical or occupational therapists can provide assistance with most motor activities and should be consulted as needed.

It is easy to incorporate music into many different motor activities. Fostering movement, dancing, or marching in parades are all ways in which music can be incorporated into motor and movement. A wide variety of music is available for young children.

Children with physical disabilities, visual impairments, or mental retardation may have some difficulties during motor activities. They may tire easily, experience confusion or frustration coordinating movements, and have limitations in strength or balance. It may be necessary to give them more time to complete activities as well as additional practice in a private setting with one-to-one attention. Physical assistance can be offered while still promoting independence.

Table 7.1

Motor Activities

Body Awareness	Coordination	Balance	Strength and Endurance	Flexibility
crawling; rolling or scooting in, under, and through things; moving while looking in a mirror; pantomiming a peer or adult; moving to music; doing the Hokey Pokey	climbing, kicking a ball, throwing and catching a ball, dancing, block building, using peg board, puzzles, buttons	walking on a balance beam, standing on one foot, kicking a ball, walking and carrying something	climbing, running, riding tricycles, pushing on scooter boards or toys, moving furniture, picking up toys, swimming and water play	moving in, under, and around things of varied sizes and shapes; simple yoga exercises; climbing; dancing

Directed Play   134

Indoor Play

When organizing inside motor activities in groups, a suggestion would be to have at least three different types of activities for the children to move through. For example, in a circular arrangement set up a balance beam, a crawl tunnel, and a climber. These three equipment pieces focus on balance, body awareness, and coordination.

Line up two or three children at each apparatus. As children complete one of the activities they move clockwise to the next. Having only two or three children at each piece of equipment reduces the amount of time they have to wait and thus cuts down on behavior problems.

Staff can position themselves in the middle of the circular arrangement to assist children as needed. If enough staff is present individual staff members can stand beside each piece of equipment. If only one staff member is present they should stand in the middle of the circle or move with the child who may need assistance to be successful.

Outdoor Play

Outdoor play is one of the best and most natural ways to promote gross motor development. Large open spaces encourage children to run, jump, ride tricycles, climb, slide, and swing. Following the philosophy of Directed Play, adults should take an active role in the play of children rather than just standing back and watching.

Outdoor play areas should contain space and equipment to promote a variety of skills, such as jumping, balance, climbing, throwing, catching, running, and riding trikes. Typical and valuable play equipment should include age-appropriate slides and swings, sandboxes, trikes, balls of various types, and climbing equipment. Areas for dramatic play with toy cars or house structures are also good. Surfaces should be appropriate to the activity—sidewalks for trikes and soft, impact-absorbent surfaces under climbing equipment. Be alert to how seasons and temperatures can affect this equipment. All equipment should be inspected periodically to be sure it is safe. Specialized equipment, like adaptive swings, is commercially available.

It is recommended that at least two or three adults be present during outdoor play. The adults should be positioned in a triangle around the play area. This positioning will allow at least one adult to see a child at all times. If adults are clustered together it can be difficult or impossible for them to see all of the children all of the time. Be aware of play areas or equipment that requires special supervision and be sure an adult is there at all times. Adults should have first aid supplies readily available and a cell phone or walkie-talkie for emergencies.

As children get older, organized activities such as ball games or chase games can be organized. This organization will get children playing appropriately and can reduce behavior problems. Games with rules in *Directed Play* include bowling, kick ball, basketball, and soccer.

General Activities

53   Simple Balance Beam

Target Objective
Increase balance, coordination, independence, following directions, turn-taking

Developmental Domains
Gross Motor, Social, Cognitive

Multiple Intelligences
Bodily

Materials
Commercially available balance beam with stands or a smooth 2" x 4" board approximately 10 feet long. For younger children the board will be on the ground; as they get older it can be raised 2–6 inches off the ground.

Preparation/Set-Up
Put the balance beam on stands for older children. Start with the beam on the floor for younger children.

Procedures

1. Have children walk heel-to-toe on the balance beam as independently as possible.

2. For children still learning to walk, provide assistance as needed.

Adaptations for Children With Disabilities

For children with physical disabilities, it may be necessary to make use of a technique called "backward chaining." This technique involves starting with the last step of the task to be completed. In this activity have children start near the end of the board and walk to the end. As they improve gradually work back until they eventually are capable of walking across the entire balance beam. Provide extra time for practice. Provide physical assistance by holding a hand or placing someone on both sides of the child for two-handed support. Another variation may be to have the children walk across by stepping side-to-side instead of heel-to-toe.

Directed Play   **136**

Standing on One Foot

Target Objective
Increase balance, coordination, concepts of right and left, following directions

Developmental Domains
Gross Motor, Language, Cognitive

Multiple Intelligences
Bodily, Logical, Linguistic

Materials
None.

Preparation/Set-Up
Large open space.

Procedures

1. Arrange children in a small circle. Tell them that they are going to play a game to see who can stand on one foot for the longest time.

2. Direct children to stand on their right foot for 15 seconds if they are able.

3. Next, have children stand on their left foot for 15 seconds. Their eyes should be kept open. Arms can come out to help with balance if needed.

4. Continue alternating feet for four to six times.

5. If children need support while trying to stand on one foot, encourage them to put their hands on the shoulder of a child beside them or on a wall or chair close by.

6. Count for the children, challenging them to stand and balance longer each turn.

Adaptations for Children With Disabilities

Standing on one foot is a prerequisite skill for kicking a ball and other activities. Give children many opportunities to practice this task. Increase with age the length of time children hold a foot up. Provide stability by allowing children to keep their back on a wall or their hand on a chair. As a variation, have children try to stand on one foot with their eyes shut. This should only be done after balancing on one foot has been mastered with eyes open. This is an important prerequisite skill for dressing and playing ball games such as kick ball and soccer.

55 Ladder Walk

Target Objective
Increase balance, coordination, counting

Developmental Domains
Gross Motor, Cognitive, Language

Multiple Intelligences
Bodily, Logical, Linguistic

Materials
Wooden ladders.

Preparation/Set-Up
Lay ladders on the ground. This activity is fun inside or outside.

Procedures

1. Lay a five- to six-rung wooden ladder on the floor.

2. Have children take turns stepping over the rungs of the ladder.

3. Have children count the rungs as they walk over them.

4. Vary the task by having children walk forward, backward, sideways, or on the side poles.

5. This activity can be made more difficult by raising the ladder off the floor.

Adaptations for Children With Disabilities

Children with difficulty completing this task can be aided with backward chaining. Have children start by walking over the last rung and then, as they become successful, gradually increase the number of rungs they walk over.

Directed Play 138

56 River Jump

Target Objective
Increase gross motor skills, counting, balance, strength, two-foot jump, number sequence 1–10, rote counting

Developmental Domains
Gross Motor, Cognitive, Language

Multiple Intelligences
Bodily, Logical, Linguistic, Naturalist

Materials
10 large "rocks" made of gray laminated paper or cardboard. Each rock should be 12–18 inches in diameter. Each rock has a number from 1–10 written on it in large print. Rocks made of carpet or heavy rubber would also work but may be hard to find or make.

Preparation/Set-Up
Arrange the rocks on the floor within easy jumping range, approximately 8–12 inches apart. The distance is dependent on age and development of children. Each rock should be taped down to reduce the chances of it sliding.

Procedures

1. Tell children they are going to play a game in which they will pretend to jump on rocks in order to cross a river.

2. One at a time, children jump from rock to rock in the correct number order. Children are to jump using both feet.

3. All the children count as a child jumps or crosses the river to the other side.

4. The number of "rocks" children jump on depends on their cognitive skills and motor abilities.

5. Vary the activity by having children jump on one foot rather than on both feet. Alternating between left and right foot upon request and while jumping is encouraged for older children.

6. For larger groups of children set out two sets of rocks so that two children can be jumping at the same time.

Adaptations for Children With Disabilities

Move the "rocks" close together. Provide physical assistance as needed. Once one child gets about halfway through, start a second child from the beginning. This activity is easily set up outside on a sidewalk or asphalt surface. Just draw the number rocks with chalk.

57 Beanbag Fun

Target Objective
Balance, coordination, problem solving, following directions, body awareness

Developmental Domains
Gross Motor, Cognitive, Social, Language

Multiple Intelligences
Bodily, Linguistic, Interpersonal

Materials
Beanbags for each child.

Preparation/Set-Up
Large open play area; music if needed.

Procedures

1. This activity can include a number of variations. As a first step, get children used to balancing a beanbag on their head while walking a short distance. As children are successful with this begin other variations on the skill.

2. Children participate in a relay race while walking with the beanbag on their head.

3. Children can move around a room walking slowly or fast or hopping. When the beanbag falls off their head they are to stop as if frozen. They must remain frozen until someone comes along and puts the beanbag back on their head.

4. Children climb up and down stairs or a ladder while keeping the beanbag on their head.

5. Play "freeze" with music while balancing beanbags on the head. When the music plays they move; when it stops they stop without dropping the beanbag.

Adaptations for Children With Disabilities

Provide considerable practice in this task for children who have difficulty with it. Larger beanbags are easier to balance. Tie the beanbags on their heads with scarves or wear beanbags under a hat. Encourage the children to be as independent as possible.

Directed Play

58 **Feet Pick Up**

Target Objective
Dexterity, coordination, body parts, problem solving

Developmental Domains
Gross Motor, Fine Motor, Cognitive

Multiple Intelligences
Bodily, Linguistic

Materials
Small and medium-sized objects, including tennis balls, marbles, crayons, stuffed animals, and blocks; a bucket or plastic tubs.

Preparation/Set-Up
Children need to take their shoes and socks off in a large motor area. Have items and buckets ready to use.

Procedures

1. Tell the children that they are going to play a game with their feet.

2. Arrange the children in a large circle and have them take off their shoes and socks.

3. Tell the children that they will have to pick up objects with their toes and/or feet working together, and then place these objects into a bucket or tub that has been placed in the middle of the group. Demonstrate the activity for better understanding.

4. Pass out the various objects to the children.

5. Children should be seated on the floor. Have them try to pick up various objects using only their toes and feet.

6. Once they have picked up an object, they are to scoot on their bottoms and place the object in the bucket or tub.

7. Make sure children try to pick up different-sized objects.

8. After several opportunities, have the children discuss how easy or hard it was to pick up different objects with their feet or how they had to move their feet to pick up an object.

9. Provide assistance in putting shoes and socks on as needed.

Adaptations for Children With Disabilities

Assist children as needed. Children with neurological disorders may have a very difficult time with this activity. Provide larger and softer objects such as semi-inflated beach balls or soft grip balls that are easier to pick up.

59 Target Throw

Target Objective
Increase motor coordination, throwing accuracy, turn-taking, following directions or routine, sensory stimulation.

Developmental Domains
Gross Motor, Fine Motor, Language, Cognitive

Multiple Intelligences
Bodily, Interpersonal, Spatial, Linguistic, Mathematical/ Logical

Materials
A variety of small to medium-sized balls; predrawn, large or medium-sized targets, such as stop signs or shapes with colors and numbers. Containers of wet mud or washable paint with bubbles, smocks, drop cloth, soap, and towels

Preparation/Set-Up
This can be a messy but fun activity that requires a large motor area inside or outside with targets taped to a wall or fence, drop cloth placed under the targets if needed. Set the throwing mark. Distance between the wall and the throwing mark will be dependent on the age of the children.

Procedures

1. Children put on their smocks and select a ball and container to dip from. They carefully dip only a third of their ball into the container picking up the texture of the mud or the paint.

2. Each child stands at a throwing mark with ball in hand. They throw the ball at the target with a shoulder rotation of arm to rear, then follow-through forward.

3. Enjoy the splat! After three or four turns, have the children examine the target to check for accuracy. Talk about accuracy and staying within the lines.

4. Provide numerous opportunities for throwing at the targets.

5. This activity can be changed and used in many different settings and situations. Some include throwing beanbags to hit over a line or shooting wadded newspaper into a basket.

Adaptations for Children With Disabilities

Shorten the throwing distance to the target. Provide throwing materials that are easily held onto, such as Koosh® balls and foam balls. Physically assist any student who is unable to perform the motor task independently. Repeat directions and give reminders frequently to maintain on-task and appropriate social behaviors.

Directed Play 142

60 Tricycle Fun

Target Objective
Increase coordination, strength, endurance

Developmental Domains
Gross Motor, Social, Language

Multiple Intelligences
Bodily, Interpersonal, Linguistic

Materials
Several tricycles of different sizes, orange cones or other materials to guide the direction of the children. Red, yellow, and green construction paper to make "stoplights" or use the stoplights created in the "Constructing a Stoplight" activity.

Preparation/Set-Up
A large, open, smooth area, such as a playground sidewalk or gym floor. Set up the cones to make a "road."

Procedures

1. Have a tricycle for each child.

2. Tell the children to ride the trikes around the road in an orderly manner and going in the same direction.

3. Set up the stoplights and show the red light at different times. Tell children to stop and have them repeat, "Red light means stop."

4. Change to the green light and have the children say, "Green means go" and then let them continue riding.

5. This activity is to simulate driving, including awareness and safety, so encourage the use of turn signals, stopping for pedestrians, and obeying the stoplights.

Adaptations for Children With Disabilities

Tricycles may need to be adapted to assist some children. A board can be attached vertically to the back of the seat to provide added support. Blocks can be placed on the pedals using duct tape. Straps for holding feet to the pedals can be created by folding strips of duct tape together with the sticky sides in. The smooth sides will be out and can be attached to the blocks or pedals by using more duct tape. Or use a different kind of transportation, like a four-wheel pedal car.

61 Flying Kites

Target Objective
Strength, coordination, understanding of wind and weather; concepts of up, down, high, and low.

Developmental Domains
Gross Motor, Language, Cognitive

Multiple Intelligences
Bodily, Linguistic, Logical, Musical, Naturalist

Materials
Commercial or handmade kites, one kite for every two children.

Preparation/Set-Up
Open, outdoor play space away from trees or power lines on a day with moderate winds.

Kites have a long and varied history and are a good way to promote cultural diversity. In Honduras and Guatemala, huge kites are flown on All Saints Day and All Souls Day. These celebrations occur in November when the winds bring in the dry season. The practice is a mixture of Native American and Spanish religious customs. Kite Day in China is on the 9th day of the 9th month of the year. On this day, kites are flown by men and boys on hills or other high places. People in Korea and Malaysia write down the misfortunes of the year on a kite. The kite is flown and the string cut so that the misfortunes of the past year can symbolically fly away and a new year can begin without old worries.

Procedures

1. Provide one kite for every two children. With adult assistance, each pair of children should work together to get the kite to fly.

2. Once the kite is flying, children can take turns holding the string. Make sure children have a solid grip on the handle when they exchange it. It is also possible to create double handles by tying an additional handle on the end.

3. Identify concepts such as up and down and high and low while the kite is flying. Also identify any colors or smells in the area.

4. The children may bore quickly once the kite is flying, so assist them in rolling up the string or running with the kite.

5. Have the children sing "Kite, Kite."

> ### Kite, Kite
> Kite, kite, soaring high,
> Reaching, reaching to the sky.
> First you're high, then you're low,
> Swooping, swirling, round you go.
> Kite, kite, fine and free,
> Dancing, dancing, just for me.

Directed Play

Adaptations for Children With Disabilities

Children with physical or health impairments may tire quickly. Be sure that all staff are aware of any specific health concerns of children. Supervise and support turn-taking.

Simple Kick Ball

Target Objective
Balance, eye-foot coordination, endurance, following directions, simple game with rules

Developmental Domains
Gross Motor, Language, Social

Multiple Intelligences
Spatial, Bodily, Linguistic, Logical

Materials
A medium- to large-sized kick ball.

Preparation/Set-Up
Have open space available.

Procedures

1. Depending on the age and ability level of the children, it may be necessary to start with only two children.

2. Set the ball on the ground and have the child run up and kick it.

3. After kicking the ball the child should run to first "base," which can be another adult, or adults can guide the child to the base.

4. The child waits while the next child kicks and they run through the bases to "home plate."

5. As other children are added to the activity they can try to catch the ball after it has been kicked.

Adaptations for Children With Disabilities

Physically and verbally direct children. Repeat the rules. Allow children to kick a standing ball if kicking a rolling one is too hard. Deflate a ball slightly to make it slower or lighter. Provide guidance while children are running the bases.

63 Preposition Obstacle Course

Target Objective
Increase motor skills, prepositional concepts, following directions, balance, coordination, endurance, flexibility.

Developmental Domains
Gross Motor, Cognitive, Language

Multiple Intelligences
Spatial, Logical, Bodily, Linguistic, Musical

Materials
Various equipment for children to walk, crawl, and climb in, on, under, over, around, behind, or through (e.g., balance beam, crawl tunnel, rolling mats, stairs, table).

Preparation/Set-Up
Arrange equipment in a large circle or in lines where children move from beginning to end and back again.

Procedures

1. Arrange children in a small group and tell them that they are going to practice moving in, on, under, over, around, behind, or through different pieces of equipment.

2. Have one to three children line up behind each piece of equipment.

3. All children should be actively participating in the activity with very little wait time occurring.

4. Children are to take turns moving in, on, under, over, around, behind, or through each piece of equipment as directed by the teacher.

5. Rotate the groups so that each child has an opportunity to interact with all of the equipment and to practice all the concepts targeted for that day. Additional staff members are to stand next to different pieces of equipment to provide assistance as needed.

6. After the children have had several opportunities to move about using the equipment, sit them in a circle on the floor and discuss what they did in the activity, reviewing what they found easy or difficult. Sing "The Bear Went Over the Mountain" (to the tune of "He's a Jolly Good Fellow").

   Repeat verses substituting "over" with other directional concepts, such as "under," "around," "in," "on top of," and "through." It is fun to sing and move at the same time, and this can be challenging for some children.

Directed Play   146

Adaptations for Children With Disabilities

Adapt equipment so that it is possible for all children to use it independently. Physically assist children as needed. Children who have difficulty with concept development and language may become quite frustrated or confused when using a variety of concepts together. Focus on one or two targeted concepts relevant to the individual child before moving on to more complex terms. Spread this activity out over a period of days or weeks. Make sure that the prepositional concepts are appropriate for the child's developmental age. For example, the concepts of "in" and "on" are much easier for a younger child to understand and perform than "over" and "through." Again, children with motor planning difficulties will also struggle shifting between concepts and body movements. Be patient and assist good performance and additional practice. Keep data on the prepositional concepts using the 0–5 data sheet to mark each prepositional movement children complete when directed.

The Bear Went Over the Mountain

The bear went over the mountain,

The bear went over the mountain,

The bear went over the mountain,

    To see what he could see.

To see what he could see,

To see what he could see,

The bear went over the mountain,

    To see what he could see.

Buddy Balance Ball

Target Objective
Cooperation, problem solving, motor planning, coordination and coping skills

Developmental Domains
Gross Motor, Language, Cognitive, Social

Multiple Intelligences
Bodily, Linguistic, Interpersonal

Materials
An assortment of different size soft balls or balloons.

Preparation/Set-Up
Have balls or balloons available.

Procedures

1. Arrange children in a group and show them the balls. Tell them they are going to have to work together to carry a ball across the room without using their hands.

2. Children choose a partner or are paired up by the teacher.

3. Give each pair of children a ball or balloon. Help them to position the ball between them using their heads, side, stomach, or back. Without using their hands they are to carry the ball to a predetermined place on the other side of the room.

4. If they drop the ball, they should stop, reposition it, and continue.

5. When all children have crossed the room, give them different-sized balls or balloons and repeat.

6. Reorganize the group and discuss what children had to do to keep the ball balanced while moving.

Adaptations for Children With Disabilities

Assist children as necessary. Be sure children are working together.

65 Balloon Bounce

Target Objective
Increase motor planning, ocular control, body awareness, following directions.

Developmental Domains
Gross Motor, Language, Social, Cognition

Multiple Intelligences
Bodily, Interpersonal, Intrapersonal, Linguistic

Materials
Large to medium-sized balloons.

Preparation/Set-Up
A large area inside or outside on a still day, one blown-up balloon per student.

Procedures

1. Divide the children into small groups consisting of four to six children per group. Give each child a balloon. Tell them to volley the balloons using their hands. Encourage them to keep the balloons in the air for as long as they can. The teacher counts for them to see how high in number they can go. If focused enough, the children should practice rote counting as well.

2. Next, the children follow the teacher commands by using two hands together, right hand, left hand, elbow, wrist, fingers, and head to volley the balloons in the air.

3. If the children appear fairly competent with the previous tasks, move them into pairs. The children pair up and volley a balloon to each other using the

body part of choice. Once they are fairly good at volleying together, they can volley with changing body parts upon command.

4. Encourage positive talk and praise between partners and peers. Give compliments and recognition of a good try or successful completion.

Adaptations for Children With Disabilities

Allow the children to begin the volley using only hands or the body part they are most successful with. Those children with physical disabilities may need assistance in maintaining the direction of the balloon. Stay with only a few body part changes. Too many changes will make it very difficult for the children with motor planning problems. The concepts of left and right are best used with children five years of age and up.

66 Broom Push

Target Objective
Increase coordination, motor planning, problem solving

Developmental Domains
Gross Motor, Cognitive, Self-Help

Multiple Intelligences
Bodily, Intrapersonal

Materials
Child-sized brooms. These can be purchased commercially or cut down from regular-sized brooms. A variety of objects of different sizes or weights to push, such as tennis balls, blocks, or empty milk containers.

Preparation/Set-Up
Have a large open area with brooms and something to push. Have a "target" on the floor for children to aim for, say, a circle made out of tape.

Procedures

1. Show children the brooms and explain what brooms are used for.

2. Show children how they can push an object across the floor using the brooms.

3. Letting them work individually, set down an object to push and identify the target on the floor.

4. The children push the object across the floor with the broom.

5. This task can be made easier or more difficult by the size, shape, weight, or even texture of the objects to be pushed.

6. This activity also can be adapted as a relay game.

149 Chapter 7

Adaptations for Children With Disabilities

Smaller brooms will be easier to use than larger ones. Provide assistance as needed. Provide lighter objects to sweep or increase the size of the target area. Children with mental retardation often enjoy doing "chores" like this.

67 Free For All

Target Objective
Increase awareness of body in space, turn-taking. This activity is especially good for young children with visual impairments.

Developmental Domains
Gross Motor, Cognitive, Social

Multiple Intelligences
Bodily, Linguistic

Materials
A large pile of pillows with mats underneath, beanbag chairs, couch cushions, or other soft items that children can jump into will be needed.

Preparation/Set-Up
Begin by having children learn to turn somersaults and roll on a mat.

Procedures

1. This activity is designed to increase children's awareness of their bodies in space. It is based on the common child characteristic of wanting to jump on a bed.

2. Jumping into something large and soft helps to increase children's spatial awareness.

3. Provide good supervision and make sure the cushions are clear before the next child jumps.

Adaptations for Children With Disabilities

Children with physical or health impairments may tire easily so provide opportunities for rest. Children with severe visual impairments may be reluctant at first; provide encouragement and physical prompts as necessary. This is a valuable activity for children with visual impairments. Provide support and encouragement as needed.

68 · Paintbrush Fun

Target Objective
Practice gross motor and fine motor skills, cooperation

Developmental Domains
Gross Motor, Fine Motor, Social

Multiple Intelligences
Bodily, Spatial, Interpersonal

Materials
Various sizes of old paintbrushes, buckets of water, paint shirts (optional).

Preparation/Set-Up
This activity is best done outside on a large cement area or wall.

Procedures

1. Arrange children in a group and tell them that they are going to paint.

2. Show children the paintbrushes and explain what they are used for.

3. Give each child a brush and bucket of water and let them experiment painting on the cement or a wall.

4. Provide suggestions as to what designs they can paint including shapes, letters or numbers, or pictures of animals.

5. Encourage children to work together to paint a large area before the water disappears.

Adaptations for Children With Disabilities

See the Fine Motor chapter for other painting activities. Provide assistance as needed. Have chairs available for resting. Step stools are good for getting up higher and promote stair climbing and balance. Make a variety of brush sizes available depending on a child's strength and fine motor skills.

69 **Weighted Blocks**

Target Objective
Increase strength, coordination, concepts of heavy and light

Developmental Domains
Gross Motor, Cognitive, Language

Multiple Intelligences
Bodily, Linguistic, Logical

Materials
Cardboard "brick" blocks, sand, zipper-lock plastic sandwich bags.

Preparation/Set-Up
Fill a number of the sandwich bags with sand and put these inside the cardboard blocks. A different number of bags or bags of different sizes can be used to vary the weight of the blocks. This activity should be conducted in a large open area and children should have their shoes on.

Procedures

1. Arrange children in a small group. Show them the blocks and tell them that some of the blocks are heavy and some are light.

2. Let the children experiment carrying the blocks to another location in the room and have them identify if the blocks they are carrying are heavy or light.

3. To foster cooperation, have two children carry a heavy block together.

4. Tell the children to build a structure using the weighted blocks.

Adaptations for Children With Disabilities

Be alert to the weights the children are carrying and don't let them try to carry more than they are able. Some children will tire easily.

70 Raking Leaves

Target Objective
Increase strength, coordination, sensory stimulation, use of objects, concept of quantity, rote memory of song.

Developmental Domains
Gross Motor, Social, Cognitive

Multiple Intelligences
Bodily, Naturalist, Interpersonal, Musical, Logical

Materials
Small plastic rakes for children; if possible each child participating should have a rake.

Preparation/Set-Up
Large open area with plenty of leaves.

Procedures

1. Have children rake leaves into a large pile. Remove any sticks or other sharp objects. Provide assistance as needed.

2. Once leaves are in a pile, children can take turns jumping into the pile feet first.

3. Point out size, shape, and color differences of the leaves. Have the children collect leaves that look the same. Leaves can also be arranged and sorted from large to small.

4. Arrange children in a small group and sing and mime "When the Leaves Are on the Ground."

Adaptations for Children With Disabilities

Physically assist with raking and jumping. Be sure that all sticks or other sharp objects are removed from the pile of leaves. Use this activity to practice classification skills by having children match or order leaves according to size, shape, or color.

When the Leaves Are on the Ground

When the leaves are on the ground

Instead of on the trees,

I like to make a pile of them

Way up to my knees.

I like to run and jump in them

And kick them all around.

I like the prickly feel of them

And the crickly, crackly sound.

---

153 Chapter 7

71 Snaky Moves

Target Objective
Cooperation, problem solving, coordination

Developmental Domains
Gross Motor, Cognitive, Language

Multiple Intelligences
Bodily, Linguistic, Musical, Interpersonal, Naturalist

Materials
None.

Preparation/Set-Up
Large open area with a clean floor, so children can take their shoes off.

Procedures

1. Tell children arranged in a large group that they are going to make and move like a snake.

2. Have each child lie down on his or her stomach.

3. When moving on the floor like a snake, each child is to grab and hold onto the ankles of another child. Each pair is then to move and join up in a similar manner with another pair, making a longer snake.

4. Have all groups join together to make one long snake that moves across the room.

5. As a related activity, have children try to roll over or curl up.

6. The group comes together and discusses how they learned to move together.

7. Children can sing "Snakes" while moving.

Adaptations for Children With Disabilities

Provide assistance in moving as needed. Teach the song prior to the activity or practice in a smaller group. Reward children with autism and behavior disorders for working together with other children. Provide a visual model for children with severe visual impairments.

> ### Snakes
>
> Snakes slither on the ground,
>
> Snakes slither all around.
>
> Some are short; some are long;
>
> Some have fangs; some have none.

72 Beanbag Toss

Target Objective Increase eye-hand coordination, targeted concepts or vocabulary	**Materials** Assorted beanbags of different colors and sizes.
Developmental Domains Gross Motor, Language, Social, Cognitive	**Preparation/Set-Up** Beanbags, containers, targets, large area set up for activity performed during small group.
Multiple Intelligences Bodily, Linguistic, Interpersonal	

Procedures

1. Beanbags can be tossed to a variety of targets. These might include a bucket or basket, targets on the floor or through a hole in a vertical target, or to another person.

2. Have enough beanbags for each child and a target for each child.

3. Children throw overhand toward a vertical target with a hole in it.

4. Children toss beanbags underhand so that they will land in a basket or bucket.

5. Children toss beanbags underhand to have them land on targets on the floor. The targets can be changed according to season or theme. Suggestions can include: snowmen, shamrocks, circles, squares, hearts, matching color to color with containers, or numerals on floor that match numerals on the beanbags.

6. Encourage children to talk to one another or the teacher while tossing the beanbags. Adults should make comments such as "That was a hard throw" or "That was a little too high."

Adaptations for Children With Disabilities

Reduce the distance between the child and the target to make it easier. Larger targets with wider openings will also be helpful. Avoid overcrowding. Make sure children are throwing the beanbags only at the targets.

73 Bounce and Catch

Target Objective
Increase eye-hand coordination, strength, social play skills

Developmental Domains
Gross Motor, Social, Language

Multiple Intelligences
Bodily, Interpersonal

Materials
Various balls of different sizes, textures, and weights, e.g., beach balls, tennis balls, rubber balls, Nerf® balls, kick balls, rubber balls.

Preparation/Set-Up
A large motor area inside or out.

Procedures

1. Begin by working with the children one-on-one to help them learn about bouncing and catching. While in a seated position with legs open or on their knees, the children drop and catch a medium-sized rubber ball. Encourage catching with both hands while bringing the ball to the chest. Once they've become proficient with bouncing and catching while sitting or kneeling, move them into a standing position. Provide many opportunities for practice.

2. Next, set up opportunities to play together in pairs. They should stand approximately six feet apart and gently bounce and catch a ball back and forth to their partner.

3. Ball activities are challenging for many young children. If they become frustrated with one another, move back into individual ball handling, with the children bouncing and catching by themselves or against a wall.

4. Bouncing and catching the ball takes consistent practice. Plan to work on ball skills over a two-week period.

Adaptations for Children With Disabilities

Some children will need considerable practice with this task. Encourage children to watch the ball as it moves into their hands. Larger balls that are semi-inflated or have increased texture will be easier to catch than smaller, smoother ones.

74 Move Like a Turtle

Target Objective
Cooperation, coordination, problem solving, strength and endurance

Developmental Domains
Gross Motor, Cognitive, Language, Social

Multiple Intelligences
Bodily, Linguistic, Interpersonal, Naturalist

Materials
A medium- to large-sized item, such as a piece of cardboard, to use as a "shell"; pictures of turtles.

Preparation/Set-Up
A large open carpeted area.

Procedures

1. Gather a small group of children and discuss what it means to work together.

2. Show the children pictures of turtles and note the shell.

3. Explain to children that they are going to pretend to be a turtle and work together to move like a turtle.

4. Have each child get in a crawling position and assume one of the turtle's four legs or the head.

5. Place the turtle "shell" over the top of them. A "shell" that is a little heavy like a gym mat will also work well.

6. The children are to move around the room keeping the shell on the turtle.

7. Provide assistance as needed for children who may be moving too fast or too slow.

8. Alternate who is the "head" and who are the legs.

9. To increase the difficulty of this activity set up an obstacle course that they must move over or through. Children who are the "head" can also tell the other children which way to go.

Adaptations for Children With Disabilities

Some will have difficulty with this activity, so provide assistance and praise for a job well done.

75 Balloon Tennis

Target Objective
Increase eye-hand coordination, socialization, concepts of up and down

Developmental Domains
Gross Motor, Social

Multiple Intelligences
Bodily, Interpersonal

Materials
Paint-stirring sticks, balloons, paper plates, glue or tape.

Preparation/Set-Up
Prepare large motor area inside, or outside if a calm day. Glue or tape paint-stirring sticks to the back of the paper plates to make tennis rackets. Blow up several medium-sized balloons. For younger children, have a balloon for each child. For older children have one balloon for every two children.

Procedures

1. Children should first practice keeping the balloon in the air using their own racket.

2. Let children take turns hitting the balloon to another child or adult.

3. As children are successful, add some kind of net or barrier and have them hit back and forth with a partner.

Adaptations for Children With Disabilities

This will be a good activity to help promote eye-hand coordination. Give children plenty of time to practice. Avoid overcrowding. Praise children for playing together.

Games With Rules

Involving children in group games is a fun and easy way to promote socialization, turn-taking, awareness of differences, motor skills, and following directions. Group games have prescribed acts and rules that children must follow, and they provide a sense of challenge for children. These games can be played inside or out. When children agree on and follow rules they are practicing a broader social/cultural concept of making "laws."

- There are many different types of group games, including:
- Games involving verbal commands—Simon Says, Mother May I
- Aiming games—Dodge Ball, Marbles, Bowling
- Race games—Musical Chairs, Three-Legged Race
- Chasing games—Tag, Duck Duck Goose, Freeze Tag
- Hiding games—Hide and Seek, Kick the Can

Some children will have difficulty with group games that have rules. These problems may be due to either motor or cognitive reasons or both. Many of these games require children to combine motor actions with a cognitive awareness of rules. This may be difficult for some children with disabilities. Give children plenty of practice in the motor actions and review the rules often. Praise children for following the rules.

Group games are also a good way to promote an understanding of cultural diversity. People all over the world play games. In fact, some games have been played by people for centuries. While some games are common to all peoples, the specific rules or other aspects of the game can vary from country to country.

Common games played by children and adults in this country actually have a long history. For example, the modern game of checkers dates back to the twelfth century. In the 1300s, game pieces were made of ivory and had elaborate decorations. Marbles is known to have been played in ancient Egypt and Rome. Darts was played by the Pilgrims while coming over on the Mayflower. Some common games and sports played in this country originated with Native Americans. For example, prehistoric Native Americans played "shinny," a game with a puck on ice that is similar to ice hockey. Native Americans also played games similar to hopscotch and hide and seek.

The way games are played also tells us something about the cultures. For example, within the Navajo culture, cheating in games may be viewed in a similar way as an April Fool's joke is viewed by other peoples. It has also been noted that in many Native American cultures competition is not stressed. Children will be urged to not compete either with other children or adults. In New Guinea, games can be played in which neither side wins. A game will end only when the two sides have reached a level of equality.

Asking children about the games they play can be an easy way to help all children become aware of the similarities and differences in games that we play. For example, children can be asked to identify the games they like to play at home. If someone doesn't know a particular game, the children can describe it to others.

Many good resource books are available that will help you plan and implement multicultural games. These include *The Multicultural Game Book* (Orlando, 1993), *International Playtime* (Nelson & Glass, 1992), and *Acka Backa Boo! Playground Games From Around the World* (Dunn, 2000).

76 Roller Ball

Target Objective
Increase gross motor skills, cooperation, balance

Developmental Domains
Social, Language, Gross Motor

Multiple Intelligences
Spatial, Linguistic, Interpersonal

Materials
Medium-sized ball, flat board approximately 3-5 feet in length, a firm object to help raise the board in the middle.

Preparation/Set-Up
Have equipment ready and available.

Procedures

1. This activity is designed for two children at a time. Tell children they are going to have to work together to balance and roll the ball.

2. With the children present, place the flat board on a firm object in the middle so that the board works like a teeter-totter.

3. The board should raise no more than 8–10 inches at its highest point.

4. Have one child sit at each end of the board.

5. Assist the children in rolling the ball to each other along the board as it is tilted.

6. Encourage the children to work together to keep the ball from rolling off the board.

7. Repeat several times and have the children try different-sized balls.

8. Children can make the board go up and down by working together.

Adaptations for Children With Disabilities

Provide extra time and assistance as needed. Make ball move slower with heavier bean-bag balls or semi-deflated balls. Play with the student rather than pairing with a peer. Praise children for working together.

77 Balloon Relay Game

Target Objective
Increase motor skills, turn-taking, cooperation, endurance, coordination, balance

Developmental Domains
Gross Motor, Social, Language

Multiple Intelligences
Spatial, Bodily, Interpersonal

Materials
Several balloons of different sizes with at least one balloon per child.

Preparation/Set-Up
Large motor area inside or outside.

Procedures

1. Divide a group of four to six children in half.

2. Have each group stand in a line with the two groups about three or four feet from each other.

3. Explain that they are going to race while doing things with the balloons.

4. Demonstrate what the children are to do for each "race."

5. For the first "race," have the children carry the balloon while walking to and around a chair placed 10–12 feet in front of them. Then, have them come back and take their place at the end of the line.

6. Repeat if needed to help the children get the idea of what is going on.

7. Next, have the children try to gently bounce the balloon up in the air while walking. Repeat.

8. Next, and as developmental age permits, have two children hold the balloon between them with their chests, hips, or knees.

9. While holding the balloon between them, they are to "race" around the chair and back.

10. This is designed to promote cooperation and interdependence.

11. Reorganize the group and have the children discuss the activity.

Adaptations for Children With Disabilities

Adapt the distance or size of the balloons as needed. Balloons are not recommended for younger children or for children who put things in their mouths.

78 Pass the Ball

Target Objective
Turn-taking, socialization, flexibility, coordination, name recognition of peers

Developmental Domains
Gross Motor, Social, Language

Multiple Intelligences
Bodily, Interpersonal, Logical

Materials
Medium-sized ball.

Preparation/Set-Up
Large motor area inside or outside.

Procedures

1. Have a group of five or six children sit in a tight circle with the teacher. Tell the children they are going to play a game of moving the ball around the circle in different ways.

2. Start the ball with one child; have him or her say the name of another child and roll the ball to that child.

3. Help ensure that each child rolls the ball to a different child.

4. Next, have the children stand up but remain in a circle.

5. Have the children turn to face the back of the person next to them and pass the ball under their legs to the person behind them.

6. Repeat the activity two or three times, going both directions.

7. Follow with the children passing the ball over their heads to the person in front of them.

8. Emphasize the concepts of forward and backward, over and under, front and back.

9. For younger children, this activity will be easier if they are standing in a line.

Adaptations for Children With Disabilities

Children with visual impairments can be easily intimidated by large groups of children. Make sure that the child is secure and aware of where other children are. Children with physical impairments may need support while sitting or standing. Reward children with autism and behavior disorders for working well with other children.

Directed Play

79 Musical Chairs

Target Objective
Following directions, directionality, following rules

Developmental Domains
Social, Cognitive, Gross Motor

Multiple Intelligences
Musical, Logical, Bodily

Materials
Chairs for all children, music.

Preparation/Set-Up
Arrange chairs and have music ready.

Procedures

1. This activity can be played in the traditional way, with one fewer chair than there are children.

2. Music is turned on and off until only one child is left with a chair.

3. As a variation, have children walk around the chairs and, when the music stops, sit on another child's lap if they don't have a chair to sit on. This promotes cooperation and togetherness.

4. Children can also sit in a circle and pass an object around until the music stops. The child holding the object when the music stops must identify it and tell something about it.

5. A variety of objects can be used, including foods, transportation items, or clothing, depending on the targeted theme or vocabulary being worked on.

Adaptations for Children With Disabilities

Children with more pronounced physical impairments have significant difficulty with this activity. With some minor adaptations a child can turn the music on and off for the whole group. Attach an adaptive switch, often used with a computer or augmentative communication system, to a tape recorder so that a child can turn the music on or off by pressing the switch. Praise children with autism or behavior disorders for playing appropriately. Provide one-to-one practice for children with mental retardation.

80 Back Stand

Target Objective
Increase motor skills, cooperation, flexibility, coordination, problem solving, following rules

Developmental Domains
Gross Motor, Social, Language

Multiple Intelligences
Bodily, Linguistic, Interpersonal, Intrapersonal

Materials
None.

Preparation/Set-Up
Large motor or movement area inside or outside.

Procedures

1. Let children choose a partner or pair them as needed. Tell children that they are going to have to work together to move from a sitting to standing position.

2. Have children sit with their backs touching and arms interlocked.

3. Have the children stand while working together. They will have to press into each other to rise.

4. Once they have stood up, have them try to sit down while still having backs touching and arms interlocked.

5. Repeat three or four times.

Adaptations for Children With Disabilities

Provide physical assistance as needed. Select specific peers to partner with. Reward children with mental retardation and behavior disorders for working together with other children.

Directed Play   164

Partner Kick Ball

Target Objective
Increase gross motor skills, stand on one foot, kicking, cooperation, problem solving, playing group games

Developmental Domains
Gross Motor, Language, Social

Multiple Intelligences
Bodily, Interpersonal

Materials
Several medium- to large-sized rubber balls, soft cloth.

Preparation/Set-Up
Set up an area where balls can be kicked, either inside or outside. Have some sort of "goal" that children can kick the ball into.

Procedures

1. Let the children choose a partner. Tell them that they will have to work together using their legs tied together in order to kick a ball.

2. Have children stand next to each other.

3. Using the soft cloth, tie the inside legs of two children together.

4. Children are to work together to kick the ball to the "goal" using their inside legs.

5. Repeat two or three times.

6. Encourage children to talk to each other while doing this activity.

Adaptations for Children With Disabilities

This activity will require balance and coordination. Pair children together who have similar levels of ability. Provide physical assistance as needed. Work one-on-one with students as needed. This activity can be very frustrating for the child whose partner has trouble organizing or completing the movement.

82 Bowling

Target Objective
Increase gross motor skills, turn-taking, counting, one-to-one correspondence, coordination, following rules

Developmental Domains
Gross Motor, Social, Cognitive, Fine Motor

Multiple Intelligences
Bodily, Spatial, Interpersonal, Logical

Materials
Commercially available toy bowling pins and balls. Pins and balls can also be made out of large plastic soda bottles, partially filled with sand, and soft rubber balls. You will need a set of bowling pins and two balls for every two or three children.

Preparation/Set-Up
Using two 10–12 foot long poles or boards (if available), set up a "bowling alley" with pins at one end and balls at the other. Arrange the 10 pins in normal fashion.

Procedures

1. This activity works best with two children at a time.

2. One child will roll the ball, and the other will count the number of pins that have been knocked down and set them up again.

3. Repeat two times, and count the total number of pins knocked down. The pins are set up again, and the children switch roles.

4. Each child should get five or six opportunities to bowl.

5. The teacher should help children set up the pins and give assistance in counting as needed.

Adaptations for Children With Disabilities

Dots on the floor may be used to identify where the pins should be placed. For some children it may be necessary to reduce the distance that the ball is rolled.

Directed Play

83 Ring Around the Rosie

Target Objective
Coordination, socialization, following directions

Developmental Domains
Gross Motor, Language, Social

Multiple Intelligences
Bodily, Linguistic, Interpersonal

Materials
None.

Preparation/Set-Up
Large carpeted area.

Procedures

1. Arrange a small group of standing children into a circle.

2. Have them sing "Ring Around the Rosie" while they walk around in a circle.

3. Vary the speed of singing: very slow, slow, fast.

4. Vary the action at the end to include such things as jump up and down, crawl, or roll.

5. Let children choose what actions they want to do.

Adaptations for Children With Disabilities

Children with pronounced physical impairments can participate by having someone assist them with their wheelchairs. Or a child can turn the music on and off using an adaptive switch attached to the music source.

84 Flag Color Tag

Target Objective
Identification and recognition of colors, following directions, playing group games

Developmental Domains
Language, Cognitive, Social, Gross Motor

Multiple Intelligences
Linguistic, Spatial, Bodily, Interpersonal

Materials
4" x 4" paper or cardboard squares of several different primary colors, string. This activity can be easily varied for children to find shapes, numbers, or letters.

Preparation/Set-Up
Punch two or three holes close to the top of the squares and lace the string through the holes to make a "belt" for each child. Each square should tear away easily from the belt. Have a large, open, indoor area or play outside.

Procedures

1. Let children pick out and name the color of the belt they wish to wear. Assist each child in putting the "belt" on and tying it.

2. Play of the game is similar to flag football and tag.

3. Select one child to be "it" and name a color for him or her to grab. Say "Go."

4. The child who is "it" chases another child with the chosen color and pulls one of the color tags off that child's belt.

5. The child being chased "freezes" when the tag is pulled.

6. Let children take turns being "it."

Adaptations for Children With Disabilities

It can be useful to limit the size of the play area in which this activity is conducted. Be alert to who is chasing whom and provide guidance as needed.

85 Basketball and Soccer

Target Objective
Increase gross motor, body in space, standing on one foot, kicking, motor coordination, balance, endurance, develop an understanding of games and rules

Developmental Domains
Gross Motor, Fine Motor, Social, Language

Multiple Intelligences
Bodily, Interpersonal, Linguistic

Materials
Basketballs and rubber kick balls and some kind of goal. Good commercially available, child-sized basketballs and soccer goals are made by a variety of toy companies.

Preparation/Set-Up
Basketball goals are set up on a wall or are placed in an open area with a flat surface. Adjust the goals to the appropriate height or distance. Basketball goals should be about four feet off the ground. The soccer goals are 10–15 feet apart.

Procedures

1. Basketball and soccer are popular sports. They are strongly encouraged within school districts and their communities. It helps to learn the basics of both games at a young age. These games promote motor skills and can be used to increase cooperation and teamwork.

2. Separate the children into two small groups, one group at the basketball goal and the other at a soccer goal. Provide each child with a ball. Allow the children to shoot or kick the balls freely into the basket or net.

3. Encourage turn-taking and waiting. After a period of time, have the children divide into pairs. One child is shooting the ball and the other retrieving and tossing the ball back to the shooter for basketball. The other pair is set up as a kicker and goalie. Promote teamwork between the pairs. Switch roles to provide all the children with a complete experience.

4. There should be little emphasis on competition or winning. However, offering compliments and giving encouragement to one another is strongly recommended, for example, "Way to go!" "You can do it!" "I'm glad you're on my team!"

Adaptations for Children With Disabilities

Children with physical or health impairments will tire easily and may have difficulty sustaining the activity or coordinating the movements required to shoot or kick a ball. Staff should provide physical support or adapted materials as needed. Consultation with a physical therapist may be necessary to best meet individual needs of children. Praise children for cooperating.

Yoga and the Young Child

Yoga is a noncompetitive activity that children can enjoy with guidance and support. Yoga involves a union between the body, mind, and spirit. Thus, there is a balance between the six developmental domains, as well as the eight intelligences. Yoga will help calm and relax children and provide a source of kinesthetic awareness by helping them to feel and think about their muscles and bodies. These activities can be very useful with children who have attention problems, such as attention deficit disorder or learning disabilities. Yoga can help increase concentration and attention to task.

Breathing is as important to yoga as balance and movement. It is impossible to have one without the other. Breathing should occur only through the nose. The exhalation should always be at least two counts longer than the inhalation. For example, if you breathe in up to six counts, then you exhale eight counts. Breathing in and out should be done slowly. For younger children, count for them as you direct them through the activities.

When doing yoga exercises, have a large, open space with enough room for children to spread out. Have the children take off their shoes and socks. Try to provide a nonskid surface. Yoga mats would be helpful for this. The environment should have soft lighting and be free of distractions. Soft, soothing music is also helpful. Children should be encouraged to take care of bathroom needs before beginning. The children are asked to not talk during these exercises unless they need assistance. The names of the positions are generally descriptive of how the pose will look and will aid children in remembering what to do.

It will be important to model these poses for the children, so practice them before working with the children. Teachers should always assist the students to ensure proper alignment and balance. Having prior experience with yoga or practice with an experienced yoga instructor would be helpful. Always consult with a physical therapist before doing any of these exercises with children who may have health or physical impairments.

The following yoga positions or poses are appropriate for young children. These are positions that are more easily learned and not as difficult as yoga poses for adults. However, most of these are poses used and practiced by adults.

Directed Play   170

The Seat

1. Have children sit cross-legged on the floor, shin to shin.

2. Make sure they are sitting on the "sits bones," or the bony protrusions at the bottom of the buttocks. Take time to explore the "sits bones" by finding them, then rocking back and forth on them.

3. While seated, have children press down through the thighs, rolling the shoulders back. Slightly tuck the chin to make the neck long.

4. Observe or become aware of tightness in the body.

5. Have them breathe in and out through the nose, six counts in and eight counts out.

6. The Seat allows a child to think about how his or her body feels. It also provides practice in how to become still.

The Table

1. Children are on the floor on their hands and knees. Knees are directly under the hips. Wrists are directly under the shoulders.

2. Their backs should be flat and stomachs parallel to the floor. The back of the head is even with the shoulders.

3. Have them breathe in through the nose six counts and out eight counts.

4. Repeat the sequence no less than three times.

5. This position is a foundation for many other poses, so spend time on it to be sure the children are comfortable with it.

The Plank

1. Children begin this position in the Table position. Children should have their hands placed on the floor directly under their shoulders with their toes tucked.

2. They should then "walk" their knees back a bit and bring the legs together approximately two inches apart.

3. They should then straighten the knees and legs to form a straight board, or "plank," in a smooth plane. Their bottoms should not be up or down but in a straight line with the rest of the body.

4. Have them move their shoulders down and away from the ears and breath in and out.

Scared Cat

1. While in the Table position have the children inhale six counts.

2. On the next exhale tip the tailbone down toward the floor; pull the stomach muscles in, and round the upper back towards the ceiling.

3. Have children tuck in their chins, dropping their heads forward.

4. Breathe six counts in and eight counts out through the nose.

5. Repeat the sequence no less than three times.

Cow

1. While in the Table position, continue to breathe in and out. On the next inhale, children tip the tailbone up, drop the belly to the floor, pull the shoulder blades into each other, and look up.

2. Breathe six counts in and eight counts out through the nose.

3. Remember to keep the mouth relaxed. Have children keep the tongue down from the roof of the mouth and lips slightly parted.

4. Repeat sequence no less than three times.

Cat's Tail

1. From the Table position, have them look behind to the right. Direct them to bring the right hip and right shoulder together.

2. Looking over the right shoulder breathe into the lower back. That is, have children think about the breathing. It is best to focus on the left, or opposite, side while breathing.

3. Return to the center Table position and repeat on the left side.

4. Continue the sequence no less than three times on each side or as needed. This is a great warm-up for the lower back and is often a favorite among children.

5. Remember to breathe six counts in and eight counts out.

Mountain

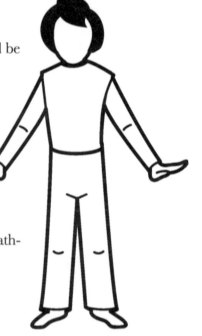

1. While standing, position the feet hip-width apart. Feet should be parallel with each other facing forward.

2. Have children press their feet down into the floor.

3. Have the children try to spread their toes apart and press into the outside of their feet while breathing in and out slowly.

4. Have them shift their weight back slightly with their shoulders, neck, and head directly over the hips.

5. The shoulders should drop and move slightly back while breathing in and out. Arms to side.

6. They will continue to press down into the feet and breathe.

Tree

1. With children in the Mountain position (standing pose), tell them to press their feet into the floor and look straight ahead.

2. Have them slightly shift their weight to their right foot.

3. They should then raise their left foot up to touch the inner thigh of the right leg. They can use their left hand to help raise their foot if needed.

4. The left knee is pointed out as if a branch.

5. If possible they should raise their hands over their heads with palms touching while continuing to breath in and out.

6. Have them move the left foot down and repeat using the right foot.

7. This is a challenging position, requiring good balance and the ability to stand on one foot.

Directed Play

Child Pose 1

1. Before beginning this pose, review body part names with the children.

2. From the Table position, have the children inhale. On the exhale, direct them to drop the bottom back toward their heels.

3. Their stomachs will rest on their thighs, and their foreheads will be touching the floor.

4. The arms are stretched reaching forward with the palms pressing into the floor.

5. The children should be breathing at least six counts in and eight counts out.

6. This is a very relaxing activity for both adults and children.

7. Repeat the breathing sequence six or seven times.

Cobra

1. Review the necessary body parts before beginning.

2. Have the children lie on their stomachs with their foreheads on the floor.

3. Legs should be parallel and hip-width apart with the tops of the feet touching the floor.

4. Hands should be placed under the shoulders, pressing into the floor.

5. The elbows should be tucked to the side of the body and pointed "toward the sky."

6. On the exhale, they should gently squeeze their buttocks and then, on the inhale, squeeze the shoulder blades back and together.

7. The shoulder action will assist them in lifting their head and chest off the floor to a cobra position.

8. Have them continue to breath in and out slowly.

9. Be careful that children do not overextend the lower back. If it hurts, they are lifting too high and should stop.

Chapter 7

Down-Faced Dog

1. Begin by having children in the Table position. They should spread their fingers wide like a paw stretching.

2. The children should press both hands into the floor and inhale.

3. On the exhale, have them straighten their knees, raising their bottoms to the sky.

4. Have them move their heads down toward (but not touching) the floor, relaxing the neck. The back of the head drops down, relaxing the neck.

5. Their heels should be flat on the floor with their hips pointing up.

6. The arms should be shoulder-width apart, with the inner crease of the elbow facing forward. Shoulders should be away from the ears.

7. Breathing should continue with six counts in and eight counts out.

8. Though this may seem like a difficult pose, young children often do this naturally in play. It can build strength and endurance and is relaxing when done correctly.

Waterfall

1. This activity will need a wall free of clutter.

2. Have the children sit directly in front of the wall.

3. Next, have them lift their legs up onto the wall and lie on their backs. They should scoot their bottoms as close to the wall as possible with the legs extending upward.

4. They should try to relax their feet as much as possible.

5. Their arms should be at their sides, approximately six inches away from the body with the palms facing up to the sky.

6. Encourage children to imagine their legs as a waterfall with water flowing down the legs and through the body while breathing slowly in and out.

7. This position is intended to increase body awareness by drawing attention to those body parts that may feel tense or different.

8. Children should come out of the pose slowly by rolling to one side and dropping the legs down.

Directed Play

Butterfly

1. Have children get in the Waterfall position.

2. Have them bring the bottoms of their feet together and slowly drop their knees down and out while moving the heels down. The legs will simulate butterfly wings.

3. Children are to breath in and out several times and move the legs straight back up into the Waterfall position.

4. Have them drop their knees and roll to side when coming out of this pose.

The Lion

1. Have children sit on their knees with their bottom resting on their heels.

2. On the inhale, have them pull their hands up to their chests.

3. On the exhale, have them lunge their arms and hands forward, with fingers touching the floor, to stand like a lion.

4. They should open their eyes and mouth as wide as they can, stick out their tongue in an exaggerated way, and give a "roar."

5. The Lion gives the often-neglected eyes, mouth, and face a good stretch.

Squat

1. Children should stand with their feet hip-width apart and with toes pointed straight ahead.

2. While exhaling, have them squat down between the feet, dropping the "sits bones" as close to the floor as possible. Their feet should be flat on the floor. For children who have trouble keeping their feet flat put a small towel or blanket under their heels.

3. They should place their elbows on the inside of their knees and press their palms together.

4. Have them breath in and out five or six times.

5. Have them stand slowly while breathing in.

Crescent Moon

1. Have children lie on the floor on their backs. Their legs should be together and straight and their arms close to their body.

2. On the inhale, have them bring their arms over their heads, pointing straight.

3. With arms and legs still on the floor, exhale and have them slowly move their feet slightly to the right. Follow by having them move their arms to the right, forming a crescent moon.

4. Have them breathe in and out several times while thinking about stretching the left side of the body.

5. Move back to the original position and then do the other side.

6. Repeat several times.

Fine Motor and Perceptual Activities

Sensory Stimulation and Integration	180
Block Play	181
Sand	185
Play-Dough or Clay	187
General Activities	188
Coloring and Drawing	195
Mazes	198
Painting	198
Scissor Activities	204
Murals	219

Sensory Stimulation and Integration

Our senses give us information about the world around us. Touch, taste, smell, hearing, and vision all guide our actions and help us understand our environment. Lesser-known sensations involve vestibular mechanism and kinesthesia. Movement stimulates vestibular sensation. Jumping, swinging, climbing, or spinning on a merry-go-round all involve a significant amount of movement that is transmitted to our brain from the inner ear. Some children may be slow to process this information and can fall or bump into things easily. Kinesthetic sensation gives us information from inside the body, such as the feelings we get from muscles and joints.

Providing children with sensory stimulation is a very old and natural practice and can easily be done with common materials. It is essential that we provide children with a wide variety of stimulation to each of the senses. This can be done in activities such as snack time, which is a natural way to promote stimulation of smell, taste, and touch. One of the suggested prop boxes listed in Chapter Two includes a variety of sensory stimulation materials.

Children enjoy stimulation of the senses, and some children may actively seek it out. Be alert to what children may be communicating to you about sensory input. For example, a child who often bites may be communicating a need for tactile or taste stimulation. Letting the child chew on something may meet this need and eliminate inappropriate behaviors. An occupational therapist once told us that children can write their own therapies, that they can tell us what they need. We need to observe children closely and be alert to what they may be trying to tell us.

Sensory integration involves our ability to take in information from our senses and combine it with our memories or knowledge to generate a behavior or response. This is a process that takes place very quickly in the brain and central nervous system.

Some children experience sensory integration difficulties. The sensory stimulation they receive from one or more of their senses is not processed easily, and it is difficult for them to understand or perform certain behaviors. The ability to attend to an activity or activity levels in general may be affected. A child who has difficulty regulating his or her attention or one who seems unresponsive to sensory stimulation may be showing signs of sensory integration problems. A child with sensory integration problems may not readily move around and explore the environment, may seem disorganized in play or engage in limited play activities, and may have difficulty calming after a physical activity or appear to be clumsy.

Children may also experience sensory defensiveness in one or more of the senses. Tactile, auditory, or visual defensiveness shows up when a child is hypersensitive to touch, certain noises, or light. Children may also have defensiveness in oral-motor (mouth), vestibular (intolerance of movements), or smell senses. Be alert and program effectively for those children who demonstrate an overly sensitive reaction to noise, touch, vision, or smell.

Directed Play   180

Block Play

Blocks are a common and enjoyable play material for young children. Blocks can be used to teach a variety of concepts and enhance many play activities. There are a variety of blocks available for children. Basic wooden blocks are very common, as are Duplos® and Legos®, bristle blocks, waffle blocks, and the large, brick-like cardboard blocks. Different blocks have different characteristics. Blocks can differ in size, shape, color, cost, and texture. They can also differ in terms of what can be built, how much space is needed, and how they need to be cleaned. Ideally, many different types of blocks should be available for children and it is reasonable to let children combine different types of blocks together in play.

Small wooden blocks have been available for many years. It is important that these blocks be of a uniform size and shape because children are learning concepts such as balance and symmetry. Small wooden blocks can be purchased commercially but are often expensive. These blocks can also be made, perhaps by a kind parent or volunteer. The blocks should be smooth and free of splinters. Covering the blocks with a nontoxic varnish can help to preserve them and make them easier to clean.

Duplo® and Lego® blocks connect and interlock. This gives children an opportunity to build things that they cannot with wooden blocks, such as cars, boats, airplanes, or animals. However, Duplos®/Legos® are small and do require more fine motor control than larger blocks. Duplo®/Lego® creations can look very realistic and have movable parts. The blocks have the disadvantage of being expensive, but they are highly durable, easy to clean, and should last for many years.

Larger, cardboard "brick" blocks are needed to build larger structures, such as a pretend post office or a house. These types of blocks require much more space than the smaller blocks in terms of both use and storage. It may also be necessary to reduce the number of children playing with these blocks at any one time to avoid overcrowding and conflicts.

Assuring Appropriate Block Play

There are five ecological factors that need to be considered to help ensure an appropriate use of blocks. These include time/stages, quantity of blocks, adequate space, other play materials, and use of language.

First, it is important to consider the developmental sequence of block play. A number of authors have noted the consistent developmental sequence in children's block play (Johnson, 1984; Reifel, 1984). In general, the literature describes block constructions increasing in complexity as children get older, reflecting advancing motor and cognitive skills. **Table 8.1** outlines six stages of block construction.

Children will gradually work through these six increasingly sophisticated stages of block construction. As children's motor and cognitive skills increase, they are able to build more elaborate constructions. Children who are four to five years old also need more time to complete their constructions than two- to three-year-old children. Older children

Table 8.1

Stages of Block Play

Stage 1   Toddlers—stacking blocks in piles, carrying blocks around

Stage 2   2–3 years—vertical and horizontal rows of blocks, vertical stacking, repetition or "do it again"

Stage 3   3 years—bridges, vertical and horizontal repetition, doing it over and over again

Stage 4   4 years—enclosures, stacking rows, bridges, vertical and horizontal combinations used to create enclosed patterns, repetition

Stage 5   4–5 years—symmetry and balance of constructions –(what is on one side will be on the other side), stacking, rows, bridges, vertical and horizontal combinations

Stage 6   5 years—more dramatic play with constructions, naming of structures, complicated three-dimensional structures

will need "Extended Time" to play with their block constructions once they are built. In addition to more time, children should be provided with other toys as "props." These might include toy farm animals, cars, furniture, or dolls.

In Stage 1 block play, children should be allowed to stack blocks and put them in piles. They may also want to carry them around. Children in Stage 1 block play will not build complex structures. At Stage 2, children create vertical and horizontal creations. These might include roads or fences. There will also be a considerable amount of repetition as the children practice their basic block skills over and over again.

At Stage 3, children create block constructions that have bridges, and these too may be repeated over and over again. New kinds of creations may be built, such as farms or houses. There is considerably more vertical building at this stage.

In Stages 4, 5, and 6, children will build elaborate block constructions based on the skills they have learned earlier. These constructions include enclosures with balance or symmetry, and children will engage in pretend play using their creations.

A second consideration surrounding block play involves the number of blocks available. It is important that each child have an adequate number of blocks to play with. This can mean that the children may need 20–40 wooden blocks each, given their developmental age. Younger children will need fewer blocks than older children. Each child needs an adequate number of blocks to avoid conflict during play. For example, a study on the effect of different quantities of blocks was reported by Bender (1978). It focused on six four-year-old boys. The boys were exposed to two block conditions: 20 blocks and 70 blocks. In the 20-block condition only two of the boys built constructions. In the 70-block condition all six boys were active participants in the block play. In the 70-block condition 83 instances of positive behaviors were observed, whereas only 19 incidents of positive behaviors were observed in the 20-block condition. No disputes were noted in the 70-block condition, but disputes were reported in the 20-block condition. *The Block Book* (Hirsch, 1984) lists the number of basic unit wooden blocks of different sizes recommended for children of different ages. On average, it is recommended that three-year-old children have about 25 blocks each, four-year-olds about 35 blocks each, and five-year-olds about 45 blocks each. The number of blocks listed here is more than what many early childhood centers or schools have available. For schools that cannot acquire more blocks because of space or financial reasons, a simple solution would be to restrict the number of children who go to the block area at any one time. Based on the age of the children, and the number of blocks available, it may be necessary to send only two children to a block area at one time.

The amount of space available for block play is the third important consideration. Ideally, the space used to build the block constructions should not be in a traffic area. This will help prevent block constructions from being knocked down accidentally and allow children an opportunity to extend their play. It will also increase the likelihood that block constructions can stay set up for the next day. It would be ideal to have four to five feet between individual children's structures. The flooring should be even. Carpeting will help to reduce the noise level. A considerable amount of shelving will also be required to store the blocks.

The fourth consideration is having an ample quantity of other toys available to combine with the blocks. Toy cars, animals, boats, or people are useful in enhancing dramatic and pretend play. Other blocks of unique sizes, shapes, or colors can add to the decorations or interesting architectural elements of the creations. Other play materials can be added to the block play based on a wide variety of themes.

Fifth, children should be encouraged to talk about their block constructions. Teachers don't need to ask children "What is it?" but rather should note interesting or special features of the structures. Noting how a sturdy foundation will help hold the structure up, or how difficult it must have been to build a "roof" promotes the children's pride in their accomplishment and encourages discussion. Older children are much more likely to engage in dramatic play with the block constructions than younger children.

Block Activities

Blocks are an excellent way to teach beginning math or science concepts. Blocks can be counted, ordered by size, and used to teach concepts such as weight and balance. A number of activities in this book make use of blocks.

Table 8.2

Some Simple Block Activities

- Pick up a block and have children find a block that looks like it.
- Have children pick up all blocks that are a certain shape (square, rectangle, curved).
- Count the number of blocks used to build a structure.
- Have children arrange blocks from largest to smallest.
- Using large cardboard blocks, have the children create cages for wild animals.
- Using wooden blocks, have children make a town. Combine with cars, trucks, and people and build roads and houses.
- Have children work together to build a tower.

---

86 Block Sorting

Target Objective
Recognition of similarities and differences

Developmental Domains
Fine Motor, Cognitive, Social, Language

Multiple Intelligences
Bodily, Linguistic, Interpersonal

Materials
Wooden unit blocks of various sizes and shapes; three to four small cardboard boxes.

Preparation/Set-Up
Large open area away from foot traffic.

Procedures

1. This activity can be conducted as a stand-alone activity or at the end of another activity. If done as the latter, it could be a part of the clean-up process.

2. Provide a small group of children with various sizes and/or shapes of blocks in a large pile on the floor. Provide a container that has a picture of the type of block to go in it.

Directed Play

3. Demonstrate how the children are to find a block and put it in the proper container.

4. Place the containers within easy reach of all children and let them begin to sort the blocks.

5. Encourage talking among the children and watch children carefully to be sure they get the proper block in the correct container.

Adaptations for Children With Disabilities

For younger or children with more pronounced disabilities begin with only two types of blocks and containers. Gradually increase to three or four different types of blocks.

Sand

Playing in sand is both fun and educational. Outdoor sandboxes are used to teach a variety of concepts in a natural way. Indoor sand tables are also good but do not offer quite the same experience as outdoor sandboxes do. When outside, children should be encouraged, as weather permits, to take their shoes off so that they can feel the sand with hands and feet. This also provides a natural opportunity to work on the self-help skills of taking off and putting on shoes.

Filling, scooping, and dumping are common sand activities. Concepts such as empty and full, heavy and light, in and out, up and down, and most and least can all be addressed with filling and dumping. It can also be fun to bury seashells or other treasures in the sand for children to find. Common materials for the sandbox include cups, buckets, shovels, sieves, and dishpans. Check the materials frequently to make sure they are clean and free from cracks.

Combining sand with other play items will enhance the play experience. Combining sand and water is an old but enjoyable activity for children that is easier and less messy to do outdoors. With sand and water children can make rivers, lakes, dams, sand castles, and can even float boats. It is essential that children be given "Extended Time" to engage in these activities. It will take time for the children to make their sand creations and time to engage in the higher-order play it can encourage. Encourage cooperation among children by having them work together. For example, one child can bury something in the sand for another to find. Some buried items might include different colored blocks, toy people, or dinosaurs.

Combining sand with other play materials, such as plastic blocks, transportation toys, dinosaurs, or toy people, will promote increased opportunities for good language experiences. The added materials create or add to the dramatic play experiences generated by the children.

As with any activity, safety is an important consideration. Review and discuss rules for sand play frequently with the children. The rules should include not throwing sand and keeping sand below eye level. Never leave children unattended at the sand and only use materials that are unbreakable.

Table 8.3

Sand Activities

- Children make footprints and have other children guess whose feet it is.
- Children fill buckets with sand then turn them over quickly to make small castles. Make several to create a town. Have three different-sized buckets to create a sequence from small to large.
- Children draw faces or other designs, such as circles, squares, stars, or diamonds.
- Children play tic-tac-toe in the sand.
- Children draw letters and numbers in the sand.

Songs Involving Sand

Let's all play in the sand,
It feels so good on our hands.
We can dig it and sift it
And shake it about.
We can spoon it in pails
And then pour it out.

Sand castle on the beach,
I built you big and strong.
A wave washed in upon the sand,
Whoops. You were gone.

Sand can be wet,
And sand can be dry.
I like both,
And I'll tell you why.
I can make castles
With wet sand,
And pouring it dry
Feels just grand.

Play-Dough or Clay

Play-dough can be made or purchased. It is a good material to promote sensory integration and other fine motor skills. This material is easily incorporated into just about any thematic unit. To enhance play, have other materials such as dull plastic knives, scoops, egg slicers, cookie cutters, garlic presses, scissors, or rolling pins handy. A helpful sourcebook for play-dough activities is entitled *Mudworks* (Kohl, 1989).

For children with orthopedic handicaps it is helpful to make the play-dough more pliable by adding a little more water to it or warming it in a microwave. All children should be encouraged to use both hands. For children with disabilities who have one side of the body affected more than the other, have them use one hand (assisting hand) to hold or press the play-dough while the other hand molds it into a shape. Provide warm-up activities for students who have difficulty controlling hand movements. Warm-up activities might include stretching out rubber bands, pressing fingers together, opening and closing fists rapidly, shaking out hands and fingers with rapid shakes, or molding clay.

Stages of play with play-dough or clay include:

1. Random manipulation—play-dough or clay is squeezed, pounded, or manipulated in an uncontrolled way.

2. Patting and rolling—play-dough is rolled into balls or thin ropes or made into "pancakes."

3. Circles and rectangles—play-dough is manipulated to make balls or boxes.

4. Synthetic manipulation—objects are made by a child putting together separate pieces of play-dough.

5. Analytic manipulation—objects are made and formed by using only one piece of play-dough.

6. Figures—objects or forms are shaped into figures (i.e. snowman, car).

Interacting with play-dough or clay is often a solitary activity for many children. Encourage them to talk to one another about what they are making or doing. Make statements about what children are doing rather than asking questions. Point out unique features of their creations or similarities between the different creations.

Simple Stove Top Play-Dough Recipe

1 cup flour

½ cup salt

2 tablespoons cream of tartar

Combine and add:

1 cup water

2 tablespoons vegetable or cooking oil

2 tablespoons food coloring (optional)

Scented oil (optional)

Mix and cook until it pulls away from the pan.

---

187   Chapter 8

General Activities

87 Pop Beads

Target Objective
Increase eye-hand coordination, visual perception, sequencing, concept of next, strength

Developmental Domains
Fine Motor, Cognitive, Language

Multiple Intelligences
Bodily, Linguistic, Intrapersonal

Materials
Commercially available pop beads.

Preparation/Set-Up
Have materials preconnected and ready to use at group setting. Have at least a dozen pop beads for each child. Children are to sit on the floor or at a table.

Procedures

1. Have children sit in a small group and do some simple hand exercises. Present the pop beads. Demonstrate how they connect and disconnect.

2. Different cognitive tasks can be presented depending on the age of the children, such as matching a sequence of color (red, blue, red, blue), having children make pop beads of various lengths and ordering by size; or making shapes (circles) or designs.

3. Once completed, pull the construction apart and leave the beads in a pile for the next child to use.

Adaptations for Children With Disabilities

Watch children for any problems with visual perception or manipulation of the pop beads. Provide physical assistance as needed. Children lacking upper body strength may be able to get the beads connected but may struggle with pulling them apart.

Directed Play 188

88 Bead Stringing

Target Objective
Increase fine motor skills, sequencing, turn-taking, concept of next

Developmental Domains
Fine Motor, Cognitive, Social

Multiple Intelligences
Bodily, Spatial, Logical, Interpersonal

Materials
Assorted sizes and colors of beads with shoelaces or strings.

Preparation/Set-Up
Have beads, strings with end knots, pattern cards. Have children do simple hand exercises before beginning.

Procedures

1. This activity should begin with children stringing beads by themselves. Point out the color, size, shape, or order of beads.

2. Gradually have children imitate a sequence of beads (e.g., red, blue, red, blue). As they master imitation, increase the number of colors in the sequence and have them copy or create a pattern.

3. A picture or example is always helpful to the children.

4. In another activity, have three children sit in a small circle on the floor.

5. Give each child a certain color or style of bead.

6. Have children, in turn, place their bead on the string and pass the string to the next child.

7. The string goes around the circle with children putting on their beads. Comment about who is putting on what kind or color of bead.

8. Have the string go around the circle several times.

9. In another activity, the children can make necklaces out of breakfast cereal or a similar food. Children enjoy making edible jewelry.

Adaptations for Children With Disabilities

Children with perceptual-motor difficulties will need beads with large openings. Children with physical disabilities will benefit from the string being held by another. Many other items can be substituted for stringing, including macaroni or cut-up straws. Physically assist children as needed.

89 Form Boards

Target Objective
Matching shapes, pincer grasp, manipulation of objects

Developmental Domains
Fine Motor, Cognitive, Language

Multiple Intelligences
Spatial, Bodily

Materials
Commercially available or homemade form boards with various shapes. Begin with circle, square, and triangle for younger children. Form boards with other shapes, such as diamonds, rectangles, and stars, are used as children get older.

Preparation/Set-Up
Form boards available with different shapes.

Procedures

1. Have children sit at a table or on the floor. Show them the target shapes and the form board and demonstrate that they are to put the shapes in the form boards.

2. Provide the materials and let children place the shape pieces in the form boards. Give children time to experiment, and only intervene if the children appear frustrated.

3. Trade boards with peers.

Adaptations for Children With Disabilities

For younger children use form boards with only two shapes and gradually increase the number of shapes on the boards. Drilling small holes and inserting short pegs to make them easier to hold can adapt shape pieces. Typical three-year-olds should have no problem with this task.

Directed Play 190

90 Nuts and Bolts

Target Objective
Identification and use of objects; increase fine motor; size differences; prepositions—on, off, around; right and left; concepts of go together and pairs

Developmental Domains
Fine Motor, Cognitive

Multiple Intelligences
Logical, Linguistic, Bodily

Materials
A large quantity of common nuts and bolts of different sizes. Larger ones are easier to handle. These are available at hardware stores or from families. Pieces of wood (holes drilled) that can be bolted together (optional).

Preparation/Set-Up
Materials available on the floor or table with trays and tubs for easy cleanup. Exercise hands before beginning.

Procedures

1. Use the nuts and bolts to address size concepts: big/little, long/short. Show the children the different nuts and bolts. Explain that these are items used to build or connect things.

2. Let children practice screwing the nuts onto the bolts and note that they go in circles, one way to tighten and one way to loosen.

3. Let children practice bolting two pieces of wood together if the wood is available. Be sure wood, such as pine, is free from splinters and has holes drilled in several places.

4. Children are to work freely, experimenting with a variety of nuts and bolts.

Adaptations for Children With Disabilities

Caution needs to be exercised with younger children. Larger nuts and bolts, including commercial plastic ones, will prevent any danger of choking and will be easier to use.

91 Lock It Up

Target Objective
Identification and use of objects, safety, increase fine motor, concepts of open and close

Developmental Domains
Cognitive, Language, Fine Motor

Multiple Intelligences
Logical, Linguistic, Bodily

Materials
Assorted locks screwed to a wooden box or board, hinges. Locks and latches can be acquired from a hardware store or could be donated by kind families. A parent might be willing to attach the locks/latches to the board or wooden box.

Preparation/Set-Up
Have materials available. Exercise hands before beginning.

Procedures

1. Children practice locking and unlocking locks and latches on a wooden board or wooden box.

2. If using a wooden box, the activity can be enhanced by having a "surprise" inside a "door" when opened.

3. Emphasize concepts of open and closed and note how the different locks and latches operate.

Adaptations for Children With Disabilities

This activity will require fairly well-developed fine motor skills and a good pincer grasp. Related activities include clothes fasteners, such as buttons, zippers and snaps.

Directed Play

92 Stone Drop

Target Objective
Perceptual-motor

Developmental Domains
Gross Motor, Fine Motor,
Cognitive

Multiple Intelligences
Bodily, Spatial, Logical

Materials
A number of small stones or pebbles; a jug
or coffee can with a wide opening for each
child; small chair.

Preparation/Set-Up
Large motor area inside or outside.

Procedures

1. Show children the small stones and the coffee can. Tell children they are going to play a game where they drop stones into a can. Demonstrate it for them.

2. Have the children place the can on the floor and set a chair next to the container.

3. Have children stand on the chair and drop the stones down into the container.

4. Repeat several times.

5. As children get better with the task, use a different container with a smaller top opening.

Adaptations for Children With Disabilities

Reducing the distance children must drop the stones will make it easier for them. Have a large coffee can with a wide opening or use some other container such as a bucket for an easier target. Allow the children to sit instead of stand.

193 Chapter 8

93 Tower Ball

Target Objective
Increase eye-hand coordination, problem solving, turn-taking, cooperation

Developmental Domains
Fine Motor, Gross Motor, Cognitive, Social

Multiple Intelligences
Bodily, Spatial, Interpersonal

Materials
Cardboard or wooden blocks; different-sized balls, such as tennis balls or larger rubber balls.

Preparation/Set-Up
Large open play area with materials available.

Procedures

1. This activity is similar to the game played at carnivals. Children try to knock down the blocks with the balls.

2. Let the children build a tower using the wooden blocks or cardboard blocks. The size of the tower will depend on the child's age and ability. If using wood blocks, the tower should not be higher than the head for safety reasons.

3. Have the children stand at a distance from the tower. This distance depends on the child's age and ability. Younger children should stand closer than older children.

4. Have the child throw the ball toward the tower to knock it down. Let children take turns throwing the balls and rebuilding the towers.

Adaptations for Children With Disabilities

Experiment with different-sized balls to see which best meets the needs of the children. Shorten the distance between the tower and the child as needed.

Directed Play

Coloring and Drawing

Coloring and drawing are important prewriting skills and provide for self-expression and creativity. Children should be exposed to a wide variety of drawing materials, including crayons, pencils, markers, and chalk. Make sure the markers are nontoxic and washable. They should also be given a variety of materials to draw on. Papers of different thickness or texture, such as construction paper, contact paper, or heavy glossy paper, should be used. Incorporate drawings into various activities as found in the Murals section. Before beginning most coloring or drawing tasks, exercise the hands so that they are warmed up and ready to work.

Children will generally progress through stages in coloring and drawing. At first, children will simply bang crayons on paper or even try to mouth them. Next, they will scribble randomly on a page and use color in a random way, perhaps using only one color per page. They begin to spontaneously draw horizontal and vertical lines but later move on to imitating them. They will begin to use several colors per picture and start staying within lines. They will progress to using color appropriately and will be able to adjust their drawing strokes to the size of the page and the area in which they are drawing. In the beginning they will imitate circular strokes and later they will be able to copy lines, circles, and crosses. Being able to imitate and copy shapes such as circles, diagonals, triangles, diamonds, and squares is important to the development of prewriting. Eventually the children will be able to color and draw small designs with detail using a variety of appropriate colors.

Remember that it is the process, not the product, that is most important. Provide the children with activities that will allow them to practice these skills and do the work themselves. Providing children with activities in which the parents or teachers do most of the work is not appropriate. See Kohl (1994) and Kohl and Gainer (1991) for sources of art activities.

When children are coloring and drawing, encourage them to talk about what they are producing. Make statements such as, "Tell me about your drawing," "What part do you like best?" or "How did you make that?" Be nonjudgmental about what they have created. Praise effort and performance often. Always encourage appropriate grasp and handedness. As a general rule, have children finish a drawing task with the same hand that they started with. Provide opportunities for rest if you see children switching hands or losing grip.

Drawing Ideas:

- Have children trace over an existing picture.
- Have children draw from a model.
- Chalk drawings outside on cement.
- Keep drawings and combine them into a book for each child.

195 Chapter 8

94 Draw a Person

Target Objective	**Materials**
Increase eye-hand coordination, recognition of body parts and body awareness	Paper for drawing; pencils, crayons, markers, or chalk. Have a couple of examples of predrawn completed figures.
Developmental Domains	**Preparation/Set-Up**
Fine Motor, Cognitive, Self-Help, Language	All materials available at a small table. Some body parts can be predrawn for some children. Exercise hands before beginning.
Multiple Intelligences	
Bodily, Spatial, Linguistic, Logical, Musical	

Procedures

1. Instruct the children to draw a person (i.e., "Draw a man or girl or boy") on white or manila construction paper.

2. The older the child the more complete the person should be. Depending on the age of the children, encourage them to add other body parts that they have not included. This may be done directly or by asking questions such as "What do we smell with?"

3. Immature drawings will often have arms and legs coming out of the head. If this is common have children draw a person in imitation.

4. Once the children are comfortable with drawing a person have them progress to drawing animals or transportation items.

5. Children sing "Head, Shoulders, Knees, and Toes" in closing.

Adaptations for Children With Disabilities

Be aware of the developmental sequence in drawing a person and have some predrawn bodies for younger children. The sequence includes:

1. Body part features added in a top to bottom progression, drawing head and face features before drawing feet.

2. Progression from being one-dimensional (a line for a leg) to two-dimensional (circle for a nose).

Directed Play

3. Body parts are attached and recognizable.

4. Picture includes head, ears, eyes, nose, and mouth (five facial parts).

5. Picture includes earlier items, adding arm, trunk, and hands (eight body parts).

6. Picture includes all previous items, adding ears, neck, and feet (11 body parts).

7. Picture includes all previous parts with additional details, such as teeth, jewelry, clothing, or eyebrows.

95 Texture Pictures

Target Objective
Sensory stimulation, awareness of textures

Developmental Domains
Fine Motor, Cognitive, Language

Multiple Intelligences
Spatial, Bodily, Linguistic

Materials
Paper, peeled crayons, and various textures that can be laid flat under paper, e.g., various grades of sandpaper, cloth, or window screen. Exercise hands before beginning.

Preparation/Set-Up
Paper can be precut and attached to the textured material.

Procedures

1. Have a small group of children sit at a table. Tell them they are going to color pictures by drawing over something else.

2. Give each child a blank piece of paper with crayons available.

3. Place a textured material under the blank piece of paper.

4. Have children color on the blank paper using the flat sides of the crayons.

5. Let children experiment with the patterns that come through.

Adaptations for Children With Disabilities

It may be helpful to tape the textured pattern to the paper and then tape both to the table for better control.

Mazes

Mazes are an excellent way to promote many skills, including prewriting, directionality, spatial understanding, awareness of left and right, and following directions. Mazes are also a nice way to promote problem solving and sensory integration. Children can complete mazes with a variety of materials that can be used to address the multiple intelligences. The size and complexity of the mazes can easily be adapted for children of different ages. Younger children need very simple mazes that include short horizontal and vertical paths, while older, higher-functioning children can complete mazes that are more complicated, with curves and corners. Appropriate mazes are often found in activity or coloring books that can be purchased for a nominal fee. Mazes can be created in various ways including:

- Using paper, crayons, or markers
- Using finger paints
- Using an easel and paintbrushes
- Creating a pattern in sand or dirt for children to trace with their index fingers
- Using chalk on a sidewalk or wall chalkboard
- Using large blocks or chairs to make a maze to walk through or small mazes that children can move toy cars or people through
- Making "raised" mazes out of dry spaghetti glued to paper

Painting

As with coloring and drawing, children should be provided with a wide variety of painting opportunities with different materials and textures. Finger painting and painting with brushes or other items such as sponges should be done often. Make sure the paints used are washable and nontoxic. Some painting activities are also included in the Motor and Movement chapter.

96 Paint Mix-Up

Target Objective
Recognition of colors, increase fine motor and gross motor development

Developmental Domains
Fine Motor, Gross Motor, Cognitive, Language, Social

Multiple Intelligences
Bodily, Spatial, Linguistic, Interpersonal

Materials
Paint easels, various sizes of paintbrushes, various colors of tempera paints in separate containers, tape or clothespins.

Preparation/Set-Up
Paint smocks, drop cloths, large pieces of paper attached to the easels.

Procedures

1. Give the two to three children at an easel the paintbrushes and two containers of paint.

2. Have the children paint with paint from one container and then the other in separate places on the paper.

3. Next, have the children mix the two paints together to create a new color. Start with primary colors that lead to other easily recognizable colors, e.g., blue/red = purple, red/yellow = orange.

4. Have the children name the color or colors they have created.

5. Let children experiment with different colors. Encourage them to trade paints and brushes with peers.

Adaptations for Children With Disabilities

This will create an opportunity for children to cooperate. Provide assistance as needed. Let children try to work out conflicts on their own before intervening.

97 Sponge Fun

Target Objective
Increase strength and dexterity, sensory stimulation, concepts of empty and full

Developmental Domains
Fine Motor, Cognitive

Multiple Intelligences
Bodily, Linguistic

Materials
Sponges cut into 2" x 2" or 3" x 3" pieces; several small containers, such as margarine tubs; food coloring with scents (optional); towels and paint smocks.

Preparation/Set-Up
Fill containers about half full of water. Put in food coloring or scent if desired. Have children put on paint smocks and have the towels and sponges available.

Procedures

1. With several children sitting at a table, give each child a sponge and two containers. One of the containers will be half full of water and the other empty.

2. Demonstrate to the children that they are to squeeze the sponge to soak up the water in one container and squeeze it into the other container.

3. Have children begin by using their whole hand to squeeze the sponge.

4. Next, have children try to squeeze the sponge using only their thumb and first two fingers.

5. Repeat by trading containers using different colors or scents.

Adaptations for Children With Disabilities

Some children may be sensitive to the texture of the sponges or will not want to get their hands wet. Introduce this gradually and praise the children for good effort.

Directed Play

98 Smelly Art

Target Objective
Sensory stimulation, recognition of different smells

Developmental Domains
Cognitive, Fine Motor, Language

Multiple Intelligences
Logical, Spatial

Materials
Assorted colors of paints, assorted things that smell (e.g., cinnamon, nutmeg, lemon extract, vanilla).

Preparation/Set-Up
Mix the "smelly" substances into the paints.

Procedures

1. Have children paint pictures at a table or easel using the "smelly paints." Pictures can relate to themes or seasons.

2. Be sure all of the children are exposed to each of the smells.

3. Have children guess what they smell.

Adaptations for Children With Disabilities

Make sure children do not try to eat the paint. Watch them closely. Provide assistance as needed. It may be helpful to tape the paper to the table.

99 Thumbprint Picture

Target Objective
Precutting, visual perception, sensory stimulation

Developmental Domains
Fine Motor, Cognitive, Language

Multiple Intelligences
Bodily, Spatial, Intrapersonal

Materials
Finger paints, precopied pictures, paint smocks.

Preparation/Set-Up
Clear and set up a large area on tile or outside that will hold a group of six to eight children, the paper, and paints. Predraw a large shape or design relevant to a concept currently being worked on in the classroom, such as a circle or the letter "P." Have children exercise hands before beginning.

Procedures

1. Set up paint and paint smocks.

2. Copy pictures and set up trays of paint.

3. Have children put on paint smocks and take seats around a table.

4. Hold up your thumb and have children model you.

5. Talk about the pictures that you put in front of the children and how the picture relates to the current theme or topic.

6. Show children how to dip their thumbs into paint and press on the pictures.

7. Encourage children to fill in whole pictures using their thumbprints to make the picture complete.

8. Set pictures aside to dry and provide assistance in cleanup as needed.

Adaptations for Children With Disabilities

Tape paper to the table to prevent movement. Place trays of paint in such a way as to encourage children to reach across their bodies and cross midline. Encourage the use of thumbs only and provide physical assistance as needed. Let children rest if they get tired.

Directed Play

Easel Painting

Unfortunately, easel painting is an activity that many children are not routinely exposed to. Adults often think of it as too messy, and few families have easels at home. It is vital that we provide children with opportunities to practice easel painting in early childhood settings. There should be at least one easel painting activity every day.

Painting at an easel is good for cognitive and motor development and is often recommended by occupational therapists. Easel painting promotes a good grasp, upper body strength and control, and eye-hand coordination, and is an opportunity for self-expression and creativity. When painting, children should be encouraged to make fluid painting strokes rather than a random filling of space.

General materials needed include easels with tray, smocks, drop cloths, drying rack, paint, and brushes. Be sure to have assorted colors of nontoxic paints and different-sized brushes for children to use. Other painting tools can include rollers, sponges, feathers, or clothespins with cotton balls attached.

Children with specific disabilities will require certain adaptations to the activities. Children with physical disabilities would benefit from having paper on the easel taped down. Children with visual impairments would be aided by having dark strips of paper surrounding the white painting paper. This provides a border and helps children know where the paper ends.

To promote communication have two to three easels arranged in a semicircle so that children can see each other. Encourage them to discuss their projects. Exercise hands and arms before beginning.

Some easel suggestions:

- Vertical and horizontal lines, mazes
- Shapes—circle, square, triangle, rectangle
- Drawing trees, flowers, animals
- Faces and bodies, people, self, friends, family
- Fire—orange, red, and yellow paints
- Beach—blue sky, brown sand, green grass, yellow sun
- Imitate or copy shapes, letters, or numbers predrawn on the paper
- Red and pink hearts for Valentine's Day
- Drawing and painting jack-o-lanterns for Halloween, holly for Christmas, shamrocks for St. Patrick's Day
- Drawing and painting houses, school, public buildings

Scissor Activities

For all scissor and cutting activities make use of heavier paper, such as construction paper. Children learning to cut will have difficulty cutting lightweight paper. Provide warm-up activities for students who have difficulty controlling hand movements. Warm-up activities might include stretching out rubber bands, pressing fingers together, opening and closing fists rapidly, shaking out hands and fingers, or molding clay. A general sequence for the development of cutting skills is: snips, strips, angles, and curves.

100 Let's Make a Mess and Clean It Up

Target Objective
Bilateral tearing, precutting, following directions, sequence of activity

Developmental Domains
Fine Motor, Social, Language, Cognitive, Self-Help

Multiple Intelligences
Bodily, Spatial, Interpersonal, Linguistic, Intrapersonal

Materials
Newspaper strips approximately six inches long and the width of one page. At least five to six strips per child, trash container.

Preparation/Set-Up
Set up in fine motor area where most cutting and gluing activities would occur. Stack the strips of paper on the table. Exercise hands before beginning.

Procedures

1. Arrange children in a small group at the table.
2. Tell children that we are going to make a mess and clean it up.
3. Give each child a strip of the newspaper.
4. Each child should grab the top edge of the length of the paper.
5. One hand moves away from the body while the second hand moves in and toward the body.
6. Children tear the paper from top to bottom across the six-inch height.
7. Let children toss the two pieces of paper freely into the air falling on the table or floor.
8. Repeat the tearing and tossing sequence no less than five times.
9. Talk about what children need to do next.
10. Direct children to work together to pick up the mess and place the pieces in the trash in an orderly fashion. Provide praise for children who are helping.

Adaptations for Children With Disabilities

Provide hand-over-hand assistance as needed. Encourage the bilateral movement of tearing. Provide smaller pieces of paper if needed.

 ## Clothespin Shapes

Target Objective
Precutting, recognition of shapes, following directions, 1:1 correspondence, hand strength

Developmental Domains
Fine Motor, Cognitive, Language

Multiple Intelligences
Bodily, Spatial, Linguistic, Logical

Materials
Eight to ten clothespins per child, precut shapes of circle, square, triangle, and rectangle on stiff cardboard with predrawn dots around the outside of these shapes.

Preparation/Set-Up
Have dotted shapes and clothespins ready. Exercise hands before beginning.

Procedures

1. Have children sit in a small group around a table or on the floor.

2. Show them the materials and tell them that they are to place the clothespins on the dots on the shapes.

3. Have children place the clothespins on the dots using a one-handed, thumbs-up position similar to what would be required when using scissors.

4. Encourage children to identify and name the shapes.

5. Once they have all the clothespins on a shape have them count the clothespins using one-to-one correspondence and tell how many.

Adaptations for Children With Disabilities

Provide hand-over-hand assistance as needed. Have shapes with a different number of dots to increase or decrease difficulty of this task. Allow opportunities for rest if children become fatigued or careless with the task.

Getting Ready for Scissors

Target Objective
Holding scissors correctly, following directions

Developmental Domains
Fine Motor, Social, Language, Cognitive

Multiple Intelligences
Bodily, Linguistic, Intrapersonal, Spatial, Interpersonal

Materials
Five-inch blunt-nosed scissors for each child. Scissors should have small loop handles and be sharp enough to cut easily.

Preparation/Set-Up
Table and chairs for small group of children. Make sure their feet are supported when seated.

Procedures

1. Present scissors to children. Point out that scissors are dangerous and need to be used with care. Encourage them to hold the scissors as you do.
2. In imitation, each child is to place his or her thumb in the smaller loop of the scissors.
3. Next, position the middle finger (not the index finger) in the larger loop.
4. Position the index finger below the scissor blade as a guide finger.
5. Practice opening and closing the scissors together and individually.
6. End the activity with praise for the effort and for using scissors correctly.
7. Repeat this activity often.

Adaptations for Children With Disabilities

Offer breaks for children who become fatigued. Provide adapted scissors and seek the assistance of an occupational therapist for children experiencing a great deal of difficulty. Provide hand-over-hand assistance with correct positioning of grip and body.

Safe With Scissors

Target Objective
Handling scissors safely

Developmental Domains
Fine Motor, Gross Motor, Language, Social

Multiple Intelligences
Bodily, Intrapersonal, Interpersonal, Linguistic

Materials
Five-inch blunt-nosed right- and left-handed scissors. Once children demonstrate control of the scissors, introduce five-inch chip-point scissors. Plastic scissors don't cut all types of paper consistently.

Preparation/Set-Up
Clear the classroom of any obstacles in and around the tables.

Procedures

1. Pass scissors to each child. Tell them to make a fist with their hand around the closed scissor blades. Pointed end should stick out of the fist toward the floor just enough so as not to jab self or others.

2. Practice holding with both hands, first left, then right. Reposition their hands as needed.

3. With scissors on the table, children practice picking them up and passing them to their neighbor by handing the scissors handle-end first. Have children practice passing them back and forth.

4. Next, have the children stand and walk to one side of the room carrying their scissors holding them by the closed blades.

5. Have children check their own safety as they slowly walk back and forth across the room several times.

6. Children then return to seats and pass the scissors back to the teacher.

7. Discuss what children just did and remind them that pointing or running with scissors is dangerous.

8. This activity should be repeated throughout the year.

Adaptations for Children With Disabilities

Provide adaptive scissors as needed. A few examples of such scissors are double-looped or spring scissors. Practice this safety routine more than once.

104 Brooms

Target Objective
Cutting on lines, task completion, constructing from an example

Developmental Domains
Fine Motor, Cognitive, Language

Multiple Intelligences
Bodily, Spatial, Linguistic, Intrapersonal

Materials
Sharp child-sized scissors; six to eight pre-drawn lines, 3/4 of the way across a piece of construction paper and placed about 2" apart; precut 12–14" brown construction paper broom "handles"; glue; pictures of or actual brooms.

Preparation/Set-Up
Have materials readily available. Make sure chairs and table are appropriate height and children's feet are supported.

Procedures

1. Arrange a small group of children at a table. Show them a broom or picture of brooms. Tell the children that they are going to make a broom.

2. Present them with the scissors at midline and give them the paper with the predrawn lines. Demonstrate how the lines are to be cut, pointing out that the children are not to cut all of the way but to stop at the end of the line.

3. Using thumbs on top, children are to cut the lines, not deviating more than 1/4" from the line. Once completed, have the children safely hand the scissors back to the teacher.

4. Present the children with the broom handles and glue.

5. Children are to glue together their cut lines and the broom handle to complete the task. Encourage children to be patient and to press the handle until the glue is dry.

6. Praise the children for good work and have them assist in cleaning up the area. Let children pretend to sweep with their brooms.

Adaptations for Children With Disabilities

Provide a finished example to model. Glue can be partially opened to help control flow for those students who have difficulty judging pressure. Some of the lines can be partially cut.

Paper Strip Collage

Target Objective
Precutting, cutting, hand positioning, task completion, color recognition, perceptual-motor

Developmental Domains
Fine Motor, Language, Cognitive

Multiple Intelligences
Spatial, Bodily, Linguistic, Logical

Materials
2-, 6-, and 10-inch-long construction paper strips of a variety of colors relevant to the season or holiday; scissors; large piece of black construction paper; glue.

Preparation/Set-Up
Provide strips on three trays divided into sizes of short, medium, and long, and scissors for each child; black paper and glue are close by and available for use after cutting is completed.

Procedures

1. Each child is to pick up five to eight strips of paper from trays naming their sizes and colors or repeating names after they've been modeled.

2. Next they are to snip/cut the strips, creating squares. Focus on hand position with the thumbs of both hands on top. This is an excellent opportunity to offer repetitive cutting practice with immediate reward for the children. The different lengths of strips allow for different levels of cutting skill.

3. Once cutting is complete, clear away the scissors and have the children sort the square pieces by color into waiting trays.

4. Children finish by gluing their cut squares into a colorful collage.

Adaptations for Children With Disabilities

Provide hand-over-hand assistance as needed. Be ready to guide or readjust a child's grip. Encourage the child to complete the cutting task with same cutting hand to promote handedness. Children with fine motor difficulties often switch hands because of fatigue or problems with crossing the midline of their bodies. Promote crossing midline by having the children reach across their bodies for the paper or glue, alternating between both hands.

106 Snipping Practice

Target Objective
Increase cutting skills using both hands

Developmental Domains
Fine Motor, Cognitive, Language

Multiple Intelligences
Bodily, Linguistic, Spatial

Materials
Child-sized scissors and a variety of precut or die-cut shapes (circle, square, triangle, rectangle) in targeted color. Scissors need to be appropriate for the children. The scissors used should have small loop handles so that the fingers do not slip through and should be sharp enough to cut easily. Scissors are to be held "thumbs up."

Preparation/Set-Up
Have all materials ready in the table area.

Procedures

1. Have a small group of children sit at a table.
2. Show them the precut shapes.
3. Have children repeat the name of the color and shapes as you show them.
4. The children select a shape by naming its color and design.
5. Show the children how to snip around the shape, being careful not to cut the shape in half.
6. Encourage children to use both hands, one to snip and one to turn the pattern, as they snip along the pattern. Encourage children to cut more than one shape.
7. Note which children have difficulty and provide physical assistance as needed.

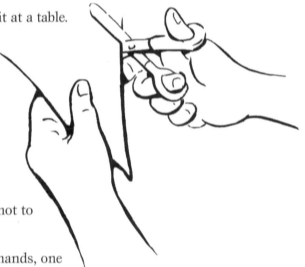

Adaptations for Children With Disabilities

Have adaptive scissors available. Let children having extreme difficulty with this task begin by tearing. Assist with hand-over-hand cutting and reposition hands as needed. Provide a break for children if they become fatigued. Provide warm-up activities for students who have difficulty controlling hand movements. Warm-up activities might include stretching out rubber bands, pressing fingers together, opening and closing fists rapidly, shaking out hands and fingers with rapid shakes, or molding clay.

107 Shape-Cutting Practice

Target Objective
Use of scissors, cutting, perceptual-motor skills, following directions

Developmental Domains
Fine Motor, Language, Cognitive

Multiple Intelligences
Bodily, Spatial, Linguistic, Logical

Materials
Four to five predrawn shapes on a variety of construction paper in 6"x 6" squares for each child, blunt-nosed five-inch scissors for right and left hands, glue, black construction paper.

Preparation/Set-Up
Have materials available.

Procedures

1. Have children sit in a small group around a table or on the floor. Discuss with the children the importance of safety when using scissors.

2. Have them choose and name the color and shape.

3. Children cut the shape out while staying on the lines.

4. After they have four to five shapes cut, remove the scissors and uncut shapes from the work area.

5. Present the children with a piece of black construction paper and glue.

6. Show them how to glue their shapes on to the paper to make whatever design they choose. The children should name the shapes as they glue them.

7. Have children assist in cleaning up the work area. Letting children pick up small pieces of paper from the floor is also good for fine motor development.

Adaptations for Children With Disabilities

Provide shapes already half-cut for children who easily become fatigued or reduce the number of shapes to be cut. Provide hand-over-hand assistance in cutting. A general sequence for the development of cutting skills is: snips, strips, angles, and curves. Have thick, dark lines for children with visual impairments. Review safety procedures often.

108 House

Target Objective
Cutting shapes with no less than 1/4" deviation; construct parts to whole; task completion, visual perception

Developmental Domains
Fine Motor, Cognitive, Language

Multiple Intelligences
Bodily, Spatial, Linguistic, Intrapersonal

Materials
Predrawn and precut (optional) shapes of large squares and triangles, markers, glue, 8" x 10" pieces of white construction paper, pictures of houses and washable markers.

Preparation/Set-Up
All materials readily available.

Procedures

1. Gather a small group of children together at a table. Tell them they are going to make a house and show them pictures of different types of houses, pointing out the different shapes that are seen (square, triangle, etc).

2. Give children the materials and direct them to make a house. Use predrawn and precut shapes as necessary to guide this activity.

3. Have children cut the necessary shapes and glue them to the paper.

4. Once gluing is completed, give them the markers and encourage them to add details to the pictures, such as people, sun, clouds, or trees. Let children be creative; be nonjudgmental in what they create. Assist them in writing their names on the back of the paper.

5. This activity can be expanded into a cooperative activity by having children create a neighborhood or a collection of all of their houses.

Adaptations for Children With Disabilities

Provide less drawing or cutting for some children or shorten the task by having them only complete the house and details. Be sure to have good contrast of black lines on white paper. Provide a sample for children to model. Provide hand-over-hand assistance as needed. This activity can be incorporated into the home and family activities in the Personal/Social chapter.

109   **Holiday Placemats**

Target Objective
Perceptual-motor, precutting, following directions, task completion, color recognition

Developmental Domains
Fine Motor, Language, Cognitive

Multiple Intelligences
Spatial, Bodily, Linguistic

Materials
Large pieces of construction paper in holiday colors, scissors, markers or crayons.

Preparation/Set-Up
Provide each child with a piece of paper, scissors, and a variety of markers or crayons.

Procedures

1. Give each child a piece of construction paper and explain to them that they are going to make placemats for the snack table. Talk about the color as it relates to the season or holiday.

2. Encourage the children to decorate the placemats with decorative lines, designs, or pictures relevant to the holiday or season. Clear away drawing materials before scissors are distributed.

3. Next, each child will take his or her scissors and snip around the outside of the mats to make "fringe." Encourage the children to hold the scissors and paper with thumbs on top. Move the assisting hand as the snipping hand goes along, turning as they reach a corner. Snipping is also a precutting activity that is strongly recommended prior to beginning cutting more complex shapes and designs.

4. Use the placemats during the week at the snack table or for a special party.

Adaptations for Children With Disabilities

Provide hand-over-hand assistance when needed. Assist students with appropriate finger placement on the scissors and hand placement while holding the paper. If the child tires easily, have them only snip half of the paper or provide smaller pieces of construction paper for snipping. This activity can be spread over two days if the drawing and snipping becomes too tiring or difficult.

213   Chapter 8

Leaf Cutting

Target Objective
Increase cutting skills on a line, visual perception, task persistence and completion

Developmental Domains
Fine Motor, Cognitive, Social

Multiple Intelligences
Bodily, Spatial, Naturalist, Linguistic

Materials
Predrawn leaves of different sizes in seasonal colors (red, yellow, green, brown) on 4" x 6" construction paper squares, brown rectangle strips for the trunk, scissors, large white construction paper (8" x 10"), glue sticks, picture of trees and leaves of fall.

Preparation/Set-Up
Children seated at a table with feet supported. Have all materials available.

Procedures

1. Show the children the picture(s) of trees in the fall, spring, or summer and note the color of the leaves.

2. Allow children to pick a variety of colors to cut depending on the season. Children are to name the colors.

3. Children cut leaves following on the line. Encourage turning the leaf while cutting with both thumbs on top.

4. Once leaves are cut, children throw away scraps and give scissors safely back to the teacher.

5. Children then glue their tree trunk and leaves to the white paper.

6. Encourage children to copy the word for the season at the top or bottom of the paper.

7. Write the name of students on the back of the page.

Adaptations for Children With Disabilities

Precut 1/2 of the leaf for the child. Make the lines of the leaves thicker and easier to see and follow while cutting. Reduce the cutting to one to two leaves. Provide hand-over-hand assistance as needed. Have children point to and name the colors. Provide adapted scissors as needed.

Apple Tree

Target Objective
Increase fine motor and language skills, completing a construction task independently

Developmental Domains
Fine Motor, Language, Cognitive

Multiple Intelligences
Spatial, Bodily, Naturalist

Materials
Precut paper, glue sticks, picture of an apple tree, completed example tree, scissors (optional). Precut or outlined pieces of the tree: one trunk, four branches, five apples, green construction paper scraps for leaves, large blue background.

Preparation/Set-Up
Have enough pieces of paper cut to make an apple tree. This will include precut brown rectangle pieces for the trunk, small brown rectangle strips for branches, small scraps of green for leaves, and small red or green circles for apples.

Procedures

1. Have a small group of children sit around you at a table.
2. Show them a picture of an apple tree.
3. Show the children the completed example of the precut and glued apple tree.
4. Distribute precut pieces and glue to each child.
5. Assist children as needed in gluing their tree together.
6. Identify the shapes and colors of the pieces being used.
7. Children should tear the green paper leaves using pincer grasp and both hands and glue these to the branches.
8. The apples should be glued on last and children should count the number of apples.
9. Older children can cut their own pieces for the tree.
10. Have lines drawn on paper to assist children in the size and shape of the pieces.
11. Cut up apples for snack.

Adaptations for Children With Disabilities

Some children will need physical assistance with cutting or gluing pieces. In addition, consider the developmental age of the children. For three-year-olds, three to five pieces of paper are enough. For four-year-olds, six to ten pieces are appropriate.

Colorful Trees—Fall

Target Objective
Cutting, perceptual-motor, following directions, color recognition, one-to-one correspondence, control of glue

Developmental Domains
Fine Motor, Cognitive, Language

Multiple Intelligences
Naturalistic, Spatial, Linguistic, Bodily, Logical

Materials
Scraps of construction paper—red, orange, brown, green; glue; large white construction paper with predrawn trunks and branches.

Preparation/Set-Up
Provide each child with a variety of scraps including listed colors; predraw or glue tree trunks and branches onto large white construction paper for each child.

Procedures

1. Provide each child with a variety of fall-colored paper scraps. Children are to tear small pieces using a reciprocal tearing motion into "leaves." Children can also cut these out if they are able.

2. Once tearing is completed and pieces are piled neatly, provide children with the predrawn or glued tree, trunk, and branches and a bottle of glue.

3. Children use the glue to dot all over the branches. Then they place the leaves on top of the glue dots. Encourage glue dots, not puddles, with the glue. One-to-one correspondence is being worked on by placing the "leaves" on each glue dot.

4. Encourage children to glue the leaves on or around the branches, falling from the tree, and lying on the ground.

Adaptations for Children With Disabilities

Provide glue bottles that are only partially opened to assist those children who have difficulty in controlling pressure when squeezing the glue. Provide hand-over-hand assistance as needed. Assist those who have difficulty tearing. Tearing is a skill that should be mastered or promoted before moving on to scissor activities.

113   Face Construction—Jack-O-Lantern

Target Objective
Cutting, recognizing facial features, shape recognition, following directions

Developmental Domains
Fine Motor, Cognitive, Language

Multiple Intelligences
Bodily, Spatial, Linguistic, Naturalist, Logical

Materials
Predrawn large pumpkins on orange construction paper. Precut or outlined triangles for eyes and nose and a variety of mouths (happy, sad, scary), scissors, glue sticks, markers, and green and brown 12" strips of construction paper.

Preparation/Set-Up
Have all materials readily available.

This is an example of a face construction activity in which the focus is on the head and face. The faces may be of the children themselves, family or friends, people in the community, animals, or holiday or seasonal characters, such as a snowman.

Procedures

1. Have children sit as a small group around a table.

2. Give each child a pumpkin and scissors.

3. Show children how to cut the pumpkin shape turning as they go. Promote thumbs on top as they cut. When holding the scissors, have the index finger be the lead finger with the thumb and other three fingers filling scissor loops.

4. Provide the facial shapes, letting children choose which mouths, noses, and eyes they want. Encourage children to speak in complete sentences.

5. Have the children practice placing the shapes on the pumpkin to check for accuracy and appearance before gluing.

6. Give children the glue sticks and let them glue the shapes in place.

7. Once complete, let the children cut their choice of the green or brown construction paper to make a stem. Have them glue the stem on the back and at the top.

Adaptations for Children With Disabilities

Have children who are able cut all the shapes. Provide precut shapes for children who have difficulty cutting. Encourage children to make positive comments about the pumpkin jack-o-lanterns created by other children.

Figure Construction—Dancing Jack-O-Lantern

Target Objective
Increase fine motor skills; visual perception; identification of shapes, colors, and body parts. Figure constructions focus on the whole body rather than just the head. Other constructions could include snowmen or other children in the classroom.

Developmental Domains
Fine Motor, Cognitive, Social, Language

Multiple Intelligences
Spatial, Bodily, Linguistic, Naturalist

Materials
Predrawn orange circles for pumpkins, washable black markers, scissors, 8" x 2" strips of black paper with dividing line drawn down the middle for legs, 4" x 2" strips of black paper for arms, predrawn or precut green or brown stems, glue sticks, string.

Preparation/Set-Up
Have all materials readily available.

Procedures

1. Have children sit at a table. Present an example of the finished product, a dancing jack-o-lantern.

2. Have the children cut out the orange circles and black arms and legs. Let them draw faces on the circles with markers. Let children be creative.

3. Have them glue the arms and legs to the back of the circle, being sure legs are down and arms are out.

4. Poke a small hole in the top of the head and insert a length of string. Tie this off so that children can make their jack-o-lantern dance by moving the string.

5. Put names on the back of each construction and play some music for the jack-o-lanterns to dance to.

Adaptations for Children With Disabilities

Provide a thicker predrawn line for some children. The circle can be partially cut out if curves are difficult. Be sure children are in a good sitting position.

Murals

Murals are a fun and excellent way to work on a variety of developmental domains and multiple intelligences at the same time. Murals are easily used with a variety of themes and integrated with literature and songs. Completing murals enhances problem solving, task completion, cooperation, and part-to-whole concepts. In addition, working on murals is good for body strength and fine motor control. Finished products are easily displayed for all to see and create a sense of pride among students. Murals are play-based activities that extend over three to five days for 20–30 minutes each day and thus make use of the "Extended Time" concept that is a part of Directed Play. Each completed mural should include a title at the top and be signed by the children who created it.

The materials often used to complete the murals include markers, scissors, glue sticks, large pieces of bolt paper, and different colors of construction paper. Other, more specific materials are used to enhance the texture or appearance of the murals and increase sensory stimulation. These might include sponges, packing peanuts, cotton balls, or paints with different smells.

Murals can be created individually or as a group. For individual murals, use smaller pieces of bolt paper approximately 18" x 24". Individual murals enable the children to develop something solely of their own creativity but don't allow them to work together with other children to create a larger project. Individual murals can be specific to a theme or topic and be completed as an individual lesson.

For group murals you need to consider how many children will be involved in the creation of the mural, what the topic is, and over how many days you will be working on it. Group murals will require large pieces of bolt paper approximately 4' x 6'. The mural should allow enough space for several children to work on it at the same time without bumping into one another. The bolt paper should be hung on a smooth surface. However, some children will do better if the mural paper is lying on the floor. In either case be sure you have drop cloths or newspaper available for messes.

With most mural activities it is necessary for shapes or designs to be predrawn on construction paper. Build in preparation time for murals. It will take some time for adults to draw the necessary shapes onto the construction paper being used for specific murals. The drawings often include the basic shapes children are learning, such as circles, squares, triangles, rectangles, and diamonds. Use a dark marker pen to draw the shapes that children will cut out. There should be enough pieces of construction paper for every child and even a couple of extras. It is helpful to have paper of different thicknesses. It is generally easier for children to cut out shapes from thicker pieces of paper. For younger children or children with physical impairments, the shapes, items, or patterns can be precut. To save time, draw the desired shapes on one sheet of construction paper and then stack several pieces of construction paper together when cutting out the shapes.

Helping children to learn to work together on the same mural will take some time and discussion. Be sure that children understand that other children are also working on the same mural and that they will need to take turns and share. Have the children take turns using step stools and be sure that they use "inside" voices; use manners, such as please and thank you; give compliments to each other; listen; and practice good safety procedures with scissors.

It is a good idea to prepare for the mural activities a day or week ahead of time. Solicit help from older students when preparing for the murals. Older students sincerely enjoy helping teachers and spending time with younger children. Murals take planning and preparation but are well worth the effort.

115 Flower Garden Mural—Flowers and Bugs

(3 Days)

Target Objective
Cutting practice, comprehension, retelling stories of facts, cooperation, task completion.

Developmental Domains
Fine Motor, Cognitive, Language, Social

Multiple Intelligences
Bodily, Linguistic, Naturalist, Interpersonal

Materials
Various colors of construction paper, scissors, markers (green, brown, yellow), glue sticks, large bolt paper, predrawn petals (round and long ovals), flower centers, tulip heads, stems (long and short), leaves, literature books about flowers and gardens, storage materials.

Preparation/Set-Up
Set up large bolt paper on a wall in a large open area. Have step stools available.

Procedures

Day 1

1. Gather children in a small group and read a story about growing flowers or flower gardens.

2. Talk about the flower and label the parts—leaves, petals, center, and stems.

3. Provide the children with the predrawn flower parts; review and name these parts and then have them construct the flowers using the glue sticks. Put names of children on the back of the flowers. When completed set the flowers aside and save for the next day.

4. Take the children to the large bolt paper (mural site) and talk about how we're going to make a garden together with the flowers we've made. Encourage the children to talk to their parents about flowers and gardens.

Day 2

1. Gather the children together in a small group at the mural site. Get out the flowers made the day before. Briefly discuss the book read the day before about gardens. Encourage the children to recall facts from the book.

Directed Play   **220**

2. Have the children discuss how they made their flowers and identify the parts of the flowers.

3. Present the children with markers and tell them to come and draw the ground and grass on the mural for the flowers to live in.

4. Once completed, use the glue sticks to glue their flowers to the mural. Be sure to note where the flowers should be (i.e., no flowers in the sky).

5. Have the children sit in front of the mural together and talk about what they have created. Encourage the children to share compliments.

Day 3

1. Gather children together at an easel with large white paper. Talk about the mural garden and ask the children what is missing—"We forgot the bugs."

2. Read a short story about bugs. Then brainstorm as a group for bugs that might be found in a garden.

3. Draw the bugs the children identify on the easel. Possible insects might include butterflies, flies, worms, ladybugs, bees, or ants.

4. Take the picture to the mural with markers. Have the children talk about which insects they are going to add to the mural.

5. Let children draw their own bugs on the mural. Discuss where they would be (on the ground, in the air). Encourage creativity.

6. Offer encouragement and praise. Provide assistance as needed. Promote discussion among the children about the bugs (e.g., "Jenny, ask Mike what he is making").

7. When completed have the children sit back and look at the mural they have created and celebrate a job well done.

Adaptations for Children With Disabilities

Provide chairs for sitting at the mural while working, drawing, or gluing. Continue to offer periods of rest to prevent unnecessary fatigue. Provide hand-over-hand assistance as needed. Monitor all children for correct posture and handgrip during the activity.

116 Healthy Teeth Mural (3 Days)

Target Objective
Tell facts about healthy teeth, retell sequence of brushing, describe function of teeth

Developmental Domains
Fine Motor, Cognitive, Language, Self-Help, Social

Multiple Intelligences
Bodily, Spatial, Interpersonal, Intrapersonal, Linguistic

Materials
Scissors, glue sticks, large bolt paper, markers, predrawn 2" x 8" strips of white construction paper, predrawn toothbrush handles on varied construction paper, white paint, three to five books on teeth and brushing teeth, small mirrors, old toothbrushes, paint smocks (optional).

Preparation/Set-Up
Set up bolt paper on wall or bulletin board. Have step stools available. Have all materials ready to use before beginning each day.

Procedures

Day 1

1. Gather children together and read a fictional story about tooth care or a dentist. Have children retell facts of story, beginning, middle, and end. Discuss what teeth are for and how we care for them.

2. Present children with the white strips and have them snip the strips into small, medium-sized rectangles to later be used as teeth. Save for day two.

3. Give the children predrawn toothbrush handles and have them cut these out. Save for day two.

Day 2

1. Talk about the book read the day before and what the children cut out. Retell facts on teeth and sequence of tooth brushing. Ask and answer "wh" questions about the topic.

2. Have children look at their own teeth and smiles in the mirrors. Encourage children to hold the mirror for a partner and encourage compliments about smiles.

3. Gather children together in a large open area. Present the cut "teeth" from previous day, glue sticks, markers, and mirrors.

4. Using the markers, have children draw a picture of themselves on the mural with open mouths. These pictures need to be big enough to include the cut teeth. Have the children glue their precut teeth within the mouths.

5. Put all materials away and have children assist in cleaning up the area.

Directed Play 222

Day 3

1. Gather children together in front of the mural. Read a new expository story about teeth or tooth care and talk about proper care of the teeth. Discuss the book or story and identify facts and sequence of events.

2. Provide the precut toothbrush handles and glue sticks. Glue these to the mural. Encourage children to draw arms and hands on their person as if holding the toothbrush.

3. Next, the children dip an old toothbrush into paint and paint on the "bristles" of the brush.

4. Children sign their mural and celebrate a job well done.

5. Have children assist in cleaning up the area.

Adaptations for Children With Disabilities

See the Personal/Social section for other activities related to dental care and the thematic units on dentists. See the suggestions for cutting and construction activities. Review vocabulary often with children with developmental delays or mental retardation.

Warm Weather Land and Sea Mural (3 Days)

117

Target Objective
Cutting, cooperation, identification and use of objects, problem solving

Developmental Domains
Fine Motor, Social, Language, Cognitive

Multiple Intelligences
Naturalist, Interpersonal, Linguistic, Spatial

Materials
Four predrawn, medium-sized triangles and one large precut triangle of various colors of construction paper per child. Precut, large squares and rectangles and 4–6" strips, glue sticks, large piece (4' x 8') of bolt paper, markers, scissors, crayons tape, pictures of water and land scenes.

Preparation/Set-Up
Prepare a large floor or wall space to work on the mural. A hallway can work well for this also. This is at least a three-day activity, so consider this when finding a space.

Procedures

Day 1

1. Gather children together in a small group for this 20-minute session. Show the children the pictures of water/land scenes, including sailboats, land, people, buildings, and sky. Tell them they are going to create a large picture or mural by working together.

2. Provide the large piece of bolt paper. Some land, sky, or water boundaries can be predrawn. Name the areas in the mural. Use natural colors, blue for water and sky, brown/green for land. Tell children you want them to complete the picture by coloring in the land, grass and trees, water, waves, sky, clouds, sun, and birds flying.

3. Let children discuss what they want to draw. Give them the materials and let each begin work on a different place in the mural. Have each child do a task that is easily completed in 15–20 minutes.

Day 2

1. The next day revisit the mural and discuss what had been done yesterday.

2. Talk about constructing sailboats.

3. Cut triangles for the sailboats. Be sure children are using the scissors correctly and safely.

Directed Play   224

4. Give the children the precut 4–6" strips and have them construct their sailboats on the floor. Then give them the glue sticks and have them attach these to the mural.

5. Use markers to draw details on the boats, such as flags, names, or numbers.

6. Have children assist in cleaning up the area.

Day 3

1. Gather the children together and revisit the mural. Identify and discuss what has been done and what could be done to finish the mural. Ask them how they constructed their boats and point out unique aspects of each child's work.

2. Children should add houses and other buildings to the land. Use squares and triangles for houses and rectangles for other buildings. Have each child construct a house or building to add to the land portion of the mural.

3. Have them complete their houses on the floor, then glue them to the mural. Again, provide markers so that children can add details.

Adaptations for Children With Disabilities

See cutting adaptations. Provide chairs for working at the mural. Allow children to rest if they become fatigued.

118 **Winter Mural** (3 Days)

Target Objective
Identification of objects, seriation, sizes, seasonal vocabulary concepts

Developmental Domains
Fine Motor, Cognitive, Language, Social

Multiple Intelligences
Bodily, Spatial, Naturalist, Linguistic, Interpersonal

Materials
Various colors of construction paper (green, light blue, white); scissors; markers; glue sticks; two to three pieces of large, colored bolt paper, paint; different-sized paintbrushes; white or clear glitter; white packing peanuts or cotton balls; predrawn circles, triangles, and tree trunks (brown rectangles, precut optional); paint smocks (optional).

Preparation/Set-Up
Prepare mural with dark blue or gray bolt paper. A good contrast color is preferred. Have step stools ready for use.

Procedures

Day 1

1. Gather children at the mural paper. Read the book *A Snowy Day* by Ezra Jack Keats. Talk about winter, cold, and snow. What does it feel like, look like, sound like? Have children retell facts about the story.

2. Provide the children with paintbrushes, white paint, glue, and white packing peanuts or cotton balls. Children are to work together to create the "snowy landscape." Include a dividing line for the sky. The packing peanuts or cotton balls add texture and work on sensory stimulation. Assist with drawing boundaries as needed. Allow this to dry overnight.

3. Have children assist in cleaning up.

Day 2

1. Have children gather at the mural and review what was done yesterday. Discuss what kinds of things are associated with winter and snow. Draw a picture of what the children identify on a board or a piece of paper.

2. Provide the predrawn (or precut) circles (small, medium, large) and tell the children they are going to create snowmen. Have the children cut the circles, then glue them together in the proper sequence on the mural.

3. Provide black or brown paper for children to cut out arms and hats. Use markers to draw in the face and other details.

4. Have children assist in cleaning up.

Directed *Play*   **226**

Day 3

1. Gather the children at the mural and review what has been done so far. Reread *A Snowy Day* or another story about winter. Tell the children that they are going to add trees to the mural.

2. Provide the predrawn (or precut) green triangles (small, medium, and large) and the brown tree trunk rectangles. Assist the children in gluing together a tree with the triangles in the proper sequence at the table. Allow to dry.

3. Provide a glue mixture in trays, glitter, and small paintbrushes. Have children carefully paint their trees with the mixture and then shake the glitter on. The glitter will add a sparkling effect to the trees. Allow to dry.

4. Wait times can be filled with looking through the books and brainstorming about other natural things we find in winter.

5. Have all children sign the mural or have a sign that says "Artwork by . . ." Put a title on the mural for all to see.

6. Glue the dried sparkly trees to the mural.

7. Have the children assist in cleaning up. As a group, sit back and look at the mural. Offer compliments to one another about a job well done.

Adaptations for Children With Disabilities

Provide examples of the trees and snowmen. Read books about winter and snow not previously read. Provide guidance as needed.

119 Pumpkin Patch Mural (3 Days)

Target Objectives
Cooperation, task completion, identification of objects, practice cutting

Developmental Domains
Fine Motor, Cognitive, Social, Language

Multiple Intelligences
Bodily, Spatial, Naturalist, Interpersonal, Linguistic

Materials
Large piece of white bolt paper, scissors, markers, glue sticks, predrawn (or precut) pumpkins of different sizes on orange construction paper, step stools, light blue paint and paintbrushes, paint smocks (optional), books about a pumpkin patch or growing pumpkins.

Preparation/Set-Up
Bolt paper attached to an open wall area, all materials available.

Procedures

Day 1

1. Gather children together and read *The Pumpkin Patch* or another similar story. Show children pictures of pumpkins and identify vocabulary words such as stem, vine, squash, and flower, and also name the colors and shapes. Retell the sequence of planting, growing, and picking.

2. Provide children with scissors and a variety of pumpkins to cut. Let children cut as many pumpkins as time allows.

3. Write the name of children on the back of the cut pumpkins and save.

4. Let children assist in cleanup.

Day 2

1. Gather the children at the mural and tell them they are going to work on creating a pumpkin patch. Pumpkins grow in large fields and need plenty of sunlight. Provide the blue paint and paintbrushes. Have children paint the sky on the top 1/3 of mural. The skyline does not need to be an even line. This may be easier for some children if the bolt paper is lying on the floor.

2. Have children assist with cleanup.

Day 3

1. Gather at the mural and discuss what has been done previously. Have children tell facts they have learned about pumpkins, including vocabulary words.

2. Give the children their cut pumpkins and let them glue them to the mural to create a pumpkin patch. Add details of stems, vines, and leaves, using green and brown markers. Connect the pumpkins together using the vines. Pumpkin leaves are large and the pumpkins grow on long, thick vines. A sun can be added to the sky by gluing on a yellow circle or using yellow paint.

3. As time permits, children can even draw jack-o-lantern faces on their pumpkins if desired.

4. Have children assist with cleanup, write their names on the mural, and add the title.

Adaptations for Children With Disabilities

Provide assistance in routine of cutting and gluing. Assist with balance if some children are standing on step stools. Conduct a field trip to a pumpkin patch to enhance this experience.

229   Chapter 8

120 # Refrigerator Mural (4 Days)

Target Objectives
Awareness of foods, diet, nutrition, cutting skills, task completion, cooperation

Developmental Domains
Fine Motor, Cognitive, Language, Social, Self-Help

Multiple Intelligences
Bodily, Spatial, Interpersonal, Linguistic, Intrapersonal

Materials
Two large sheets of bolt paper approximately 4' long and 2' wide, glue sticks, scissors, markers, fliers or advertisements from grocery stores, a small piece of sticky putty, pictures of refrigerators, books about foods, small pieces of paper and crayons.

Preparation/Set-Up
Hang one of the large sheets of bolt paper vertically on an open wall. The second piece of bolt paper will be the refrigerator door and will be attached last.

Procedures

Day 1

1. Gather the children together and show them the pictures of refrigerators. Talk about what they are used for and what kinds of foods can be found in them. Also stress that children should never get inside a real refrigerator.

2. Read a book about foods or food groups and have children talk about what foods they like.

3. Gather the children at the mural. Have them talk about and design what the inside of the refrigerator should look like. There should be several shelves, and a freezer section is often on the top. Once it is decided how it should look, have them use the markers to draw the inside of the refrigerator on the mural. Designate which child draws what shelf or drawer.

Day 2

1. Gather the children together at a table and review what was discussed the day before.

2. Pass out the grocery store fliers or advertisements, scissors, and glue sticks.

3. Have children cut out pictures of foods that can be found in a refrigerator. These might include fruits and vegetables, milk and pop containers, or condiments.

4. Try to have children cut out a wide variety of foods.

Directed Play **230**

5. Have the children gather at the mural and glue their pictures "on the shelves." Have the children organize these foods according to food groups on the shelves.

6. Have children assist with cleanup.

Day 3

1. Gather the children at the mural and discuss what they have done so far. Ask them what is missing on the refrigerator. The door! Tell children they are going to make the refrigerator door.

2. Get the second large sheet of bolt paper and lay it flat on the floor. Using a strip of construction paper, create the door handle by making two folds on either end of the strip and glue it to one side of the door.

3. Have the group gently pick up the door and position it appropriately in front of the open refrigerator. Designate a child to staple or tape the door to one side of the refrigerator.

4. Use the sticky putty on inside of the door handle to help hold the door shut. Given the weight of the paper, you may need to use several pieces of sticky putty at the top portion of the door.

Day 4

1. Have children gather at the mural and discuss what they have done.

2. Tell them that families often have things on the door of the refrigerator and ask them what kinds of things are on their refrigerators.

3. Explain that one of the things that many people have on their refrigerator door is a picture of family members.

4. Give each child small pieces of paper and have them draw pictures of their family, pets, or other objects that might be found on refrigerator doors.

5. Once drawn, have the children glue these to the outside of the refrigerator door.

6. Have children sign their names on the mural and assist with cleanup.

Adaptations for Children With Disabilities

See the foods and eating activities in the Personal/Social chapter and the grocery store dramatic play activity in the Thematic chapter for related activities. Provide assistance as needed. Repeat the names of foods and talk about what children like to eat.

121 **Space Mural** (4 Days)

Target Objectives
Concepts of space, including planets, stars, sun, moon, gravity, top/bottom, rotation, cutting practice, recognition of shapes, task completion, estimation

Developmental Domains
Fine Motor, Cognitive, Language, Social

Multiple Intelligences
Bodily, Spatial, Interpersonal, Linguistic, Naturalist, Logical

Materials
Books on space, predrawn planets in three sizes, triangles to make stars or predrawn stars, rectangles and triangles to make a spaceship, markers, scissors, glue sticks, song card of "Twinkle, Twinkle," black paint,
silver or gold glitter (optional), glue, newspapers, precut yellow circles, step stools or chairs.

Preparation/Set-Up
Have all materials readily available for each day.

Procedures

Day 1

1. Gather a small group of children together and read a book about space. The book should have clear, large pictures of planets, stars, moon, and sun. Name the shape and color of these objects.

2. Tell the children they are going to make a space mural that will also include rocket ships.

3. Present children with predrawn planets (white, blue, or gray circles of different sizes). Children are to cut out the circles. Write their names on the back and save for the next day. As time permits, children can draw shapes or designs on their planets.

4. With the large bolt paper placed on the floor, have the children color or paint in the "space." This will involve the use of black markers or black paint. If black paint is used, glitter can be sprinkled on to simulate distant stars.

5. As a variation, instead of painting or using markers, children can estimate how many pieces of black construction paper will be needed to cover the bolt paper. The black construction paper can then be glued or taped onto the bolt paper and counted.

6. Put in an out-of-the-way place to dry for the next day.

Directed *Play*   232

Day 2

1. Hang the painted bolt paper. Gather the children together and read a book about space, earth, gravity, stars, etc. Discuss what was done yesterday.

2. Have children use glue sticks to glue their cut planets onto the mural. This can be done in a random fashion or you can place a large sun on the mural and have the children place their planets as if they are rotating around the sun.

3. Have children place small moons around the planets. This can be done by cutting out small circles or using a hole punch on white paper. These should be glued around several of the planets.

4. Have children assist with cleanup.

Day 3

1. Have predrawn or precut (optional) triangles, four per child, to make stars or have predrawn stars to be cut out. If the predrawn triangles are used, have children glue the pieces together to make stars. Put children's names on the back of the stars.

2. Have a glue mixture available and, using newspapers to protect the table, have the children "paint" the glue on their stars. Then, sprinkle some silver or gold glitter over the stars.

3. Set the stars aside to dry. Gather the children together and read a book about space. Discuss what has been done on the mural so far.

4. Let the children glue their stars onto the mural.

5. End the activity by singing "Twinkle, Twinkle."

6. Have children assist with cleanup.

Day 4

1. Have predrawn rocket ships or predrawn rectangles and triangles to make a rocket ship.

2. Gather the children together at the mural and read a book about rockets or spaceships.

3. Give the children the predrawn shapes and let them cut them out; then construct the rockets.

4. Children glue these on to the mural as if flying through space or landing on a planet.

5. Use markers to add details to the rocket ships, such as flags, numbers, letters, or even astronauts.

6. Finish the activity by having each child sign the mural. Praise the children for a job well done.

Adaptations for Children With Disabilities

Use precut shapes as needed for some children and provide one-to-one assistance as needed. See the rocket activity in the sociodramatic play section.

122 Ocean Mural (4 Days)

Target Objectives
Understand ocean concepts, increase vocabulary, perceptual-motor, understanding of deep/shallow and large/small, cooperation, task completion

Developmental Domains
Fine Motor, Cognitive, Language, Social

Multiple Intelligences
Bodily, Spatial, Interpersonal, Linguistic, Naturalist

Materials
Washable blue paint (light and dark), paintbrushes, books on oceans or fish, large bolt paper, salt and spoons, predrawn fish of different sizes, construction paper, scissors, glue sticks, paint smocks (optional), stools or chairs to stand on, and predrawn black, white, or gray whales.

Preparation/Set-Up
Large bolt paper hung in a hallway or wall. Drop cloth prepared as needed. Materials ready for each day.

Directed Play 234

Procedures

Day 1

1. Gather together in a small group and read a book on oceans or fish.

2. Using a question/answer format, have children work on answering "wh" questions and identify or name things found in the ocean or sea. Talk about the mural and all that will be a part of it.

3. Go to the mural and tell the children they need to paint the water. Have them put paint smocks on. Remind them that the water in the ocean is salty. Have children put a spoonful of salt into their paint. Provide a small cup of paint and paintbrush for each child.

4. Children are to paint the entire area and can use different variations of blue. Explain that the blue would be lighter near the top of the water (because of the sunlight) and darker near the bottom.

5. Let the mural dry until the next day and have children assist in cleanup.

Day 2

1. Gather children together and read another book about oceans or fish. Encourage children to look at the rocks and plants on the bottom of the ocean and have them list things that they see.

2. Move to a table and have the children freely cut and construct rocks, plants, and caves. Provide glue sticks and markers for details.

3. Next, the children gather at the mural and glue their rocks, caves, or plants to the lower portion of the mural.

Day 3

1. Have predrawn black, white, or gray whales; glue sticks; markers; and scissors ready.

2. Gather the group together and talk about what has been done so far. You may be able to find audiotapes of whale songs that can be played as well.

3. Read a book about whales or have pictures of whales. Explain that these are the largest mammals in water and that there are different types of whales.

4. Have children move to a table and let them choose from the predrawn whales. These should be fairly large in size, at least 8" x 10". They are to cut out the whales.

5. After cutting, have them add eyes or small fins to the side using the markers.

6. Have the children go the mural and glue their whales in the ocean.

Day 4

1. Have predrawn fish of different sizes, color, or shapes.

2. Have the children gather and talk about what they have done so far. Read a book about fish in the ocean and have pictures available for children to look at if they wish.

3. Have children sit at the table and cut out different kinds of fish. Children should be encouraged to cut out at least three to five fish each.

4. Have them take their fish to the mural and glue them to the mural using glue sticks or cotton swabs dipped in glue. Encourage children to be conservative with the glue and to wait a few moments to let the glue dry before gluing on another fish. This is a good opportunity to help children learn to control drips and not to add too much glue.

5. Once all fish are glued on, have the children step back and admire their work. Make positive comments about what you see.

Adaptations for Children With Disabilities

This mural can be stretched as far as your creativity will take you. Other ideas can include cutting and adding sea sponges to the mural, or jellyfish, shipwrecks, treasure, or people scuba diving. For younger children, the bolt paper can be painted on the floor. Older children should be encouraged to paint with the bolt paper hanging as this promotes better motor coordination and strength. Provide one-to-one assistance as needed. See cutting adaptations.

123 **Traffic Signs and Safety Mural** (3 Days)

> **Target Objectives**
> Safety, understanding traffic signs, cooperation, increase vocabulary, cutting, task completion
>
> **Developmental Domains**
> Fine Motor, Cognitive, Language, Social
>
> **Multiple Intelligences**
> Bodily, Spatial, Interpersonal, Linguistic
>
> **Materials**
> Literature about traffic and safety signs; set of sign cards, including stop sign, traffic light, yield, railroad crossing, and school crossing; large bolt paper; markers; scissors; predrawn traffic signs (at least 10–12" high); toy people and transportation items (cars, trucks, trains); red stop sign; strips for posts; yellow yield sign.
>
> **Preparation/Set-Up**
> Large bolt paper hung on the wall. All materials ready.

Procedures

Day 1

1. Gather children together and show them the safety sign cards. Identify and name each sign and explain what it means. Talk about what the action signs tell us to do.

2. Present the toy transportation items to the children and have them act out moving these items and then responding with the correct action when shown a particular sign (e.g., stop on red light or stop sign, slow with yellow light or yield sign).

3. Have them gather at a table and cut out the predrawn stop sign from red construction paper and add a strip for the post. Have them glue the post to the sign. For children who are able, encourage them to copy or print "STOP" on the sign using markers. Save the signs for the next day.

Day 2

1. Gather children together at a table and review the sign cards with particular emphasis on the yield sign.

2. Present the predrawn triangles (yield signs) and have the children cut these out. Give them a strip for the signposts.

3. Have children construct the yield signs, making sure the top of the triangle points down.

4. For children who are able, have them copy or print "YIELD" on the sign. Save the signs for the next day.

237 Chapter 8

5. Have children gather at the mural (either on the wall or the floor). Using markers, have the children draw vertical and horizontal lines for roads. The "roads" will require two parallel lines approximately 2" or 3" apart. Include corners for turning and intersections. It may be helpful to show them a model of this predrawn on smaller paper.

Day 3

1. Have predrawn circles in red, yellow, and green and predrawn rectangles in black or gray. These will be used to create stoplights.

2. Have children gather at the table and look at pictures of stoplights and discuss what the lights mean.

3. Present the materials to the children and have them cut out the circles and rectangle and then glue these in the proper order to create the stoplight.

4. Once completed, have children glue the stop sign, yield sign, and stoplight on the mural. Encourage patience. The children need to wait until one item is dry before they attempt to glue another.

5. Once completed, children can use the toy transportation items and people to play on the mural. Have each child sign the mural and assist with cleanup.

Adaptations for Children With Disabilities

Have words such as "STOP" and "YIELD" in dots so that they can be traced. See the Thematic chapter for other safety activities and the Motor and Movement chapter for the tricycle activity. Review the vocabulary words and actions often.

School Mural (3 Days)

> **Target Objectives**
> Identification of objects related to schools, increase vocabulary, cooperation, perceptual-motor skills, part/whole relationships
>
> **Developmental Domains**
> Fine Motor, Cognitive, Language, Social
>
> **Multiple Intelligences**
> Bodily, Spatial, Interpersonal, Linguistic
>
> **Materials**
> Fiction and nonfiction books about school; pictures of schools; predrawn bus; school crossing sign with strip for the post; large rectangles, squares, and triangles for school buildings; markers; crayons; scissors; large bolt paper.
>
> **Preparation/Set-Up**
> Hang the bolt paper and have step stools available. Have all materials ready.

Procedures

Day 1

1. Gather children together and read a book about school, e.g., *Froggy Goes to School*. Retell events of a day at school. Talk about making a mural of school and have children name items that might be included.

2. Talk about how children get to school and list the variety of ways we travel to school. Target the school bus and describe what it looks like.

3. Present children with bus-making materials. Have children cut out the predrawn school bus and the wheels, then glue the wheels to the bus. Finish by having them draw on the doors and windows. Have them draw in a driver and children.

4. Write names on the backs of the buses and save. Have children assist with cleanup.

Day 2

1. Have predrawn shapes ready with glue sticks, markers, or crayons.

2. Gather children and look at pictures of schools or read a book about school. Talk about what schools look like in terms of size, shape, color, number of doors, windows, sidewalks, etc.

3. Have children sit at a table and present materials to make a school building. This should include the same color pieces of construction paper. Have each child work on his or her "section" of the school building by using markers or crayons to add details such as windows, doors, or children looking out of windows.

4. Once each child has completed his or his section, gather at the mural and have the children glue their sections together to make a completed school building. They can be glued side by side or in different levels.

5. As time permits, children can use markers to draw roads that lead to school or draw sidewalks that people walk on.

6. Have children assist with cleanup.

Day 3

1. Gather children together and discuss what has been done so far. Read another book about schools. Introduce a completed school crossing sign and tell children that they are going to make one.

2. Provide the predrawn school yellow crossing sign for the children to cut out and a strip for the post.

3. Have children glue the sign to the post. Next, they draw in the lines and the children on the sign.

4. Get the completed school buses and gather at the mural.

5. Have the children glue their buses and school crossing signs to the mural.

6. Review rules for school safety and school bus safety.

7. Add final touches, such as a flagpole and flag, people, additional sidewalks, etc.

8. Have children sign the mural and compliment one another for a job well done.

Adaptations for Children With Disabilities

See the Thematic chapter for related activities. Provide one-to-one assistance as needed.

Garden Mural—Corn, Tomatoes, and Watermelon (4 Days)

Target Objectives
Identification of and naming of objects, foods, colors, shapes, science concepts, cooperation, problem solving, cutting, and construction

Developmental Domains
Fine Motor, Cognitive, Language, Social

Multiple Intelligences
Bodily, Spatial, Interpersonal, Linguistic, Naturalist

Materials
Pictures and literature on gardens and plants specifically depicting corn, tomatoes, and watermelon; large bolt paper; predrawn circles and ovals for corn, tomatoes, and watermelon on yellow, red, and green construction paper; long green strips of predrawn "stalks"; green yarn; scissors; markers; predrawn leaves on green construction paper; stapler or tape; brown and blue washable paints; large paintbrushes

Preparation/Set-Up
Hang bolt paper. Have all materials readily available.

Procedures

Day 1

1. Gather the children together and read a book about plants and gardens. Show them the pictures of the corn, tomatoes, and watermelon, making note of what these plants look like and their color, shape, etc.

2. Provide the predrawn circles on red construction paper and let children cut out the "tomatoes." Show them pictures of tomatoes and note that these can be different sizes. Each page of construction paper should have at least five to six "tomatoes." Cutting circles can be challenging for some children, so have precut circles available as well.

3. Collect the cut red circles and save in an envelope or baggy for the next day.

4. Have children gather at the bolt paper and provide the brown washable paint and paintbrushes. Have them paint the lower 2/3 of the bolt paper in brown to represent the dirt.

5. Allow to dry until the next day and have children assist in cleanup.

6. Provide some tomatoes for children to taste. Tomato plants also have a very distinctive smell, so, if possible, bring in some tomato leaves for children to feel and sniff.

Day 2

1. Gather the children together and talk about what was done the day before. Read another book on gardens and plants.

2. At a table, provide children with predrawn large ovals (watermelons) to be cut out. Let children cut out more than one if they wish.

3. Have children use red markers to draw some small lines on the watermelon.

4. Save the cut watermelons.

5. Have children gather at the mural and use blue paint and large brushes to paint the top 1/3 of the mural. This will represent the sky.

6. Have children assist with cleanup.

7. Provide watermelon for snack. Save the seeds for other activities (see Farms in the Thematic chapter).

Day 3

1. Gather at the mural and talk with the children about gardens. They have worked on creating the tomatoes and watermelons, now they will work on the corn.

2. Provide the predrawn long ovals on the yellow construction paper and have children cut them out.

3. Provide the predrawn corn stalk leaves on green construction paper. These leaves are usually long and narrow with a point at the end. Have the children cut these out and save.

4. Using markers let children draw squares on their yellow "corncobs" if they wish.

5. Have children assist with cleanup.

6. Have corn for snack.

Day 4

1. Gather the children together and review what has been done. The final steps will be to create the tall cornstalks, the branches and leaves for the tomatoes, and the vines for the watermelon. These will all be glued to the mural.

2. Construct the mural, using the top, middle, and bottom of the surface. The cornstalks are near the upper middle to top of the mural, the tomato plants in the middle to lower middle, and the watermelons on the bottom of the mural setting, on the ground.

3. Next, they cut the predrawn cornstalks and glue them at the top of the mural with the leaves and corncobs included.

Directed Play

4. Provide predrawn or precut leaves for the tomato plants and thick green markers for drawing the vines. Have the children cut the leaves then go to the mural and draw the vines. Glue the leaves to the vines.

5. Staple or tape green yarn on the bottom of the mural to represent the watermelon vines. Once attached, have the children glue their watermelons touching the string.

6. Have all the children sign the mural and assist with cleanup. Praise the children for a job well done.

Adaptations for Children With Disabilities

Provide precut shapes for children or provide hand-over-hand assistance in cutting. Allow children to rest if they become tired.

Bad Weather Mural (3 Days)

Target Objectives
Weather concepts relevant to geographical area, science concepts, safety in storms, weather vocabulary, cooperation, cutting and construction

Developmental Domains
Fine Motor, Cognitive, Language, Social

Multiple Intelligences
Bodily, Spatial, Interpersonal, Linguistic, Naturalist

Materials
Books and pictures relevant to stormy weather in your geographic area; dark markers; large paper for listing; white, gray, and black construction paper; scissors; cotton balls; glue; gold glitter paint pencils (optional); water paints and brushes; large bolt paper; yellow markers.

Preparation/Set-Up
Materials available for each day. Hang bolt paper for mural.

Procedures

Day 1

1. Gather a small group of children together and read a book about storms, such as *Storm Book*. Talk about what we see and hear when it storms, including the concepts of dark clouds, heavy rain, lightning, thunder, wind, or tornados.

2. Discuss safety procedures for storms. Record a list of safety preparations, including actions (e.g., stay off the phone, get away from windows, go to the basement) and materials (e.g., radio, candles, flashlight).

3. Have the children gather at a table and tell them that they are going to create a stormy weather mural. The focus for day one will be on dark clouds. Provide books or pictures for reference.

4. Provide the children with predrawn large clouds on gray, black, and dark blue construction paper and let them cut these out. Allow for a variety of shapes and sizes.

5. Glue pulled and stretched cotton balls over the cut-out clouds. Once dry, let children use black, gray, or dark blue markers on the cotton to give additional darkness to the clouds. Save for the next day.

6. Have children assist with cleanup.

Day 2

1. Gather children together and read a book about stormy weather. Discuss what was done the day before.

2. Have children glue their clouds to the upper part of the large, prehung mural paper. It is okay if clouds overlap.

3. Provide children with yellow markers or chalk and have them draw lightning strikes. These should be drawn top down using a zigzag motion.

4. If available, have children trace their lightning strikes with gold or silver glitter paint pencils.

5. Review safety procedures regarding lightning.

Day 3

1. Gather at the mural and read a book about storms relevant to your geographical area and review safety procedures.

2. Practice a tornado drill (or a drill relevant to your area). For a tornado drill, have children assume a turtle position with knees on floor, forehead to the floor, chest to thighs, and hands covering the back of the head and neck. Talk about listening for directions.

3. Have children regroup at the mural and review what was done previously. Have children use black or gray chalk to draw tornados. Start at the top and, beginning with larger circles, have them draw in a spiral motion down, gradually making the circles smaller. These should close when they touch the "ground."

4. Once completed, have children use water paints and small brushes to add rain to their storm. This can include dashes for pelting rain, dots for drops, and even "puddles" on the ground.

5. Have children sign their mural and assist with cleanup.

Adaptations for Children With Disabilities

Physically assist children as needed. Repeat directions and model vocabulary. Provide support while working and climbing the step stools. Praise the children for working together. Let children try to resolve conflicts before intervening.

127 Feelings and Emotions Mural (4 Days)

Target Objectives
Name and recognize facial expressions of happy, sad, angry, and afraid

Developmental Domains
Fine Motor, Cognitive, Language, Social

Multiple Intelligences
Bodily, Spatial, Interpersonal, Linguistic, Intrapersonal

Materials
Books and pictures about facial expressions and feelings; predrawn heads on white, yellow, dark brown, and light brown construction paper; paper scraps that correspond to hair colors; glue; scissors; step stools, tempera paints and brushes; paint smocks; drop cloths; crayons.

Preparation/Set-Up
Large piece of bolt paper hung on a wall or bulletin board.

Procedures

Day 1

1. Gather together a small group of children and read a story that targets happy feelings. Talk about facial characteristics; for example, when smiling, cheeks rise and eyes are open wide.

2. Have the children brainstorm a list of events or things that make them feel happy. The teacher should record this list with words and pictures as needed for understanding. This is a good time to help children see that different things make different people happy.

245 Chapter 8

3. Have the children move to a table and give them the predrawn heads in a variety of colors. Let children draw happy faces by adding smiles and happy eyes.

4. Provide the children with scraps of paper, scissors, and glue and let them cut hair to glue to the heads.

5. Save for the next day. Have children assist with cleanup.

Day 2

1. Gather children at the mural paper, pass out the happy faces created the day before, and review what was discussed about facial expressions. Review things that make us happy.

2. Have the children trim the excess paper around their head carefully to not cut the hair off. Then, glue their faces on the mural to make a "crowd." Children can glue their faces anywhere on the mural.

3. Have the children sit in a small circle and read a short book about feeling sad. Help them to understand that sad is the opposite of happy and show them pictures of faces that are sad. Talk about the story and allow the children to talk about things that make them sad.

4. Play a happy/sad game with a short list of happy and sad situations. Ask questions such as "How did the little boy feel when his favorite toy was broken?" Children name the feeling as happy or sad.

5. Move to the mural and have the children paint sad faces, allowing for level of development and creativity. Show them pictures of sad faces.

6. Have children assist with cleanup.

Day 3

1. Gather together as a small group and read a story about feeling mad or angry. Show the children pictures of people who are angry or mad and note how their faces look. Review the story and have the children talk about why someone would be mad.

2. Allow children to share stories about what has made them mad in the past, but limit the time to five or six minutes. Emotions are powerful and children can talk about them for a long time. If there are more stories, have the children talk about them while working on the mural.

3. Move to the mural and have the children use crayons to draw complete faces of people who look mad. Have an example for them to look at. Encourage children to talk about things that make them mad and how they feel when they are mad. Peer conversation is strongly encouraged.

Directed Play

Day 4

1. Gather children together and read a story about feeling afraid, such as *There's a Nightmare in My Closet*. Discuss events of the story and any personal experiences children have about being afraid. Record a list of things children identify that have made them feel afraid.

2. Move to a table and let the children construct faces of people who are afraid. Let the children draw faces on white, yellow, or brown construction paper and have them use markers to add facial details and hair. Have an example of a face of someone who is afraid for children to model. Be sure to point out how the mouth and eyes look.

3. As children complete their faces, let them move freely to and from the mural to glue their faces on. This provides an opportunity to work on turn-taking, manners, independence, and multiple-step directions.

4. Have children sign the mural and assist with cleanup.

Adaptations for Children With Disabilities

For younger children, have all four heads predrawn. As another option for this activity, take photos of children making these faces and let them cut them out and glue them to a mural. This could be done individually or as a group mural. Have children identify the pictures of other children making these faces. For older children, move on to secondary emotions such as lonely, tired, bored, or frustrated. An understanding of facial expressions and emotions is very important for children with autism, emotional and behavior disorders, and mental retardation. Review these concepts often. Start each day asking children how they feel. Encourage each child to name at least one feeling and then discuss it. See the Personal/Social chapter for related activities on emotions. Repeat this activity several months later.

128 Together Mural—People of the World (3 Days)

Target Objectives
Awareness of similarities and differences in people, uniqueness, individuality, togetherness, belonging, peoples of other cultures

Developmental Domains
Cognitive, Social, Language, Fine Motor

Multiple Intelligences
Linguistic, Spatial, Bodily, Intrapersonal, Interpersonal

Materials
Books that discuss a variety of cultures, such as *Elmer the Elephant* or *Children of the World*; predrawn heads on 8" x 10" construction paper; small mirrors; scissors; construction paper in skin colors; glue sticks; markers; crayons; colored pencils in a variety of colors.

Preparation/Set-Up
Have specific materials available for each day.

Procedures

Day 1

1. Gather children together in a small group and read *Elmer the Elephant* or another book about being unique or an individual.

2. Have children answer "wh" questions about feelings and events of the story. Have children identify and name the title and author and encourage them to use vocabulary such as same, different, belonging, group, individual, and special.

3. Encourage children to look at their own faces and identify the color of their eyes, skin, and hair.

4. Move to a table and have children color the skin tones and draw details of their own faces on predrawn heads. Then have children cut out their faces, being careful to cut around the hair.

5. Save heads/faces for the next session and explain to the children that these will be part of a people mural.

Day 2

1. Gather children at the mural with glue sticks and the faces created the day before. Have them glue these to the mural.

2. Return to a small group and read *Children of the World* or another book about people of different cultures. Be sure to use language children will understand.

Directed *Play*   248

3. Generate a list of how we are the same and a list of how we are different. Identify special qualities in people. Use vocabulary words such as acceptance, friend, trust, and the names of countries. Point out that differences are not bad.

4. Move to a fine motor area and have children construct a face of a child from another country or culture.

5. Provide construction paper in varied skin tones with predrawn heads, scraps of construction paper, scissors, and glue. Have children draw or glue on facial parts.

6. Add the faces to the mural.

7. Have children assist in cleanup.

Day 3

1. Gather at the mural and have children glue on the faces from the day before if not already done.

2. Have books and pictures available about other cultures and peoples. Be sure that the books and pictures show people as they are now, not how they were in the past. Talk about what children see in the pictures.

3. Show and discuss the lists of same and different and note that we are more alike than different.

4. Let children add any final touches to the people mural using markers or crayons. Have them sign the mural at the bottom.

Adaptations for Children With Disabilities

Provide extra time or practice in cutting and drawing. Provide assistance as needed. Support children while climbing and working on the stools. Repeat directions and redirect children as needed.

Table 8.4

Other Mural Ideas

Faces and Places

Jungle

Fruit Orchard

Desert

Moon

Rainforest

Transportation

Weather Contrasts

City

Seasons—Winter, Spring, Summer, and Fall

Holiday or Seasonal Murals

Letters of the Alphabet:

A—apple, alligator, ape, abacus

B—bird, bamboo, baby

C—cat, clouds, car, camel

D—dog, daisy, dime, dinosaur

E—elephant, eggs, ears

F—fish, flute, fiddle, frog, fire, fox

G—goat, guitar, grass, gorilla, giraffe

H—hamster, house, horn, hand, hippo

I—island, igloo, ice, iguana

J—jungle, jack-o-lantern, jellyfish, jaguar

K—kitten, kangaroo, kite, knot

L—leaves, lamb, lemon, lion

M—monkey, mountain, map, mermaid

N—nuts, nickel, nine, newspaper, newt

O—oval, ocean, oak tree, ostrich

P—piano, pine tree, pond, panda

Q—quarter, quilt, quail, question mark

R—rose, rabbit, round, rain, raccoon, river

S—sheep, square, six, smile, seal, snake

T—triangle, toad, turkey, tiger, telephone

U—ukulele, umpire, universe

V—valley, vine, violin, volcano, vegetables

W—watch, worm, wave, wash, walrus

X—x-ray, xylophone

Y—yarn, yard, yellow, yawn, yak

Z—zigzag, zebra, zoo, zero, zip code

Directed Play

Readiness and Preacademic Activities

Cognitive Skills	252
Prereading	272
Prewriting	280
Premath	286
Time and Seasons	296
Computers	303

Cognitive Skills

Colors and Shapes

129 Shape Matching

Target Objectives
Recognition and discrimination of shapes, fine motor skills

Developmental Domains
Fine Motor, Cognitive

Multiple Intelligences
Spatial, Linguistic, Bodily, Musical

Materials
Paper, glue sticks, precut shapes.

Preparation/Set-Up
Have shape outlines drawn on paper and matching precut shapes—circle, square, triangle, diamond, and rectangle—in a variety of sizes.

Procedures

1. Have children sit at a table. Tell them they are going to work at cutting and gluing shapes.
2. Give each child a paper with the shape outlines.
3. Have the precut shape pieces on the table within easy reach of each child.
4. Have each child glue the matching precut shape over the outlined shape on the paper.
5. The number of shapes to be glued on the paper depends on children's developmental age and knowledge of the shapes.
6. This activity can be modified for seasons or holidays. For example, at Halloween shapes can be pumpkins or black cats or for Valentine's Day the shapes can be hearts or flowers.
7. Conclude the activity by singing, "Draw for Me," paired with actions.

Draw for Me

Draw a circle,

Round as can be.

Draw a circle

Just for me.

Draw a square,

Shaped like a door.

Draw a square

With corners four.

Draw a triangle,

With corners three.

Draw a triangle

Just for me.

Adaptations for Children With Disabilities

Limit the number of shapes to be glued until children show mastery and then gradually increase the number of shapes on the paper. Keep data on recognition of shapes using the data collection form discussed in the Observation and Assessment chapter. Ask children to tell you the name of the shape they are gluing. Have a checklist of the names of the shapes and mark the ones children identify correctly. Be sure to ask for each shape at least five times. Make sure the children's feet are supported when they sit on a chair. Use smaller chairs and tables or place a block under their feet.

Color/Shape Sorting

Target Objectives
Recognition and discrimination of colors or shapes

Developmental Domains
Cognitive, Language

Multiple Intelligences
Logical, Linguistic, Interpersonal, Bodily, Musical

Materials
Colored paper (laminated)—red, blue, green, yellow, white, black, orange, brown, and purple—cut in all the same shape—circle, square, diamond, triangle, rectangle, and oval. Bowls for each color or shape, marked with a diagram of the color or shape. Have at least five to ten items for each color or shape.

Preparation/Set-Up
Have shapes or colors in a pile with bowls available. Bowls can be matching or nonmatching.

Procedures

1. Have individual children sort colors or shapes into the correct bowl by saying, for instance, "Put the same color/shape together."

2. The number of colors or shapes and corresponding bowls used will depend on the child's developmental level and will gradually increase with child success.

3. Have children sort the same color into a bowl, then shift category and sort the same shape.

4. Children should name the color or shape as they sort.

5. As an adaptation, divide children into pairs.

6. Have one child pick up a color or shape and the other child pick up the matching bowl.

7. Have children take turns picking up the color or shape or the bowl.

8. Conclude the activity by singing "Color Rhyme," paired with actions.

Adaptations for Children With Disabilities

Provide matching color bowls and/or tape a picture of the shape on the bowls. Give children lots of time to practice. Keep data on child performance using the data collection form provided. Give children extra opportunities to practice the colors or shapes they are missing most.

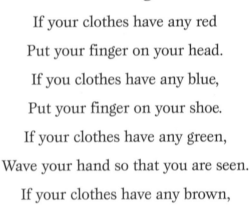

Color Rhyme

If your clothes have any red

Put your finger on your head.

If you clothes have any blue,

Put your finger on your shoe.

If your clothes have any green,

Wave your hand so that you are seen.

If your clothes have any brown,

Turn your smile into a frown.

If your clothes have any white,

Stamp your feet with all your might.

131 Shape, Color, or Emotion Bingo

Target Objectives
Child will identify and match shapes, colors, or emotion pictures

Developmental Domains
Cognitive, Language, Social, Fine Motor

Multiple Intelligences
Logical, Linguistic, Interpersonal, Bodily, Spatial

Materials
Several bingo cards in a 3' x 3' square and assorted items that differ by color, shape, or emotional expression:

- Shapes—circle, square, triangle, rectangle, diamond
- Colors—red, green, blue, yellow, black, white, pink, or orange,
- Emotional expressions—happy, sad, surprised, scared, or interested

Note: Young children will tend to focus their attention on only one dimension at a time (centration). The pictures of emotions, colors, or shapes should only differ by one attribute. Shapes should be the same color and differ only by shape; colors should be the same shape; pictures of emotional expression should differ only by facial expression.

Preparation/Set-Up
Cut out small shapes, colors, and/or pictures of emotional expressions and create approximately eight to ten bingo cards out of laminated paper. Be sure the pictures of shapes, colors, and emotions are exactly the same as on the bingo cards, counters, buttons, or markers.

Procedures

1. Gather a small group of children in a semicircle on the floor.

2. Introduce the activity, identify the name of the game, and identify each of the items.

3. Demonstrate how the game is to be played.

4. Let children choose a bingo card.

5. The activity is played as in traditional bingo—a child or an adult calls out picture names and children cover the appropriate box on their card.

255 Chapter 9

6. Children say "Bingo" when their bingo card is filled.

7. For a more challenging activity, children can use more than one card at a time or use a combination of categories on one card (e.g., colors and shapes).

Adaptations for Children With Disabilities

For children with learning needs, offer cards with four, eight, and 12 items to compare. Young children with physical disabilities may benefit from having small pieces of Velcro® attached to the items and bingo cards. Children with visual impairments will need larger cards and items with light and dark contrast. Watch children closely to see which items give them the most difficulty. Give children ample opportunities to practice this activity. Watch each child carefully and note which of the shapes or colors they match correctly and incorrectly. As children become more proficient with shapes, the bingo cards and tokens can become more difficult or complex.

Classification, Discrimination, Seriation, and Memory

Same and Different

Target Objectives
Discrimination of objects, categories, same and different

Developmental Domains
Cognitive, Language, Social

Multiple Intelligences
Linguistic, Interpersonal

Materials
Various common items arranged by category. Items can be toys or real objects, as appropriate. For example:

- Transportation—boat, plane, car, truck, train
- Foods—apple, banana, bread, milk, cookie, hotdog
- Animals—dog, cow, horse, pig, bird
- Clothes—shirt, pants, sock, shoe, hat
- Colors—red, blue, black, green, white
- Shapes—square, circle, triangle, diamond (shapes all the same color)

Preparation/Set-Up
Have materials available.

Procedures

1. This activity is designed to help promote awareness of the concepts "same" and "different."

2. Have children sit on the floor in a semicircle around you. Tell the children they are going to identify things that are the same and different.

3. Show the children all the items in one category (e.g., foods) and discuss that although the individual items look different they are all part of the same category.

4. Show all the items in each category but show only two categories of items on the first day.

5. Have children say the name of each item in each specific category.

6. Using items from two different categories, show the children three items, two from one category and one from the other category (e.g., two foods and one shape).

7. Ask the children "Which one is different?"

8. Provide assistance as needed and name the object and its category, then name the two that are the same and their category.

9. Repeat the activity at least 10 times, varying the objects each time.

10. When the children demonstrate an understanding of the concept of same and different, let children choose a partner and continue the activity.

11. Have children take turns showing objects for another child to identify and name.

12. With success, gradually increase the number and variety of objects used.

Adaptations for Children With Disabilities

Children with developmental delays will need a considerable amount of practice in this activity over a period of time. Record their performance on a checklist with two columns—same and different. Record the child's performance each day in this activity by marking a plus or minus for correct and incorrect responses. Present two or more objects at least 10 times.

(133) This Goes With This—Classification

Target Objectives
Increase classification skills, recognition of objects, categories

Developmental Domains
Cognitive, Language, Fine Motor

Multiple Intelligences
Linguistic, Logical, Bodily

Materials
Real or toy items in different categories, including colors, shapes, foods, transportation, animals, kitchen utensils, or clothing, in separate containers. Containers should have a picture on the outside showing the category of that container or box. Objects can include:

- Colors—red, blue, black, white, orange, green, yellow blocks
- Shapes—square, circle, triangle, diamond (shapes all the same color)
- Transportation—boat, plane, car, truck, train
- Foods—apple, banana, bread, milk, cookie
- Animals—dog, cow, horse, pig, bird, cat, lion
- Clothes—shirt, pants, socks, shoe, hat, coats, mittens
- Kitchen—pan, spoon, cup, plates, measuring cups

Preparation/Set-Up
Have all materials available. Depending on the developmental age of the children, present at least two categories of materials.

Procedures

1. Show a small group of children a category of objects and have the children name each item.

2. Show the children the picture of that category of items on the box or container and say that all of these objects are to go in that box.

3. Repeat with other sets of objects.

4. Let children practice sorting objects by category by placing an item in its correct box.

5. While children are sorting, explain why items are similar or different. Note commonalities in the appearance of items and why similar items go together.

Directed Play

6. Make note of which categories of objects individual children have the most difficulty with.

7. Vary the categories of objects presented and gradually increase the number of categories of objects presented at one time.

Adaptations for Children With Disabilities

Begin with colors and shapes and gradually work up to classification of items by size or use, such as transportation, household, food, or clothes. Be sure the colors and shapes differ in only one dimension. The children need to know the name of all the objects. Start with two sets of objects at first and limit the number of objects displayed if needed. Provide verbal or physical prompts as needed. Have older children classify objects by texture or classify living and nonliving things or what is real and what is not.

Describe Common Objects

Target Objectives
Recognize and describe common objects, use of language

Developmental Domains
Language, Cognitive

Multiple Intelligences
Linguistic

Materials
Common objects, such as books, puzzles, blocks, eating and cooking utensils, clothing.

Preparation/Set-Up
Have materials available.

Procedures

1. Arrange children in a small group and tell them that they are going to talk about different objects.

2. Present common objects one at a time and describe something about each one.

3. Then, have the children describe the objects in as many ways as they can.

4. This can be prompted with questions such as "What is it made of?" "What do you use it for?" "What color is it?" "Who can use it?" or "What does it feel like?"

5. Review each of the objects and the comments children made.

Adaptations for Children With Disabilities

Encourage children to speak in complete sentences. Let children manipulate and explore objects. Begin with simple, common objects, such as a spoon, brush, or crayon. Keep track of which items children can and cannot describe. Model appropriate sentence structure and word use.

135 # Instrument Memory

Target Objectives
Short-term memory, patterns, and sequence, auditory memory

Developmental Domains
Cognitive, Language, Social, Fine Motor

Multiple Intelligences
Logical, Musical, Interpersonal

Materials
Various toy musical instruments.

Preparation/Set-Up
Instruments available in a small group area.

Procedures

1. Show a small group of children the musical instruments and name them.

2. Play each one to show what kind of sound it makes.

3. While children watch and listen, play one to five musical notes on one of the instruments.

4. Have children imitate the pattern by singing or clapping.

5. Repeat two or three times with different instruments.

6. Let children choose a partner, give each group an instrument, and have the groups sit two to three feet away from one another.

7. Have children take turns playing and imitating a pattern.

8. Let each child play three or four times before trading.

9. Musical instruments such as drums, sticks, or bells are preferred instead of instruments that go in the mouth.

10. Trade instruments after a few turns.

Adaptations for Children With Disabilities

Help children to limit how many notes they make or to alternate a loud sound and a soft sound. Assist children as needed. Limit sequences to one to three notes, depending on developmental age.

Directed *Play*   **260**

136 Memory Game

Target Objectives
Matching, discrimination, categories, memory

Developmental Domains
Cognitive, Language

Multiple Intelligences
Linguistic, Logical, Bodily

Materials
Various common items or pictures arranged by category. Items can be pictures, toys, or real objects as appropriate. For example:

- Transportation—boat, plane, car, truck, train
- Foods—apple, banana, bread, milk, cookie
- Animals—dog, cow, horse, pig, bird
- Clothes—shirt, pants, sock, shoe, hat
- Colors—red, blue, black, white cut-out circles
- Shapes—square, circle, triangle, diamond (shapes all the same color)

Preparation/Set-Up
Materials should be assembled and arranged by categories in small bags with the name of the category written on the front.

Procedures

1. Children sit on the floor in a small group around the teacher.

2. Tell the children that they are going to play a memory game and that they must identify which object is missing.

3. Show children the objects and identify the name of all the objects within each category, then name the category.

4. Put the items from one category on the floor and tell the children that you are going to hide one item.

5. Have them shut their eyes and hide one of the objects behind you.

6. Children are to guess which object is missing and then tell which category it is in. Repeat.

7. Let children choose a partner. One child will "hide" an object behind his or her back, and the other child must guess which object is missing.

8. Children should take turns "hiding" and "naming" objects.

261   Chapter 9

9. Trade categories of items after three or four opportunities for each group.

10. Children can practice naming all objects in the category bags and tell why the objects go together.

11. Given the developmental age of children, you may need to start with two objects and then gradually work up to more objects.

Adaptations for Children With Disabilities

Children should be given an adequate amount of time to explore the objects. Children with visual impairments should be provided with objects with distinct tactile qualities. Children with physical disabilities may benefit from objects having Velcro® attached to improve stability. Children should be encouraged to identify and name the objects using complete sentences. Use the data collection form in Chapter Four to record the number of times children correctly identify the objects.

137 Preposition Directions

Target Objectives
Following one-, two-, and three-step directions, understanding prepositions, memory

Developmental Domains
Cognitive, Language, Gross Fine Motor

Multiple Intelligences
Linguistic, Logical, Bodily

Materials
Various common objects, such as a ball, cup, plate, or toys.

Preparation/Set-Up
Have materials available.

Procedures

1. Begin with two to three children sitting in a small group. Tell them you are going to give them some directions and that they are to do what you say.

2. Start with one-step directions that focus on prepositional concepts, for example, "Put the ball under the chair."

3. As children are successful, move on to two-step prepositional commands that require a shifting between concepts, for example, "Put the ball under the table and the cup beside the chair."

4. Vary the directions to include the concepts: in, on, under, beside, behind, between, and in front of.

5. As children are successful move up to three-step directions. Be sure to pause briefly between each direction to give children time to think about what you have said.

Adaptations for Children With Disabilities

Assist children with verbal and physical prompts as needed. Repeat the directions several times while the child is performing them. For older children, add the concepts of: top/bottom, front/back, through/around, or left/right. Make use of a lot of repetition. Don't make directions complex—keep them simple. Use the data collection form in Chapter Four to record prepositions or one- or two-step commands.

Stop and Go

Target Objectives
Following directions, short-term memory, listening

Developmental Domains
Cognitive, Language, Social

Multiple Intelligences
Linguistic, Bodily, Interpersonal

Materials
None.

Preparation/Set-Up
Large motor area or outside space.

Procedures

1. Tell a group of children that they should move when you say "Go" and stop when you say "Stop."

2. Direct children first to walk and then vary directions to have them crawl, jump, hop on one foot, or dance.

3. The children are to stop when they hear "Stop" and not move until they hear "Go." Vary the time intervals between directions.

4. Children can take turns giving the instructions.

5. This activity can also be done using riding toys, such as trikes and wagons.

Adaptations for Children With Disabilities

Praise children when they follow the proper directions. Have an adult stand next to any child having difficulty.

(139) Cold

Target Objectives
Increase awareness of seasons, recognition and use of objects, cognitive and language concepts related to cold

Developmental Domains
Cognitive, Language, Social

Multiple Intelligences
Logical, Linguistic, Bodily, Naturalist

Materials
Water, ice, snow (if available), pans, drawing materials, access to refrigerator/freezer, towels.

Preparation/Set-Up
Tile floor or covered floor area.

Procedures

1. Early in the day, have children pour water into a container and place the container outside in the winter, if it is below freezing, or in the freezer of a refrigerator.

2. Set a timer for one hour. After the timer rings, have a small group of children get the container.

3. Check to see if the water has turned to ice.

4. If so, have each of the children hold the ice in their hands and then pass it to another child.

5. Discuss things that are cold: snow, sleet, icicle, ice, or frost.

6. In a related activity, have children bring snow inside or watch an ice cube as it melts into water. Have the children draw or paint snowflakes or a snow person.

7. Follow the activity by reading a story such as "Frosty the Snowman" to the children.

8. End the activity by asking children what other things are cold. This might include things we eat (e.g., ice cream).

Adaptations for Children With Disabilities

Assist children in touching and holding the ice. Some children may be very sensitive to the cold. Don't force it.

Directed Play **264**

Large and Small

> **Target Objectives**
> Increase awareness of size comparisons, concepts of large and small, classification of items
>
> **Developmental Domains**
> Cognitive, Language, Fine Motor
>
> **Multiple Intelligences**
> Linguistic, Logical, Bodily
>
> **Materials**
> Various items presented in pairs that vary only by size, such as large and small shoes, gloves, pans, books, blocks, dolls, trucks, or cups.
>
> **Preparation/Set-Up**
> Have all materials available.

Procedures

1. Arrange children in a small group and tell them that you are going to talk about things that are large and small.

2. Show children all the items and point out the differences in large and small items.

3. Hold up a large item and have children take turns selecting its smaller mate then name the size of each item again.

4. Next, hold up a small item and have the children take turns selecting the large mate, then tell the size and name of the objects.

5. In another activity, have children take turns placing all the large objects in one pile and all the small objects in another.

Adaptations for Children With Disabilities

Be sure objects used differ only by size. You may need some items that have very pronounced size differences. Children with developmental delays will need more one-to-one attention and practice. Use the data collection form in Chapter Four to record children's responses matching large and small items.

141 Smallest to Largest

Target Objectives
Classification, seriation of objects, concepts of large and small

Developmental Domains
Cognitive, Language, Fine Motor

Multiple Intelligences
Spatial, Bodily, Logical, Naturalist, Linguistic

Materials
Four to six common objects of different sizes, such as sticks, spoons, cups, shoes, leaves, rocks, and pictures of circles, squares, and triangles. For younger children these items should differ only by size. For older children they can differ in more than one dimension.

Preparation/Set-Up
Have all materials available.

Procedures

1. Have a small group of children sit on the floor or at a table.

2. Show the children the objects and explain the size differences.

3. Tell the children that they are to put the objects in order from small to large; demonstrate what they are to do.

4. Give each child a group of objects. The number of objects depends on a child's developmental age—younger children get two to three objects, older children four to six objects.

5. Have children arrange the objects from smallest to largest in a left to right progression.

6. Children identify and name the smallest and largest objects.

7. If children master smallest to largest then switch and go from largest to smallest.

Adaptations for Children With Disabilities

Work individually with children while arranging the objects by size. Record on a data sheet the child's correct and incorrect responses each day. If children order the objects incorrectly, help them put the objects in the correct order, praise them, and repeat, using the same objects.

Directed Play   266

What's Wrong With This Picture?

Target Objectives
Visual discrimination, recognition of objects, increase sentence use

Developmental Domains
Cognitive, Language, Social

Multiple Intelligences
Logical, Linguistic, Interpersonal

Materials
Commercially produced or handmade "What's Wrong" pictures or cards. You can also use photographs taken of children or objects in the classroom. These pictures should begin with obvious things that are wrong and gradually move to pictures that require greater discrimination skills. Examples can include a teddy bear with a leg missing, a duck wearing a hat, or a football that has wings.

Preparation/Set-Up
Have pictures available.

Procedures

1. With children arranged in a small group tell them that they are going to play a game in which they have to find what's wrong with different pictures. Show them the "What's Wrong" pictures one at a time.

2. Have children take turns naming what is wrong with each picture by using a complete sentence.

3. Let children take turns showing pictures to one another.

4. Pictures can have more than one thing "wrong" in them. The children will be challenged to find all of the mistakes.

Adaptations for Children With Disabilities

It may be helpful to have two pictures, one that is "right" and another that is "wrong." Assist the children in seeing the differences between the two pictures. Children with mental retardation can have difficulty in selective attention. Help them to focus on the most relevant aspects of pictures. It is important that the pictures be simple and not too "busy." Use a barrier, such as a box, around the part that's "wrong" in the picture.

Find What's Missing

Target Objectives
Problem solving, part-whole relationships, identification of objects

Developmental Domains
Cognitive, Language, Fine Motor

Multiple Intelligences
Linguistic, Spatial, Bodily

Materials
Erasable markers, pictures of common objects covered with contact paper, wet and dry paper towels to wipe pictures clean. Pictures should have one or more missing parts. The pictures might include a car with no wheels, a table missing a leg, a boat without a sail, a dog without a tail, a bird without a beak, etc.

Preparation/Set-Up
Have all materials available.

Procedures

1. Have a small group of children sit at a table. Make sure their feet are supported.

2. Show the pictures to the children and explain that something is missing in each picture. Give them an example and demonstrate how they are to draw in the missing piece(s).

3. Provide erasable markers of different colors.

4. Give each child a picture to complete.

5. Encourage children to talk about their pictures.

6. Erase drawings and trade pictures with other children in the group.

Adaptations for Children With Disabilities

Provide pictures with only one part missing and then increase difficulty with pictures that have more than one item missing.

Moving With Directions

Target Objectives
Following one-, two-, three-, and four-step directions, short-term memory, understanding prepositions, motor planning

Developmental Domains
Cognitive, Language, Fine Motor, Gross Motor

Multiple Intelligences
Linguistic, Spatial, Bodily

Materials
Common classroom or home objects.

Preparation/Set-Up
Large motor area.

Procedures

1. Arrange children in a small group.

2. Tell them that they are going to practice following directions.

3. Begin first with a single direction, such as "Touch your nose."

4. Increase to two simple directions, such as "Touch your nose and then stand on one foot." Pause between commands to give children time to "process" what you have requested.

5. Increase to three-step commands as children are able.

6. It is easy to incorporate prepositional concepts into this activity, such as "Put the ball on the table, crawl under the table, and walk around the chair."

7. Let children take turns giving one-, two-, or three-step directions to other children.

Adaptations for Children With Disabilities

Say directions slowly, with a short pause between each direction. Repeat directions two or three times and have children repeat them back to you. Keep data on child performance by recording the number of directions they complete successfully on the 0–5 data sheet.

145　Scavenger Hunt

Target Objectives
Recognition and discrimination of common items, following directions, receptive language

Developmental Domains
Cognitive, Language, Fine Motor, Gross Motor, Social

Multiple Intelligences
Interpersonal, Intrapersonal, Bodily, Linguistic

Materials
Assorted materials in the classroom or playground setting. There should be at least one of each item for each child to find. Ideas for materials to be "found" can include:

- Specific objects such as crayons, balls, sticks, pictures of individual students
- Classroom items or toys
- Something round (or other shapes)
- Something green (or other colors)
- Something that we wear
- Something that we eat
- Something that makes sound
- Something that smells
- Something that grows
- Something that makes music

Preparation/Set-Up
The items to be found should be scattered around the classroom or outside play area. Items should be easy to find and spread out in a relatively small area.

Procedures

1. This activity is based on the traditional scavenger hunt idea of finding certain objects.

2. Show children the items and name them.

3. Children will be directed to find an object by its description or function. As children become more accustomed to the activity, have them gradually seek more than one object at a time.

4. Children can look for objects individually or in pairs.

5. Try to set up the activity so that each child finds an object that contributes to the group. For example, each child can find a piece of a puzzle.

6. Repeat two to three times with items hidden in different places.

Directed Play　270

Adaptations for Children With Disabilities

Children with physical disabilities may need assistance in moving around the classroom, and items should be placed where they are easily seen and reached. Children with mental retardation may require a smaller group of children initially so that the other children don't distract them. Assist with task completion as needed.

Go Fish

Target Objectives
Recognition and discrimination, turn-taking

Developmental Domains
Cognitive, Language, Social

Multiple Intelligences
Logical, Linguistic, Interpersonal

Materials
This activity can be played with a commercially available deck of "Go Fish" cards or number cards. However, depending on the developmental age of children, the cards can be adapted to include only colors, shapes, or pictures of the children themselves.

Preparation/Set-Up
Sit on the floor or at a small table.

Procedures

1. A small group of children play "Go Fish" in the traditional manner.

2. For younger children it may be necessary to start in pairs.

3. Teachers should play along with the children, modeling turn-taking, reviewing rules, and helping to identify card names.

4. The game can be adapted by having cards based on different colors or shapes or facial expressions or by using cards that have pictures of the children in the class. Hence, children may ask, "Do you have green?" "Do you have a square?" or "Do you have a picture of Kate?"

Adaptations for Children With Disabilities

Encourage children to speak in complete sentences. Limit the number of cards available for some children. Increase or decrease the size of the cards as needed.

Prereading

Listening Activities

Listening activities provide children with opportunities for practicing auditory discrimination and auditory memory skills. Children identify the sound and the source of the sound. Listening activities and sources can include:

- Marching to music with the children stopping when the music stops.
- Animal sounds made by an adult or recorded on a tape or CD. Children listen, then identify.
- Familiar body sounds, such as sneezing, coughing, clapping, crying, laughing, or snoring. Children listen, identify, and imitate.
- Environmental sounds, such as a dog barking, car horn, telephone ringing, door slamming, doorbell, vacuum, water running, rain, thunder, wind blowing, or waves on a beach.
- Musical instruments—children repeat beats on a drum (e.g., one beat, pause, two beats) or tambourines, bells, castanets, maracas, or cymbals. Address concepts such as loud and soft. Have children imitate the rhythm.
- Speech sounds—say two speech sounds and have children tell you if they are same or different.
- Hide a loud clock or some other sound device and have children find it.
- Make use of rhymes and songs with finger plays.
- Have children repeat sequences of numbers. Begin with two numbers and gradually increase how many numbers they are to repeat (e.g., "2, 4," then "5, 8, 3"). Use with musical rhythms or song, clap as you count, or vary pitch.
- Have children listen to speech synthesis or augmentative communication devices.
- Have children close their eyes while you make a sound with a bell or instrument. Have children guess what part of the room you are in or how far away you are. Count the steps moving toward the sound.

147 Different Sounds

Target Objectives
Recognize the source of different sounds and objects, listening, auditory discrimination, turn-taking

Developmental Domains
Cognitive, Language

Multiple Intelligences
Linguistic, Musical, Naturalist

Materials
Empty coffee cans with lids and small amount of different materials, such as sand, water, beans, sticks, leaves, or rocks in separate containers.

Preparation/Set-Up
Have materials available.

Procedures

1. Show a small group of children the various materials and introduce the activity by telling them that they are going to listen to different sounds and guess what makes the sound.

2. Pour one of the containers into the empty coffee can and put on the lid.

3. Shake the can and have children listen to the sound it makes, then guess as a group what's inside.

4. Pour material from a different container into the can, shake, and have children listen and then name what they are hearing.

5. Next, choose one child from the group and have the other children close their eyes.

6. Help the child pour one of the containers into the can, put the lid on, and shake it.

7. Children are to guess what is in the can.

8. Give each child an opportunity to pour a material in the can to shake.

9. Children can also create different rhythms with different materials.

10. Different amounts of materials can also be put in the can to make different sounds. Encourage children to listen to the pitch of the sound.

11. Have children discuss what kinds of sounds different objects made.

Adaptations for Children With Disabilities

Repeat several times using the same items and materials. Make note of any sounds children have problems with. Use the data collection form to record children matching sounds to their source.

What's That Sound?

Target Objectives
Improve listening skills, follow directions, recognition of objects

Developmental Domains
Cognitive, Gross Motor, Language

Multiple Intelligences
Linguistic, Bodily, Musical

Materials
Have a variety of laminated pictures of objects that make sounds. These can include an alarm clock, various musical instruments, a car horn, sirens, a telephone, or various animals. Have the sounds of these objects available on a cassette tape or CD.

Preparation/Set-Up
Tape several pictures on the floor that correspond to the sound recordings.

Procedures

1. Gather children in a small group and tell them they are going to match pictures of objects to the sounds they make.

2. Show them the pictures of various objects on the floor and name each of these things.

3. Working individually around the group, have a child move and stand on the correct picture after listening to a sound that is presented.

4. Repeat this activity several times to give all children opportunities to match a picture with its sound.

Adaptations for Children With Disabilities

Provide extra practice as needed. Repeat the names of the pictures for children several times.

Reading Stories

Reading stories to children is one of the most important things we can do to promote cognitive and language development. Books expose children to different ideas, recognition and identification of objects and events, time sequences, and daily living skills. Children have a natural interest in books and should be encouraged at school and at home.

To get the most of what books have to offer it is important that you read to children and have a wide assortment of literature available for them. Teachers and parents should establish a literacy-rich environment with pictures, words, and assorted books available. Books and stories should address a wide range of topics. Include books that focus on things children are curious or concerned about, such as moving, divorce, disabilities, or death of a pet or family member. Such stories help encourage discussion and reduce fears or anxieties in the children. Using books and stories in this way is known as bibliotherapy. There should also be books and pictures available for children of different developmental levels. This can include simple, sturdy cardboard picture books for very young children, as well as higher-level language books for older children.

It is important to use caution when choosing books and stories for young children. Older books, such as those published before 1970, may contain negative or inappropriate stereotypes. Make sure that books you use contain current, culturally relevant information. You can preview or check out books from public libraries or from university curriculum resource centers. Garage sales or flea markets are a source of inexpensive books, or books can be homemade.

Books and stories fit nicely into any thematic unit. Read stories to children before beginning a thematic unit to introduce words and concepts. Read stories again at the end of activities to reinforce language concepts and comprehension.

Stories should be read daily to the children. Have a scheduled, routine story time every day for independent reading or for whole group reading. Select books that correspond to the theme of the day or week. It may be helpful to add pictures to some stories or books to help children see and understand what is going on. Make sure children are in a comfortable position while listening to stories and be sure that they can see the pictures. Give children time to look and touch the pictures as you read the story. Read and reread stories. Children should enjoy being read to and show an interest in retelling the story or drawing pictures about it. Whenever possible use literature to enhance an activity.

Vary your voice as you read the story to correspond to different characters. Ask questions about characters, plot, time sequence, and events. Ask who, what, when, where, and why questions. Try to ask open-ended questions rather than close-ended questions. Open-ended questions are those that cannot be answered with a single word response. For example, "What happened to Jack and Jill?" is different than "Did Jack and Jill fall down the hill?" Don't stop too often or you'll lose the meaning of the story. Be engaging and excited about what is being read.

When reading, point out to children pictures on the front and back cover. Assist them in learning to visually scan from left to right by pointing to the top left side of each page in the book. Point to pictures and have the child say the word. Encourage the children to talk about the stories in complete sentences. After reading stories, focus on story comprehension by asking and discussing with children what the story was about, who the main characters were, and what the sequence of events was (what happened first, next, and last).

If there is an interpreter for children who are deaf, be alert to how fast you are reading. Remember that signing takes longer than speaking.

Matching Objects to Pictures

Target Objectives
Identification and discrimination of objects

Developmental Domains
Cognitive, Language, Social

Multiple Intelligences
Linguistic, Interpersonal, Spatial

Materials
Have pictures or drawings of common everyday or toy items. Items used can be relevant to the theme or concepts being taught (i.e., furniture and house items when learning about homes).

Preparation/Set-Up
Have materials available.

Procedures

1. Arrange children in a small semicircle seated on the floor.

2. Introduce the activity by telling children that they are going to play a game of matching pictures to objects.

3. Show the children the real or toy objects and have them repeat the names of these objects and their function.

4. Arrange the objects on the floor in front of you. Show the children a similar picture and have them point to and name the matching object.

5. Repeat for all pictures and objects.

6. Let the children choose a partner.

7. Give each pair two or three of the common objects and pictures.

8. One child shows the picture, and the other must match it with the correct object.

Adaptations for Children With Disabilities

This is a good activity for children who may need augmentative communication devices. It is important for all children to identify pictures as symbols for something else. Use the data form to record the pictures and objects that are matched correctly. Have a list of the objects and pictures and put a plus sign when children match them correctly. When matched incorrectly, help children to match them appropriately, praise them, and repeat. Make sure pictures are easy to see and have good contrast (black on white).

Sequencing Pictures

Target Objectives
Sequential order of events, time concepts

Developmental Domains
Cognitive, Language, Social

Multiple Intelligences
Logical, Linguistic, Interpersonal

Materials
Commercially produced or handmade pictures or photographs of simple events.

Preparation/Set-Up
Have materials available.

Procedures

1. Have children arranged in a small group.
2. Tell them that you are going to show them pictures and that they need to identify which pictures come first and last. Demonstrate one or two times.
3. Show the children two-step pictures of sequential action (e.g., a whole apple or cookie and a half-eaten apple or cookie). Describe which came first and which came last.
4. As children are able, increase to four- to five-step pictures of sequential events (e.g., whole cookie, half-eaten cookie, empty plate; buy groceries, make cookies, bake cookies, eat cookies). Identify what comes first, next, and last.
5. Give each child a set of the sequential pictures and have them put them in order from left to right. This can be done individually or with a partner. Have children retell what they have done.

Adaptations for Children With Disabilities

Have children say first, next, and last while pointing to pictures in the correct order. Keep data on each presentation of items and note the number of correct and incorrect responses. Provide children with eight to ten opportunities to do this activity at one sitting. Some children will require additional practice in a one-to-one setting with this activity prior to implementing it in a group.

151 Group Story

Target Objectives
Increase cooperation, creativity, story sequencing, using complete sentences

Developmental Domains
Language, Social, Cognitive

Multiple Intelligences
Interpersonal, Linguistic

Materials
Chalkboard or dry erase board.

Preparation/Set-Up
Have materials available.

Procedures

1. Arrange children in a small group.

2. Tell children that they are going to make up a story.

3. Each child will have a chance to say something to contribute to the story.

4. Have the children select a topic and give them an introductory sentence to get them started.

5. Let children take turns saying a sentence or let them add a sentence as they think of it. Draw or write what the children say on a board.

6. Assist children in saying complete sentences as necessary or give them ideas of what to say. Use pictures to prompt ideas.

7. Provide the children with time to think about what they want to say.

8. Continue until the children run out of ideas.

9. Repeat if desired with a new topic.

Adaptations for Children With Disabilities

Provide assistance as needed. You may want to select the topic and encourage children to add words or ideas. Limit story to three to four events within a small group, with a clear beginning and ending to the story.

Directed Play

Alphabet

 ## Alphabet Letters

Target Objectives
Recognition of letters

Developmental Domains
Cognitive, Language

Multiple Intelligences
Linguistic, Spatial, Musical

Materials
Alphabet cards or pictures.

Preparation/Set-Up
Have alphabet cards available.

Procedures

1. This will be a good activity for kindergarten-age children.
2. Show the children the pictures of the letters one at a time and have the children verbally imitate the name of the letter.
3. Sing the "ABC" song, paired with movement.
4. Let children choose a partner.
5. Distribute the letter cards to the children.
6. The children take turns showing and naming letters.
7. Provide letter lines for the children to use as a reference. Learning to rely on reciting the alphabet while pointing to the letters will help them find the name of a letter if they cannot recall it from memory.

Adaptations for Children With Disabilities

Encourage verbal imitation and the letter sign by giving the letter and then having the children repeat it. This is good practice for recognition and name recall. Have a sheet of paper with the letters of the alphabet written down the page. Each time you ask the child "What letter is this?" record with a plus or minus correct or incorrect responses. For incorrect responses, prompt the correct answer, praise the child, and repeat. Keep data each day using the 0–5 data collection form. Put extra emphasis on letters in a child's name.

Prewriting

Most children will need assistance in developing their ability to hold and use a pencil correctly. For some children it will be necessary for them to increase the strength and coordination in their hands before beginning these tasks. Suggested activities can include rolling and molding play-dough, using a squirt bottle, using tweezers to pick up something, rotating the hand (such as opening a jar), opening and closing clothespins, and practicing snaps, buttons, and zippers. Most children benefit from activities such as opening and closing hands quickly or shaking their hands before writing.

Prewriting skills are enhanced by having children practice drawing and writing in a vertical position. This might include drawing on an easel, wall-mounted chalkboard, or slant boards, or even drawing with soap on the bathtub wall.

Holding a pencil or crayon correctly involves the use of a three-finger tripod grasp. Encourage children to use their thumb and index (or pointer) finger to press about an inch from the tip of point. The middle finger should be positioned under the pencil. The web should be open with the pencil resting comfortably. Have children bend their ring finger and little finger into the palm so that they can rest their hand on the table.

Prewriting begins with an understanding of shapes and lines. Start by ensuring that children can imitate a horizontal scribble, a vertical scribble, and a circular scribble. Next, see if a child can imitate horizontal, vertical, and circular lines. If a child is successful in this, have them copy a horizontal and vertical line and a circle. Gradually introduce imitating and copying a cross, square, left/right diagonals, X, triangle, and diamond. Let children practice drawing in sand, shaving cream, flour, salt, or with finger paints.

153 Get Ready to Write

Target Objectives
Prewriting, correct posture for writing. Assist in holding a pencil in a mature tripod grasp.

Developmental Domains
Fine Motor, Gross Motor, Cognitive

Multiple Intelligences
Bodily, Spatial, Linguistic, Intrapersonal

Materials
Paper (8" x 10"), pencils or other types of writing utensils.

Preparation/Set-Up
Child-sized table and chairs so that feet are supported and hands and arms rest easily on the table.

Procedures

1. Have a small group of children sit at a table. Explain to the children that sharp pencils can be dangerous and must be used appropriately. You should check to be sure children are sitting correctly, with their feet on the floor.

2. Adjust or change their position if necessary. Encourage children to sit back in their chairs and move the chairs up to the table. Have the children look at how they are sitting at the table.

3. Encourage children to lean slightly forward resting both arms on the table.

4. Praise the children for sitting properly.

5. Present the pencils at midline for each child and let them take the pencil from you using one hand. The hand they choose with is the hand they are to write with.

6. Children should be shown how to pinch the end of the pencil with the thumb and pointer finger about one inch above the point, with the sharp end of the pencil pointing up.

7. Have them rotate the pencil to the open web space of the hand using their other hand if necessary.

8. Next, they are to position their middle finger under the pencil to complete the three-finger, or tripod, grasp.

9. They should be bending the ring finger and little finger into the palm of the hand and resting their arms and hand on the table.

10. Let the children practice drawing by giving some suggestions of what to draw. Check the alignment and position of the children while they are drawing to be sure they are maintaining the proper position.

11. Monitor the children carefully to ensure that they maintain the proper grasp.

12. They should end this activity with the same hand they started with.

Adaptations for Children With Disabilities

Provide larger paper and tape it to the table if necessary. Repeat this activity frequently and monitor the position of the children while writing. Provide bigger pencils if needed or adaptive writing materials such as grips, vibration pens, or other motivational aides.Allow for breaks if they get tired. This will help the children avoid switching hands or holding the utensil incorrectly.

154 Drawing Dot-to-Dot

Target Objectives
Prewriting, perceptual-motor

Developmental Domains
Fine Motor, Cognitive

Multiple Intelligences
Spatial, Bodily, Logical

Materials
Paper, crayons or markers, tape (optional).

Preparation/Set-Up
Have ready predrawn or commercially available dot-to-dot pages. Some should just have outlines, others a sequence to follow, such as numbers or the alphabet.

Procedures

1. Give children dot-to-dot pages to complete. Be alert to developmental age. Younger children should get only two to three dot pages, arranged in simple vertical or horizontal patterns. Older children can get more elaborate patterns with letter or number sequences.

Adaptations for Children With Disabilities

Use large dots that are easy to see. Hand-to-hand assistance may be needed for some children. Vary tools, such as crayons, markers, paints, or chalk. Gradually increase the number of dots and distance between the dots as children are successful.

155 Sandpaper Letters

Target Objectives
Recognition of letters, sensory stimulation

Developmental Domains
Fine Motor, Language, Cognitive

Multiple Intelligences
Linguistic, Bodily, Spatial

Materials
Sandpaper, scissors, glue, cardboard or construction paper.

Preparation/Set-Up
A fine grade of sandpaper will be the easiest to cut. Predraw the letters onto the sandpaper

Procedures

1. If children are able, have them cut out letters of alphabet that have been predrawn on the sandpaper.

2. Next, have them glue the sandpaper letters to the cardboard or construction paper.

3. Have the children close their eyes and then trace the letters with their pointer and middle fingers.

4. They are to try and guess what letters they are tracing.

5. Encourage children to say the name of each letter or imitate the name when given.

Adaptations for Children With Disabilities

Have dark solid lines drawn on the sandpaper for children to cut. Make the sandpaper letters large and easy to cut. Use adaptive scissors if necessary. This would be a good prekindergarten activity. Cut the letters for the children and just have forms for tracing with fingers. Provide additional opportunities for naming letters. Begin to pair sounds with letter names.

Easy and Fun Ways to Learn to Write Letters and Numbers

Children enjoy writing in a variety of textures. Get some cookie sheets or large cafeteria trays and let children practice writing in:

- Wet or dry sand
- Cornmeal or millet
- Dry or prepared pudding
- Foamy soap (not for children under three)
- Shaving cream (not for children under three)
- Birdseed
- Lotion (not for children under three)

Make writing letters fun and use a variety of utensils and surfaces:

- Markers—fat, thin, scented or with bright colors
- Chalk—various sizes and shapes
- Wiggle pens
- Colored pencils large or small
- Variety of crayons with many colors, sizes, and shapes
- Cardboard
- Tag board
- Construction paper
- Dry erase boards
- Magna-doodles
- Sensory trays with play-dough or sand

Sequencing and Tracing Letters and Numbers

Using predrawn or copied letters or numerals on paper or tag board, have children glue a variety of materials with specific qualities or quantities to the symbols. For example, the letter "M" can be glued with marshmallows or the number "7" can be glued with seven marshmallows. This is a good way to link letters and numerals together. Some items easily glued are beans, noodles, marshmallows, seeds, buttons, rice, paper strips, glitter, yarn, string, or wood shavings.

Sequencing letters is a challenging skill for young children. It is suggested that you have a number line available at all times to use for reference. Alphabet and 0–20 number strips can be found at most teacher supply stores or bookstores. They work well when attached to sentence strips with the alphabet on one side and the numbers on the other side. Each child should have one of these available for use.

Magnetic letters in upper and lower case are another way to help children learn to sequence. Have them sequence the uppercase letters and then the lowercase letters. Always start on the left side and move to the right. Magnetic numbers can also be sequenced in following a 0–5, 0–10, and 0–20 order while moving from left to right.

Use alphabet and number cards in a variety of sizes for sequencing. It is good to have number cards that have the numeral and a quantity of objects corresponding to the numeral.

Alphabet and number puzzles are fun to use when sequencing. Children may want to put pieces in randomly but encourage them to follow the proper sequence. Use this time also to review the concept of next. Some ideas for sequencing include:

- Painting letters and numbers in sequence at an easel or with finger paints.
- Using wooden or foam letters or numbers for children to sequence on the floor or at the table from left to right.
- Building letters and numbers using play-dough by first having children roll the play-dough into long "snakes."
- Using wood, foam, or magnet letters, in both upper and lower case, for the children to match.
- Using the wood, foam, or magnet letters, have children copy or construct simple words. Have a picture and/or word cards available for reference.
- Using pushpins to press an outline into precopied letters and numbers. Use large recycled Styrofoam meat trays for the backing.
- Making letters and numbers with Wikki Stix® or pipe cleaners at the table. Provide letter and number cards for reference.
- Letting a child trace or write letters on another child's back and have that child guess what letter was drawn.
- Having children trace letters or numbers with their eyes closed.
- Painting letters and numbers on varied surfaces with water, outside.

Directed *Play*

- Using masking tape or colored taped on the floor or chalk outside to make large letters or numbers and then have children:
  - Trace the letters and numbers with their feet
  - Walk, hop, jump, crawl, or ride a tricycle on the letters
  - Drive their cars and trucks over them
  - Walk toy animals over them
- Making sets of tactile alphabet or number cards for each child using large note cards with:
  - Glue and sand
  - Glue and glitter
  - Color glue
  - Puff paint
  - Glue and yarn
  - Glue and cornmeal
  - Glue and rice
  - Letters cut from sandpaper and glued to cards

Games Involving Letters and Numbers

- **Scrabble**: Use tiles to match letters, sequence the alphabet, and build words.
- **Alphabet Bingo**: Can be purchased or handmade.
- **Number Bingo**: Will need a variety of cards. Adapt the number or difficulty to the age of the children.
- **Go Fish**: Simple card game with number or letter cards.
- **Shell Game**: Using three plastic cups with small objects, such as pennies, hide an object under a cup while the child is watching. Have children take turns guessing where the object is after the cups have been scrambled. If they guess correctly, give them two pennies; if they guess incorrectly, give them one penny. Ask them how many pennies they have, to encourage counting and one-to-one correspondence. This is also a good activity for attention and concentration.
- **I Spy**: Look for requested letters in books. Promotes attention and eye tracking. Be sure they move from left to right on a page. Start with books with large print and gradually move to pages with smaller print. At first, look for letters anywhere on the page. Gradually move to more challenging concepts, like finding a word that begins with a certain letter.
- **Memory**: Can be played with letter or number cards. Organize the cards into columns. Limit the number of cards to 10 pairs each or fewer. Too many cards will be overwhelming and distracting. Use a variety of cards to promote generalization with different print. Increase the number of cards as children become proficient.
- **Guess the Letter**: Using a small bag with wooden letters, have children reach in the bag to identify letters only by their feel. Have letter cards available for reference. If they guess wrong, offer a choice, such as "Is it the letter 'B' or 'F'?"

- **Hide and Seek**: Using sand or another substance, bury letters or numbers for children to find.
- **Before and After**: Using foam, wood, or paper letters or numbers, present a letter or number and have children name the letter or number that comes before or after it. Have a number or letter line available for reference.
- **What's Missing**: With a sequence of letters or numbers, remove one or more and have the children identify which one(s) are missing. Start with a few letters or numbers at first and have letter or number lines available for reference. Children can take turns hiding and finding the letters.

Premath

Numbers

 ## One-to-One

Target Objectives
One-to-one correspondence, premath, counting

Developmental Domains
Cognitive, Language, Fine Motor

Multiple Intelligences
Linguistic, Bodily, Logical-Mathematical

Materials
Several pieces of paper with from one to ten dots or circles on each page; glue or glue sticks and materials to be glued, such as cotton balls, cereal, or dry pasta.

Preparation/Set-Up
Have materials readily available on the table.

Procedures

1. Have a small group of children sit at a table and tell them that this activity involves counting.
2. Depending on the developmental age of the children, present each child with the predrawn paper and demonstrate how they are to glue their items on the dots or within the circles from left to right or top to bottom.
3. Have each child count out the number of cotton balls or other material they need to correspond with the number of dots on the page.
4. The children glue the items directly on the dots or circles on the page from left to right or top to bottom.
5. Write the numeral corresponding to the number of dots on the page and have the children touch and count how many.

Adaptations for Children With Disabilities

Have the children point to the dots while counting them. Give them several opportunities to practice this. Provide lower quintiles of one to three or one to five. Make sure they are starting on the left and moving to the right when counting.

157 Pick Up and Hold

Target Objectives
One-to-one correspondence, rote counting, number concepts 1–10, size comparisons.

Developmental Domains
Cognitive, Language, Fine Motor

Multiple Intelligences
Logical, Bodily

Materials
Assorted small-sized objects (e.g., buttons, balls, small blocks, straws), number cards with numeral and quantity.

Preparation/Set-Up
Have materials ready in containers.

Procedures

1. Arrange children in a small group and tell them they are going to try to pick up and hold as many as 10 items in their hand.

2. Give each child a number and have them take turns picking up and holding the objects in one hand and then tell how many they are holding.

3. Have all the children count as a child picks up objects. Note that the bigger the number the harder it is to hold the items.

4. Let each child have at least three turns.

5. Talk about what numbers have more or less, then discuss which items were easier to hold.

Adaptations for Children With Disabilities

Give children extra opportunities to practice this task. Provide cups to hold quantities of items. Practice rote counting.

Number Clap

Target Objectives
Counting, one-to-one correspondence, number concepts 1–10

Developmental Domains
Cognitive, Language

Multiple Intelligences
Linguistic, Logical, Bodily

Materials
Several sets of cards with numbers one to ten and matching quantities of dots.

Preparation/Set-Up
Have materials available.

Procedures

1. Have children arranged in a small group on the floor.
2. Tell them that you will show them different number cards and that they are to clap their hands the same amount as shown on the card.
3. Demonstrate by holding up a "two" card and telling them how to clap two times.
4. Present cards several times in random order.
5. As children demonstrate success, have them divide up into pairs. They should take turns showing cards and clapping.
6. Children can vary what they do besides clapping. They can stomp their feet, spin around, or hop up and down.
7. Observe children closely to see who is having difficulty clapping the correct number of times.

Adaptations for Children With Disabilities

Have children touch and count the dots with your assistance. Provide many opportunities for practice.

159 Number Rabbits

Target Objectives Recognition of numbers, counting, one-to-one correspondence **Developmental Domains** Cognitive, Fine Motor, Language **Multiple Intelligences** Linguistic, Logical, Spatial, Bodily, Musical	**Materials** Precut rabbit pictures with large numbers (1–10) written on them, glue, cotton balls. Use white rabbits with black numbers. Make sure that the numbers are in large print. **Preparation/Set-Up** Materials readily available.

Procedures

1. The children sit at a table. Have glue and cotton balls available for each child. Tell the children they are going to glue cotton balls on the bunnies.

2. Provide each child with a numbered rabbit picture.

3. Children glue the matching number of cotton balls on the numbered rabbit.

4. Repeat with several rabbit pictures.

5. Next, sequence the rabbits one to five or one to ten while practicing rote counting.

6. Conclude the activity by singing "Tired Bunnies," paired with actions.

Adaptations for Children With Disabilities

Assist the children in counting the number of cotton balls glued on each rabbit. Predraw dots on the rabbits showing the correct number so that the children can match the quantity using one-to-one correspondence. Keep data on child performance by recording the numbers children identify correctly and incorrectly on the data collection form.

> ### Tired Bunnies
>
> Come my bunnies, it's time for bed.
>
> That's what mother bunny said.
>
> But first I'll count you just to see
>
> If you've all come back to me.
>
> Bunny 1, bunny 2, bunny 3, oh dear.
>
> Bunny 4, bunny 5, yes, you're all here.
>
> You're the sweetest things alive.
>
> My bunnies, 1, 2, 3, 4, 5.

289 Chapter 9

160 Puzzle Fun

Target Objectives
Increase problem solving, part-whole relationships

Developmental Domains
Language, Social, Cognitive

Multiple Intelligences
Linguistic, Interpersonal, Spatial

Materials
Pictures from magazines, workbooks, or photographs; poster board or cardboard stored in labeled plastic sandwich bags. At least two to three puzzles for each child.

Preparation/Set-Up
Cut up magazine pictures mounted on poster board or cardboard into ten puzzle pieces. The number of pieces and the size of the puzzles will depend on the picture and the developmental age of children. Pictures can be associated with the current theme or vocabulary in the classroom. The puzzle pieces can be cut into squares, strips, or diagonals.

Procedures

1. Have a small group of children sit at a table or on the floor.

2. Present them the puzzle pieces and demonstrate how to complete the puzzles.

3. Let children work as partners to put the puzzle pieces together and tell what they have created.

4. For older children the puzzle pieces can include words.

Adaptations for Children with Disabilities

Provide a border if necessary. Start with two-piece puzzles and increase difficulty gradually. Practice with the puzzles no less than three times before completing with a partner.

161   Number Hunt

Target Objectives
Recognition of numbers

Developmental Domains
Language, Cognitive, Social

Multiple Intelligences
Logical, Linguistic

Materials
Three sets of cards with numbers written on them from one to ten. Numbers should be large, with good contrast.

Preparation/Set-Up
With children out of the room, arrange the number cards around the room. Depending on the developmental age of the children, the cards can be partially hidden to make them harder to find.

Procedures

1. This activity will operate like a scavenger hunt. Show and tell the children what they are to look for. Give the children several opportunities to find the number cards.

2. The children take turns hiding and finding the number cards.

3. In a separate, but related, activity, have cards with pictures of different numbers of objects (e.g., two cars, three blocks, four leaves).

4. Children are to find a quantity of objects in the room to match the numeral on their number card.

5. Conclude the activity by singing "I Can Count," paired with actions.

Adaptations for Children With Disabilities

Provide assistance in helping children find cards or objects in the room. Be alert to the developmental age of the children. Make sure number cards have a good contrast (black on white) and are not too "busy."

> *I Can Count*
>
> One, two, three, and four.
>
> I can count even more.
>
> Five, six, seven, and eight.
>
> My lady fingers stand up straight
>
> Nine and ten
>
> Are my two thumb men.

Measurement

162 Measuring Things

Target Objectives
Recognition and use of objects,
number concepts, measurement,
estimation

Materials
Various items used for measurement: tape
measure, yardstick, ruler, stopwatch,
balance scale, bathroom scale.

Developmental Domains
Cognitive, Language

Preparation/Set-Up
Have items readily available.

Multiple Intelligences
Spatial, Linguistic, Logical, Bodily

Procedures

1. Arrange children in a small group sitting on the floor around you.

2. Introduce the concept of measurement and say that it is used to see how long
   things are or how much things weigh.

3. Show children each of the measurement items and give them time to explore
   them.

4. Using these tools, take turns measuring children's height and weight. Record
   the results on the board.

5. Using a balance scale, have children take turns weighing simple objects in the
   classroom. Encourage them to guess which items will weigh more.

6. Next, children can take turns running a short distance; use the stopwatch to
   time how fast they run. Let other children watch the hands go around on
   the watch.

7. Use a bathroom scale to weigh the children.

8. Record the weight and height of each child to compare with a later time.

Adaptations for Children With Disabilities

Measurement can be an abstract concept for young children. Do not be overly
concerned if they have trouble with these concepts. However, exposing them to
opportunities using measurement is an excellent way to reinforce other skills and
concepts.

Directed Play

Big Feet, Little Feet

Target Objectives
Linear measurement, recognition and use of objects, seriation, concept of largest and smallest

Developmental Domains
Cognitive, Social, Language

Multiple Intelligences
Bodily, Interpersonal, Intrapersonal, Linguistic, Spatial

Materials
Rulers.

Preparation/Set-Up
Have items readily available.

Procedures

1. Arrange children in a small group sitting around you. Have them take off their shoes and socks.

2. Show children the rulers and explain that they are used to measure things.

3. Have each child extend their legs out so that their feet are in the middle of the circle.

4. Ask children to identify who has the biggest feet and who has the smallest feet and record this for them.

5. Have children compare the size of their feet to a partner sitting next to them and continue this until everyone has compared the size of their feet. Comparisons can be done by pressing the bottoms of their feet together or by placing their feet next to each other and measuring with the ruler. Record the measurement for them.

6. Have the children sit side-by-side from the largest to the smallest feet.

Adaptations for Children With Disabilities

Provide assistance as needed. Pair with a cooperative peer or adult.

164 Which Holds More?

Target Objectives
Measurement of volume, problem solving, estimation, number concepts, same and different, most and least.

Developmental Domains
Cognitive, Language, Social

Multiple Intelligences
Logical, Linguistic, Interpersonal, Spatial

Materials
Four small plastic containers of the same size, color, and shape (e.g., two margarine tubs); various other small plastic containers, such as bowls, cups, and water bottles.

Preparation/Set-Up
Have materials available. Take the necessary precautions if using water.

Procedures

1. Arrange children in a small group at a water/sand table or a sandbox. Tell them they are going to guess which holds more.

2. Fill two margarine tubs to the top with water or sand. The amount in the tubs should be identical in terms of volume. Ask the children which would hold more. Identify and name the concept of "same."

4. Hold up a red cup and a blue cup and again ask which would hold more. Let the children point to and name the container they think would hold the most.

5. Pour the contents of the margarine tubs into each of the cups using one-to-one correspondence. Each tub pours into one of the cups. Fill the cups to capacity and again ask the children which holds more. Have them point to and name the cup they think holds the most.

6. Show the children the margarine tubs. Point out similarities and differences in the volume of the tubs. Using the second set of margarine tubs, pour the contents of one cup into one of the tubs and the contents of the second cup into the second tub. Identify if the amount of water or sand in the tubs is the same or different. Identify and name which of the cups held the most and the least.

7. Repeat this process several times using different containers. Once this activity has been performed several times, ask the children to put the containers in order by capacity.

Adaptations for Children With Disabilities

Recognize that many young children do not have the capability to "decenter," that is, the ability to look at more than one aspect of something. Point out differences in size

Directed Play **294**

and shape and give children many opportunities to practice this activity. Start with very obvious differences in size and shape of containers. Repeat this activity using bigger containers. Monitor child performance using the data collection form.

How Many Spoonfuls?

Target Objectives
Counting, measurement, estimation, problem solving, eye-hand coordination, cooperation

Developmental Domains
Cognitive, Language, Social, Fine Motor

Multiple Intelligences
Logical, Linguistic, Spatial, Interpersonal

Materials
Spoons of the same size and shape for each child; four or five various small containers, such as plastic cups or small butter tubs; sand; board or paper; marker.

Preparation/Set-Up
All materials available.

Procedures

1. Arrange children in a small group around a table or a sand table. Show them the containers and spoons and tell them that they will fill each container with sand using the spoons.

2. Show a container and ask them how many spoonfuls they think it will take to fill it. Let each child make a guess and record their answers.

3. The children take turns putting a spoonful of sand into the container while counting the number of spoonfuls together. Record the results and compare to the guess.

4. Repeat this process for three or four different-sized containers.

5. In closing, compare all of the recorded guesses and results to confirm which containers took the most spoonfuls and who guessed correctly.

Adaptations for Children With Disabilities

Use different-sized spoons as a variation. Assist with motor skills and counting as needed.

Time and Seasons

It is important for children to learn vocabulary words associated with time and seasons: today, yesterday, tomorrow, morning, afternoon, night, minute, hour, day, week, month, year, clock, calendar, next week, last week, now, early, late, never, always, long ago, birthday, fall, summer, spring, winter.

  Simple Calendar

Target Objectives
Time concepts, days of the week, seasons

Developmental Domains
Language, Cognitive, Social

Multiple Intelligences
Linguistic, Logical, Bodily, Musical

Materials
Simplified board calendar; cards with pictures and words that include days, months, weather, and seasons and with Velcro® or a magnet on the backs.

Preparation/Set-Up
Have materials ready.

Procedures

1. Arrange children in a small semicircle.
2. Each day, introduce the calendar; tell children the name of the day and the month and anything that might be significant about the day. Encourage the children to repeat the day and month.
3. Tell and show what day yesterday was and what day tomorrow will be.
4. Have children tell you what the weather is like today (sunny, rainy, cloudy, cold, hot).
5. Review any seasonal activities associated with the month.
6. Conclude by singing, "Count the Days," paired with movement.

> ***Count the Days***
>
> Come along and count with me,
> There are seven days you see.
> Monday, Tuesday, Wednesday, too,
> Thursday, Friday, just for you.
> Saturday, Sunday, that's the end.
> Now let's say them all again.

Adaptations for Children With Disabilities

Daily repetition is suggested to aid in memory and recognition. Young children do not need a lot of emphasis on day, week, month, or year until they reach kindergarten or first grade. This activity is just to introduce and practice time concepts and to discuss daily weather.

 ## Day and Night

Target Objectives
Time concepts, day and night, identification and use of objects

Developmental Domains
Cognitive, Language, Self-Help

Multiple Intelligences
Linguistic, Logical

Materials
Objects and pictures of objects that are associated with either day or night. For example, Night—sleep, pajamas, bed, blankets, robes, slippers, moon, dark; Day—sunrise, light, sunglasses, suntan lotion, school/work. Large day and night pictures.

Preparation/Set-Up
Have materials available.

Procedures

1. Tell a small group of children that you are going to talk about day and night.
2. Show the children pictures of objects associated with day or night and discuss why and what we do with them.
3. Let the children choose a partner.
4. Children sort objects or pictures into the categories of "day" or "night." The children work together to sort the items. Trade objects or pictures with another group and repeat the sorting task.
5. Conclude by singing "Night Time."

Adaptations for Children With Disabilities

Provide extra time and practice. Watch children as they sort items to be sure that they are sorted correctly. Make sure to partner children with a cooperative peer and provide praise for their cooperation.

Night Time

Before I jump into my bed,

Before I dim the light,

I put my shoes together,

So they can talk at night.

I'm sure they would be lonesome,

If I tossed one here and there,

So I put them close together,

For they're a friendly pair.

168 Our Day

> **Target Objectives**
> Awareness of self; time concepts—first, next, last, morning, afternoon, evening, night; identification and use of objects
>
> **Developmental Domains**
> Fine Motor, Social, Language, Cognitive, Self-Help
>
> **Multiple Intelligences**
> Linguistic, Bodily, Intrapersonal, Interpersonal, Musical
>
> **Materials**
> Common home and body care items, including bedding, toothbrushes, combs, clothes, backpacks, dishes, and foods.
>
> **Preparation/Set-Up**
> Create a little "home setting."

Procedures

1. This activity should focus on a child's day "miniaturized" into 20–30 minutes.

2. First guide the children through the sequence of their day by role-playing the events for them. Encourage them to imitate as you go.

3. Next, the children should pretend to get up, dress, eat, go to school, eat lunch, go home, eat dinner, and go to bed.

4. This routine will provide many opportunities to review and practice skills such as brushing teeth and hair, dressing, eating, or bus safety. Join in the play if you are invited.

5. As the role play continues ask children how they do things at home or what time of day it is when they do something and try to incorporate this into the play.

6. Bring the group of children back together and review the order in which things happen in a day (e.g., breakfast, lunch, dinner).

7. Conclude by singing "The Sun," paired with actions.

> ### The Sun
>
> Over there the sun gets up,
> (Raise arms)
>
> And marches all the day.
> (Wave arms over head)
>
> At noon, it stands right overhead;
> (Arms straight up)
>
> At night, it goes away.
> (Lower arms)

Directed Play 298

Adaptations for Children With Disabilities

This activity will provide children with mental retardation and children with visual and physical impairments an opportunity to practice daily tasks. Extra time can be taken to give them an opportunity to tie shoes, brush teeth, or fasten buttons or snaps. Provide picture schedule depicting the time of events (e.g., morning = eat breakfast). This activity can be done over four days with each day focusing on a particular time of day (morning, afternoon, evening, night). See the Home and Family activities in the Personal-Social chapter for related activities.

Time, Seasons, and Multiple Intelligences

Introducing children to time concepts and identification and use of objects is easy to do by incorporating activities organized by seasons. It is also fun to identify activities by the different multiple intelligences.

Table 9.1

Fall and Multiple Intelligences

Intrapersonal	Have children dress for fall and look at themselves in a mirror. Identify what clothes they wear in the fall that they do not wear in the summer.
Interpersonal	Children play a simple game of tag football. Children work together to gather leaves that look the same.
Linguistic	Read a book about fall, such as *Fall Harvest* or *Pumpkin Pumpkin*. Write a book together about a fall walk—what we saw and what was collected. Discuss the weather of the day: sunny, foggy, rainy, cold, windy, or cloudy.
Logical	Children sort and count fall leaves by shape, color, and size. Seed Math—Children use pumpkin seeds to match quantity of seeds with number (one through ten). Collect or purchase a variety of nuts and have children classify nuts by same or different. Measure how tall children are and how much they weigh. Measure again in the spring to compare.
Spatial	Children make fall leaf mosaics. Painting fall trees and leaves with sponges at an easel. Children color or paint jack-o-lantern faces on orange paper.
Bodily	Children move like falling leaves. Children help rake a pile of leaves to jump and roll in. Children throw and kick a football.
Naturalist	Children take a fall walk and collect fall items such as leaves and nuts. Children take a field trip to a pumpkin patch. Children roast pumpkin seeds for snack. Children talk about how to keep warm: movement, extra layers of clothing, or build a fire.

Chapter 9

Table 9.1 continued

Musical:

Song "Little Leaf," paired with movement:

Song "Autumn," paired with movement:

Little Leaf

Little leaf, little leaf,

fly, fly, fly.

The cold wind will take you up

to the sky.

The cold wind will take you around

and around.

Then slowly, slowly, you'll

fall to the ground.

Autumn

Leaves are floating softly down.

They make a carpet on the ground.

Then swish, the wind comes

whistling by,

And sends them dancing to the sky.

Table 9.2

Winter and Multiple Intelligences

Intrapersonal	Intrapersonal: Children put on winter clothes and look at themselves in a mirror. Children make a "feeling" snowperson with markers or chalk. Snowpeople can have faces that reflect happy, sad, mad, or afraid.
Interpersonal	Children dress babies or one another for winter. Have children discuss what kinds of clothes they wear in the winter as opposed to the summer. Children build a snowman or snow fort by working together.
Linguistic	Read the story "Frosty the Snowman." Sequence pictures of a snowman: build, dress, and melt. Discuss the weather of the day: sunny, foggy, rainy, cold, windy, or cloudy.
Logical	Construct snowpeople with numbered balls.
Spatial	Children draw snowpeople with white chalk on dark paper. Children paint snowpeople on an easel using circular strokes. Children construct a snowperson out of precut pieces of paper that can include hat, scarf, carrot, buttons, etc. Using folding and cutting children make snowflakes.

Directed Play

Table 9.2 continued

Bodily   Rolling or sledding in the snow. Skating to rhythm or making angels in the snow. Catch snowflakes on tongues or faces. Shoveling snow.

Naturalist   Children make bird feeders using corncobs, peanut butter, and birdseed on a string. Children roll or sled in the snow. Discuss changes in animals and plants in the winter. Children play with snow on trays, add food color as it melts.

Musical:

Sing "I'm a Little Snow Person" or "Frosty the Snowman."

Sing "Winter," paired with movement:

Winter

When it is winter I run

Up the street, and I make the ice

Crackle with my little feet.

Crickle, crackle, crickle,

crackle, crickle,

crackle, crickleee

Sing "Winter Weather," paired with movement:

Winter Weather

Let's put on our mittens

And button up our coat,

Wrap a scarf snugly

Around our throat,

Pull on our boots,

Fasten the straps,

And tie on tightly

Our warm winter caps.

Sing "Chubby Little Snowman":

Chubby Little Snowman

A chubby little snowman had a

Carrot nose;

Along came a bunny, and what do

You suppose?

That hungry little bunny, looking

For his lunch,

Ate that snowman's carrot nose,

Nibble, nibble, crunch.

Table 9.3

Spring and Multiple Intelligences

Intrapersonal Children dress for spring and look at themselves in a mirror.

Interpersonal Children plant and care for a garden together, each assuming daily chores.

Linguistic Discuss the weather of the day: sunny, foggy, rainy, cold, windy, or cloudy.

Logical Match pictures of baby animals to adults and count legs, wings, horns, etc.

Spatial Draw spring flowers and trees. Puzzles of flowers or trees. Cut and paste paper flower petals or leaves on stems using one-to-one correspondence.

Bodily Fly a kite or blow bubbles in the wind.

Naturalist Plant flower or vegetable seeds. Water and sand play. Visit a zoo. Feed ducks at a pond.

Musical:

Sing "The Rain," paired with movement:

The Rain

Pitter-patter, raindrops,

Falling from the sky;

Here is my umbrella

To keep me safe and dry.

When the rain is over,

And the sun begins to glow,

Little flowers start to bud,

And grow, and grow, and grow.

Sing "Pitter Patter," paired with movement:

Pitter Patter

Pitter, patter falls the rain

On the roof and windowpane.

Softly, softly it comes down,

Makes a stream that runs around.

Flowers lift their heads and say,

"A nice cool drink for us today."

Sing "Eency, Weency Spider," paired with movement:

Eency, Weency Spider

An eency, weency, spider

Climbed up the waterspout.

Down came the rain and washed the spider out.

Out came the sun and dried up all the rain.

And the eency, weency spider

Climbed up the spout again.

Table 9.4

Summer and Multiple Intelligences

Intrapersonal Put suntan lotion on self. Children talk about what they like about summer.

Interpersonal Put suntan lotion on one another.

Linguistic Discuss the weather of the day: sunny, rainy, hot, windy, or cloudy. Follow instructions to make ice cream.

Logical Compare smells and colors of different plants. Sort various objects by winter or summer. List all the things people do on vacation. Count the number of birds that come to a birdbath.

Spatial Make drawings in sand or mud. Let children make flower arrangements from artificial flowers.

Bodily Swimming and water play. Play T-Ball, tennis, or soccer. Throw and catch a beach ball. Run and jump in a lawn sprinkler.

Naturalist Water and sand play outside. Tend to a garden by planting, pulling weeds, or watering. Climb a small tree. Look under rocks for different insects. Go fishing or feed ducks at a pond.

Musical:

Have a parade outside using musical instruments.

Computers

It may seem strange to think of a computer as a toy for play. But think of how a young child uses a crayon or blocks as toys. At first the use of these toys is crude, but they use these toys in more complex ways as their cognitive and motor skills increase.

It is important that we provide young children with appropriate computer experiences. Some children, particularly those from lower-income homes, may not have computers available at home. It is important that we expose children to different software programs at school, as this may be their only opportunity to use computers. Computer programs can be fun and educational, and learning computer skills is important for school and later job success.

Using the Computer

A first consideration in the use of computers with young children is to give them time to explore the parts of the computer, such as the keyboard, mouse, and monitor. For some younger children you won't even have to turn the computer on, just let them practice pushing the keys or the buttons on the monitor. Children will need some time to explore the different parts of the computer. Simple software programs that require a single key press will help children understand the cause and effect of pressing keys. For example, a talking word processing program can be used. When children press a key the computer will say the letter or number and the child will see it on the screen. Children can be assisted in typing in their names or can make up words.

One good way to help get children involved in technology is to use adapted battery-powered toys. This is a very good way to help younger children understand cause and effect and how adaptive switches can be used to operate toys, such as cars or animals. It is fairly easy to construct a battery interrupter that permits a child to turn on/off control of battery-operated toys without changing the toys themselves. Such devices can be used with a variety of toys. Instructions for creating a battery interrupter can be found in Vanderheiden, Bradenberg, Brown, and Botterf (1988). Battery interrupters can be created using inexpensive materials, such as speaker wire, phone plugs, and a copper wafer. Information on such adaptations may also be available from state technology projects (see Appendix B).

It is important to note that many of the skills needed to use a computer are at least at a four- or five-year-old's level. For example, children below the age of three will find it difficult to visually track an object across the monitor and press the correct key at the correct time. Such a skill is a form of one-to-one correspondence that many children will not yet have mastered. Children younger than five years of age will not reliably recognize numbers and letters.

Table 9.5

Skills Needed by Young Children to Use Computers or Augmentative Communication Systems

Cognitive Skills:

Means-ends causality

One-to-one correspondence

Symbolic representation
(pictures represent real objects)

Reliable yes/no response

Form discrimination

Sustained and selective attention

Motor Skills:

Range of motion

Reliable press and release

Visual tracking and scanning

Eye-hand coordination

Children using computers should be positioned so that they are at eye level with the computer monitor. It is also important that their feet are supported. Basic computer tables are not always appropriate for young children. If possible, it may be useful to sit the computer on the floor, as this provides a natural and easy way for children to access it.

Particular attention needs to be given to how children respond to the computer stimuli. The traditional keyboard will be difficult for children, as most will not yet have knowledge of letters and numbers. Software programs usually require the use of the keyboard. It can be helpful to block off keys the children won't be using or highlight keys that they will press to make it easier for them to find. Yellow stickers with large letters written on them can be placed on the keys children need to press. This makes finding these keys easier and will increase the child's speed and success using the computer.

Many software programs today make use of a mouse to operate the program. Using the mouse will take practice for children and will be particularly difficult for young children with perceptual motor difficulties.

Separate, keyboard-like input devices are also available for young children. Many of these have been developed for toddlers or children with physical impairments. These keyboards may have letters displayed in alphabetical order or have larger keys to press. One disadvantage is that children must look away from the computer screen to use these devices.

One of the best means of computer access for young children is a touch screen (Rettig, 1986). With touch screens, children need only touch a spot on the monitor screen to use the software. They can maintain their attention on the monitor without having to look away from the screen. Unfortunately, there are not a lot of software programs available that provide this means of input, but it is worth finding these programs as they become available.

Software

A wide variety of software programs have been developed for young children. Teachers should always preview software before purchasing it. Advertising can lead you to believe that the software will be good, but you will want to try it to know for sure. Curriculum resource centers at universities, technology access projects, or public libraries may be good places to preview software programs. Be sure to choose software that is interactive. This means that the children should be responding to computer stimuli frequently. A software program that makes children wait while it reads a long paragraph, for example, will not be popular with children. It may be possible to check out or preview software programs through state technology assistance projects. A listing of state technology projects is in Appendix B.

Table 9.6

Questions for Previewing Software

- What is the age level of the software?
- Can speed or difficulty of items presented be changed?
- How will this software fit into the total curriculum?
- Does the program present the same stimuli every time or is there some variety in presentation?
- Can children use input devices other than the keyboard (e.g., mouse, touch screen, voice, single switch)?
- What do children need to do to operate the software independently? What keys need to be pressed and in what order?
- Are the screen displays "busy"? Are there objects or words on the screen display that are distracting or that children won't understand?
- Does the software keep data on child performance?
- Is the program interactive, that is, does the child make frequent responses to computer stimuli?
- What is the reinforcement for correct responses and the feedback for incorrect responses? The "reward" should be something enjoyable and should include both auditory and visual stimuli. The feedback for incorrect responses should not be too discouraging. It is possible for software to deliver feedback for incorrect responses that is rewarding for children. In addition, see if the reinforcement or feedback can be changed in any way.

Be prepared for children to want to change software programs frequently. As with other playthings, children will want to "try something new." Some children may access two or three software programs in a 10-minute period. Children who are four to five years old will spend more time working with a single program than will two- to three-year-olds.

As with other toys and playthings, software programs need to be selected based on various developmental domains, including social, language, and cognitive skills. Teachers would be wise to select programs that address a wide variety of skills and concepts. In addition, software programs should be selected that can be used in conjunction with thematic units. Look for software that is easy for children to use. Screen displays should be simple and stimuli on the screen should not be abstract. Try to use software that allows you to alter what is presented and how fast it is presented and that elicits both auditory and visual stimuli.

Do not be concerned if you do not have the latest computer system. Young children do not need the most up-to-date technology. While new computer systems can provide some good experiences, older computer systems and software can be very functional and affordable. However, be on the lookout for new technology that can assist children in ways not possible in the past. For example, Dacta has developed LEGO® CAD software that allows children to create virtual 3-D LEGO® creations on the computer screen without actually building them. Software such as this could be used by a child with physical disabilities who might have a great deal of difficulty building LEGO® creations with the bricks. The child could build these constructions on the computer.

Web Sites

There are a number of web sites that offer children and families access to computer-based activities without having to purchase software programs. For example, www.pbskids.org offers a variety of activities relating to Sesame Street® characters, Teletubbies®, and other shows seen on PBS.

Adaptations for Children With Disabilities

Adaptations will depend on the specific disability. Young children with physical disabilities will need assistance in inputting information into the computer. Adaptive switches or larger keyboards can be very helpful. It can also be helpful to slow down the speed of some software functions, as it can be very difficult for these children to respond to stimuli quickly.

Children with visual impairments will need assistance in computer output. Speech synthesis, enlarged print, or screen magnification can all assist children with visual impairments. By adding speech or making the screen display larger, these children can access any software program. It may not be necessary to purchase additional hardware or software, as some computers come with this software in their system. Moving the monitor closer or increasing the contrast can also be easy adaptations. Also, it can be useful to put the Braille alphabet on the keyboard. Put each Braille letter on the corresponding letter on the keyboard. When children use a "talking" program, such as a speech-based word processing program, the children can enhance their knowledge of Braille while learning touch-typing.

Young children with mental retardation or attention difficulties will not need any special hardware modifications. Software should be chosen to provide repeated practice on basic concepts. Screen displays should be simple and not too distracting. It should be easy for these children to see what they are to respond to. Try to find software in which screen displays do not change quickly.

Children with hearing impairments can benefit from special software and hardware. Software programs that teach sign language or finger spelling can be helpful. Speech recognition units can allow these children to see their vocalizations, and this can aid in learning speech. Software for children with hearing impairments needs to be chosen based on visual quality. Look for good, clear screen displays that don't change too quickly.

Thematic Units

Thematic Units and Cultural Diversity	310
Community Awareness	311
Post Office	314
Doctor's Office	318
Safety	323
Bus Safety	332
Fire Safety	335
Water Safety and Boats	349
Veterinarians	357
Farms and Animals	362

Thematic Units and Cultural Diversity

An understanding and appreciation of diversity is an important part of early childhood education. Many activities can be generated around the theme of diversity, which can help children learn more about people from backgrounds different from theirs. Young children are aware of individual differences among other people and need to learn that these differences are not bad.

Cultural diversity needs to be seen in a broader way than simply focusing on racial or ethnic differences among peoples. It should be recognized that cultural diversity includes such things as age, gender, verbal and nonverbal language, region of the country in which we live, religions, disabilities, or socioeconomic status.

Recognize that young children are still learning about individual differences in others. This awareness tends to follow a developmental sequence, with children understanding differences in gender by age two, differences in race by age three, and differences due to disabilities by age four. Be prepared to answer questions children may have about other people.

Provide examples and discuss how even common things, such as clothing, music, transportation, foods, or toys and games have similarities and differences among cultures. Some ways to promote diversity awareness:

- Have families visit your school to cook ethnic foods or show different clothing or toys.
- Have children play games from around the world. Numerous books have been published in this area and can be found in local libraries.
- Examine books and other print materials to be sure that they do not contain gender- or racially-biased content.
- Be sure to provide appropriate playthings, such as foods and dolls that reflect cultural diversity. Commercial toy companies have been producing plastic ethnic foods and dolls with appropriate facial characteristics and hair for many years.

A Note About Holidays

It is not uncommon for schools to organize thematic units around the calendar and the observance of holidays. However, when examined from a multicultural perspective, holidays can pose a problem for school staff. Some authors have suggested that it is unfair to observe some holidays and not others, and certainly we run the risk of offending some people by not recognizing a holiday they observe. There are also concerns that when schools observe a holiday it represents only a superficial effort at promoting true cultural awareness.

Almost every day, in some part of the world, people are observing a holiday. True cultural awareness means that we look at why a holiday is being celebrated. Holiday celebrations may or may not have a religious significance. For example, the Fourth of July celebrates American independence; Cinco de Mayo in Mexico also celebrates independence.

Directed Play   310

We need to consider what holidays are important to the families in our schools and in our community. We should have an understanding of why these holidays are important. Families can be asked what holidays are important to them and they can be invited to come and discuss the significance of the holiday with students. Holidays should be seen as a way to help all of us learn something of other cultures.

Community Awareness

 ## People Who Build and Fix Things

Target Objectives
Community awareness, identification and use of objects, occupations

Developmental Domains
Cognitive, Language

Multiple Intelligences
Linguistic, Intrapersonal, Interpersonal, Musical

Materials
Pictures and objects associated with occupations that build or repair things, such as plumber, mechanic, electrician, carpenter, or TV repairman.

Preparation/Set-Up
Have pictures or materials available.

Procedures

1. Show a small group of children pictures of people in occupations who build or fix things.

2. Have as many tools or objects associated with these occupations as possible for children to see and manipulate.

3. Name occupations and the objects that go with them.

Adaptations for Children With Disabilities

Give children extra opportunities to handle and manipulate objects. Identify key characteristics about these objects such as size, weight, or use. Encourage children to repeat concepts. Promote the understanding of "go with." For example, "The hammer goes with the carpenter." Sing the popular children's song "Johnny Hammers With One Hammer."

170 People Who Keep Us Safe

Target Objectives
Recognition of people involved in safety

Developmental Domains
Cognitive, Social, Language

Multiple Intelligences
Linguistic, Intrapersonal

Materials
Pictures of and objects associated with people who keep us safe—police, firefighters, ambulance drivers, TV newspeople, crossing guards.

Preparation/Set-Up
Have pictures, toy people, or toys available.

Procedures

1. Arrange children in a small group seated on the floor.

2. Show children the various pictures of people who help keep us safe.

3. Identify each of occupations and explain what these people do and where they work.

4. Let children ask questions or tell what they know about these people.

Adaptations for Children With Disabilities

Provide individual attention for children as needed. Encourage children to repeat the names of these occupations. Help children to understand that either men or women can do these jobs.

171 Different Hats

Target Objectives
Associate hats with different occupations, community awareness, discrimination of objects

Developmental Domains
Cognitive, Language

Multiple Intelligences
Linguistic, Intrapersonal, Interpersonal

Materials
Hats or pictures of hats that correspond to different occupations, pictures of people in different occupations not wearing hats.

Preparation/Set-Up
These materials may be purchased commercially or can be teacher-made.

Directed *Play*   312

Procedures

1. Arrange children in a small group and tell them they are going to match the hats people wear to their jobs.

2. Show the children pictures of people in different occupations. These can include: construction workers, soldiers, cooks, cowboys, football and baseball players, nurses, firefighters, and astronauts.

3. Point out the kinds of hats these people are wearing.

4. Show the children pictures of people in different occupations who don't wear hats.

5. Children take turns matching a hat to a person.

6. Conclude by singing "Hats on Everyone."

Adaptations for Children With Disabilities

Provide extra time for practice. Point out key characteristics between the hats. Repeat or demonstrate directions to the task as needed.

Hats on Everyone

Hats on police officers,

Starchy and blue.

Hats on firefighters,

Shiny and new.

Hats on marchers

In a band.

Hats on astronauts

When they land.

Hats on farmers,

Made of straw.

Hats on artists,

When they draw.

Hats on babies

Out in the sun.

Hats on almost everyone.

Occupations and the Multiple Intelligences

Teaching children about different jobs is an important part of community awareness. The following list shows different occupations as they can be linked to different multiple intelligences. Talk to children about these professions. Make time to visit some of these people in the workplace so that children acquire a better understanding of what these people do.

Occupations and Multiple Intelligence Activities

Intrapersonal	Clergy, Teacher, Psychologist
Interpersonal	Teacher, Child Care Provider, Waiter/Waitress, Hairdresser, Cashier, Doctor, Nurse, Clergy, Psychologist, Social Worker, Receptionist, Small Business Owner
Logical-Mathematical	Banker, Accountant, Construction Worker, Bookkeeper, Scientist, Chef, Mechanic, Architect, Computer Programmer, Engineer, Carpenter, Small Business Owner
Linguistic	Teacher, Lawyer, Judge, Editor, Politician, Librarian, Mail Carrier, Pharmacist, TV and Newspaper Reporters, Actor
Spatial	Artist, Pilot, Photographer, Astronaut, Hairdresser, Florist, Architect, Engineer, Carpenter
Bodily	Military Personnel, Construction Worker, Firefighter, Athlete, Astronaut, Hairdresser, Plumber, Mechanic, Dancer
Musical	Musician, Dancer, Singer, Entertainer
Naturalist	Park Ranger, Zookeeper, Lumberjack, Fisherman, Florist, Farmer/Rancher, Veterinarian, Landscape Architect

Post Office

Teaching children about their community is a necessary component of early childhood curriculum and programs. The activities associated with this play theme should be conducted over a period of two to three weeks. Various activities that cross developmental domains and multiple intelligences will be presented to children. Materials used depend on the specific activity. As a part of the activities during the week, arrangements should be made for children to visit a post office.

172   Something About Mail

Target Objectives Increase awareness of what is involved in mail, mail delivery, names	**Materials** Various pieces of mail, including large and small packages; post office pictures.
Developmental Domains Cognitive, Language, Social	**Preparation/Set-Up** Have materials ready at the group setting.
Multiple Intelligences Linguistic, Interpersonal	

Procedures

1. Have children sit in a semicircle on the floor.

2. Show the children several different types of mail, including standard-sized envelopes and magazines. Explain to children that people send mail to other people for many reasons. Pass the mail around for children to touch and examine.

3. Discuss the shape, size, and weight of these items.

4. Show the children different stamps and address and return address labels.

5. Have the children point to the address on the mailing label.

6. Show the children pictures of a post office and letter carriers and discuss how the mail is delivered. Have the children name the post office and letter carriers.

7. Ask children who they would send mail to.

Adaptations for Children With Disabilities

Provide assistance as needed. Repeat vocabulary often, especially among children with mental retardation.

315   Chapter 10

173 My Mailbox

Target Objectives
Increase awareness of names, language, socialization

Developmental Domains
Fine Motor, Language, Social

Multiple Intelligences
Interpersonal, Bodily

Materials
Cardboard boxes; red, white, and blue paints; pictures of mailboxes; small and medium-sized paintbrushes; paint smocks (optional).

Preparation/Set-Up
Have materials readily available at the group setting.

Procedures

1. Introduce the activity by telling children that they are going to make mailboxes like letter carriers use.

2. Show the children pictures of the large mailboxes commonly found on street corners.

3. Have the children work in two small groups to paint the boxes to look like a mailbox and assist them in cutting a hole for the letters to be placed in.

4. Save the completed mailboxes for a later activity.

Adaptations for Children With Disabilities

Provide assistance with painting and cutting as needed. Encourage children to name what they are doing, what color paint they are using, and where on the box they are painting (top or bottom). Provide chairs for sitting while painting if the children get tired.

Directed Play

Deliver the Mail

Target Objectives
Prewriting, personal/social

Developmental Domains
Language, Social, Cognitive, Fine Motor

Multiple Intelligences
Linguistic, Interpersonal, Intrapersonal

Materials
Crayons or markers, three envelopes per child, name cards for students.

Preparation/Set-Up
Have all materials available at the table.

Procedures

1. Arrange children in a small group and tell them that they are going to send letters to other children in the class.

2. Have children address letters to three other children in the class by having them write the first name of children on envelopes.

3. Provide models or outlines for children to imitate or trace if needed.

4. The children should take turns "delivering" the mail to the other children by having them walk around and give the envelopes to each child.

5. For children who are not able to write letters for names, a picture or symbol may be used and will be matched to a symbol that each child has.

Adaptations for Children With Disabilities

Provide an outline of the name on the envelope that a child can trace over. For older children have them write out names several times. Watch them to be sure they write correctly. Provide hand-over-hand assistance in writing or provide models of the names for children to imitate.

Doctor's Office

 ## Doctors and Nurses

Target Objectives
Recognition of people and objects, community awareness

Developmental Domains
Language, Social, Cognitive

Multiple Intelligences
Linguistic, Intrapersonal, Bodily, Interpersonal

Materials
Pictures of a doctor's office, toy doctor materials, children's storybooks about doctors.

Preparation/Set-Up
Have all materials readily available.

Procedures

1. Show a small group of children pictures of a doctor's office, including equipment and people.

2. Discuss why we have doctors, what kinds of doctors there are, and the purpose of some of the equipment.

3. Have children name objects in pictures and answer simple who, what, where questions.

4. Read a book or books about visiting a doctor's office and have children discuss their past visits to the doctor.

5. Ask children to talk about their visits to a doctor's office.

Adaptations for Children With Disabilities

Have realistic doctor objects or toys to match with pictures. Encourage children to talk about their visits to the doctor. Work to increase vocabulary related to doctors and nurses. Promote conversation between peers.

176 Doctor's Office

Target Objectives	Materials
Identification and use of objects, personal/social	Commercial doctor toys, blocks (optional), classroom furniture.
Developmental Domains	**Preparation/Set-Up**
Social, Cognitive, Language, Fine Motor	Set up the dramatic play area with appropriate props.
Multiple Intelligences	
Linguistic, Interpersonal, Spatial, Bodily	

Procedures

1. Present the doctor toys to small groups of four or fewer children.

2. Blocks can also be added to allow children to build parts of the office.

3. Be sure to have enough toys for all the children in the group. Let children bring in room furniture to the set-up.

4. Assist children in setting up the doctor play and make sure that each child has a role to play. Roles can include doctor, nurse, patient, and/or receptionist.

5. Adults should provide children with considerable freedom in this activity.

6. Help children understand how or why equipment or people do what they do.

7. Make simple statements such as "The baby looks hurt" to help guide the play, or volunteer to be the patient.

8. Make yourself available to redirect the play if it gets off topic. Assist peers if conflict arises.

Adaptations for Children With Disabilities

Provide scripted language or conversation between characters or a picture schedule of sequenced events when visiting a doctor's office. The doctor theme promotes empathy, and this is a good activity for children with behavior disorders or autism.

177 # Visit the Doctor

Target Objectives
Increase community awareness, recognition of objects

Developmental Domains
Language, Social

Multiple Intelligences
Linguistic, Intrapersonal, Interpersonal

Materials
Class lists, name tags for children.

Preparation/Set-Up
Prior arrangements for field trip, with transportation, permission slips, and parent
volunteers.

Procedures

1. If possible, arrange a field trip to a doctor's office.

2. If a doctor visit is not possible, a local nurse might be a good option.

3. It might also be possible for the doctor or nurse to visit the classroom and bring samples of items that they use.

4. Have the doctor or nurse explain his or her job and the equipment used.

5. Encourage children to ask and answer questions.

6. Practice naming new objects.

Adaptations for Children With Disabilities

Children with speech or language delays may be reluctant to ask questions. You may want to help them think of a question to ask. Provide a visual schedule or pictures of a child being examined in a doctor's office.

Directed *Play*

(178) Doctor Play

Target Objectives
Identification and use of objects, language, personal/social

Developmental Domains
Cognitive, Language, Social, Self-Help

Multiple Intelligences
Linguistic, Interpersonal, Spatial, Bodily

Materials
Commercial doctor toys, blocks (optional), ace or cloth bandages.

Preparation/Set-Up
Dramatic play area with materials available.

Procedures

1. After the visit with a doctor or nurse, repeat the dramatic play activity.

2. Have the children again play with the doctor toys and assign roles for each child. You may want to assign these roles.

3. The adult should point out things seen on the field trip and children should be encouraged to incorporate this information into their play.

4. Adults should be a part of the play, for example, by acting as the patient or receptionist.

5. Allow the children to bring classroom furniture into the setting.

Adaptations for Children With Disabilities

Provide scripted dialogue and more teacher-guided play with assistance as necessary. A picture schedule of events can be helpful. Role playing is an important way to promote positive social interactions.

179 # Doctor Puzzles and Drawing

Target Objectives
Identification and use of objects, fine motor, problem solving, turn-taking

Developmental Domains
Cognitive, Fine Motor

Multiple Intelligences
Spatial, Logical, Linguistic

Materials
Doctor/hospital puzzles, paper, crayons.

Preparation/Set-Up
Play area with pictures, puzzles, and crayons available.

Procedures

1. Give small groups of children puzzles that have a doctor theme.

2. In addition, give children pictures of doctors and nurses to color.

3. Encourage children to show one another their pictures and talk about them.

4. Give children compliments for a job well done.

Adaptations for Children With Disabilities

Puzzles adapted with pegs or knobs (drill small holes in puzzles and use dowel rods as pegs). Use a variety of puzzles ranging in size from 6–20 pieces and adapted coloring materials, such as paper taped to table and larger crayons or markers.

Safety

 ## Safe and Dangerous

Target Objectives
Increase children's understanding of safety, identify objects that are safe or dangerous

Developmental Domains
Language, Cognitive, Personal-Social

Multiple Intelligences
Logical, Linguistic, Intrapersonal

Materials
Have various pictures of things that are safe and things that are dangerous. Real items can also be shown to children. Dangerous materials can include such things as fire, guns, stove, busy streets, wild animals, electric socket, etc. Safe materials can include such items as a teddy bear, picture of grandma, dolls, baby blanket, or cups.

Preparation/Set-Up
Have all pictures or items available.

Procedures

1. Show a small group of children pictures and/or items that are safe and dangerous.

2. Hold up each item and have children say which items or pictures are safe and which are dangerous.

3. Collect all the pictures and have children divide the pictures into a "safe" category and a "dangerous" category.

Adaptations for Children With Disabilities

Provide extra time and practice sorting the pictures. Repeat this activity several times over a week period. Revisit it again at a later date. Send home pictures that can be practiced. Encourage parents to label items in their home that are safe or dangerous.

Helping Me Be Safe

Target Objectives
Safety, recognition and identification of self and parents, child's address and phone number

Developmental Domains
Cognitive, Language, Personal-Social

Multiple Intelligences
Linguistic, Intrapersonal

Materials
Phone numbers, parent names, addresses of children.

Preparation/Set-Up
Have information on parent's names, phone numbers, and addresses for all children. Names and addresses should be printed on sentence strips for visual reference.

Procedures

1. This will be an activity that should be repeated many times. It can also be divided up into smaller units.

2. With children arranged in a small group, review their full names, their addresses, phone numbers, and the names of their parents. Use name and address sentence strips for reference.

3. With older children, especially those of kindergarten age, discuss strangers, emergencies, full names of parents, and not answering the phone or the door when no one is home.

Adaptations for Children With Disabilities

Go over this information many times. You may want to collect data on individual information for some children. Use the 0–5 data sheet for this purpose. Practice identifying names, addresses, and phone numbers.

182 I'm Lost

Target Objectives
What to do if lost

Developmental Domains
Cognitive, Language, Personal-Social

Multiple Intelligences
Linguistic, Logical, Musical, Intrapersonal

Materials
Pictures of common places in which to get lost, such as wooded areas, or a shopping mall, park, or neighborhood.

Preparation/Set-Up
Have materials available.

Procedures

1. Show a small group of children pictures of common places and ask them to name these places.

2. Discuss what being "lost" means and what to do if they get lost.

3. The first rule is to "Stay where you are." Discuss why it is important not to walk away from where you are. Practice a sequence of Stop, Look, Listen.

4. If children are in a public place they can look for assistance from police, security guards, cashiers in stores, or even mothers with babies.

5. Practice having children say their name and the name(s) of parents.

6. Children should practice listening for someone calling their name.

7. Have children engage in some role play. Have one child pretend to be lost and another child pretend to be a police officer. The lost child is to tell the police officer he or she is lost, and the officer asks questions about name and address.

8. Conclude by singing "If You Get Lost."

Adaptations for Children With Disabilities

Work with children individually. Review this activity often. Use dolls to act out steps in the activity.

If You Get Lost

If you get lost someplace in town,
Don't talk to a stranger.
Look for a police officer
To keep you out of danger.
Tell her what your name is
And where your house is too.
She will help you get back home,
Or bring your mom to you.

183 Warning Sounds

Target Objectives
Awareness of warning sounds in the environment, auditory discrimination

Developmental Domains
Cognitive, Language, Self-Help

Multiple Intelligences
Logical, Linguistic, Intrapersonal

Materials
A sound recording of police/fire siren, train whistle, microwave timer, shouts of alarm, smoke alarm, car horn. The recording may be homemade or purchased commercially.

Preparation/Set-Up
Have sound recording available.

Procedures

1. Describe warning sounds to a small group of children. Tell children that when they hear these it means something important.

2. Have the children repeat the sound and what it means.

3. Play the sounds and have children identify what the sounds are and what they mean.

4. This activity can be expanded into practicing drills, such as fire drills.

Adaptations for Children With Disabilities

Repeat this activity several times over the course of the year. Provide extra time and practice.

Warning Signs

Target Objectives
Recognition of dangers, identification of objects

Developmental Domains
Cognitive, Language, Self-Help

Multiple Intelligences
Linguistic, Intrapersonal

Materials
Pictures of various warning signs: stop sign, crosswalk, exit, poison, railroad crossing, stoplights.

Preparation/Set-Up
Have pictures available.

Procedures

1. Arrange children in a small group. Tell the children that there are pictures and signs that warn us of dangers.

2. Show the children the pictures and tell the children what the danger is and describe what is on the sign.

3. Discuss where you see such signs.

4. Walk around the school or outside to look for real warning signs. Have the children name them.

5. Children can also complete warning sign puzzles if available.

Adaptations for Children With Disabilities

Work with children individually as needed. Repeat this activity several times. For younger children reduce the number of signs you start with. Work most with common signs such as stop signs, exit signs, stoplights, and crosswalks. Introduce new signs as these are mastered.

185 Stop Sign

Target Objectives
Identification of a warning word/sign, color recognition, fine motor skills, coloring an entire space

Developmental Domains
Cognitive, Language, Fine Motor

Multiple Intelligences
Spatial, Linguistic, Intrapersonal

Materials
Red and yellow crayons, precut stop sign on paper, black markers, tape (optional).

Preparation/Set-Up
Have crayons and precut stop sign on the table. Have a completed example to show children.

Procedures

1. Tell a small group of children that they are going to make a stop sign.

2. Have the children sit at a table around you. Show the children a picture of a stop sign.

3. Give each child a precut stop sign. The word "Stop" should be outlined on the sign.

4. Have the children use red or yellow crayons to color the stop sign. Use a black marker to trace the word "Stop."

5. Count the corners and sides of the sign using one-to-one correspondence.

6. When all children have completed coloring, ask them to describe the stop sign.

7. Save these for use in other activities.

Adaptations for Children With Disabilities

Provide assistance with one-to-one correspondence as needed. Tape the paper down for children who may have difficulty holding it. Have children speak in complete sentences when discussing what a stop sign means.

186 Red Light, Green Light

Target Objectives
Turn-taking, color recognition, social skills, understanding games with rules

Developmental Domains
Cognitive, Language, Social, Gross Motor

Multiple Intelligences
Interpersonal, Logical, Linguistic, Bodily

Materials
Red, green, and yellow tag board circles glued to tongue depressors; large area for children to spread out.

Preparation/Set-Up
Have premade "lights" available and clear the large space of any obstacles.

Procedures

1. Arrange children in a group and tell them that they are going to play the game Red Light, Green Light.

2. Pick a child to be the first one to hold up either a red or green light.

3. Have the children take turns showing lights while the rest of the group moves or stops to the correct light. Children can say what to do or have other children respond to the light without verbal direction.

4. Adults should move with the group.

5. Children can walk or crawl on hands and knees as "cars."

6. Add the yellow light (slow movement) once children are good at stop and go.

Adaptations for Children With Disabilities

Adults should position themselves with any children having behavior problems to assist them in the activity. All children can participate. Assist those children with physical disabilities by helping them move about independently.

187 Constructing a Stoplight

Target Objectives
Identify and understand stoplights; recognition of objects and colors; the meaning of stop, go, and slow down

Developmental Domains
Cognitive, Language, Fine Motor

Multiple Intelligences
Linguistic, Spatial, Bodily, Intrapersonal

Materials
Red, yellow, and green construction paper; scissors; white paper rectangles; glue sticks; stoplight pictures.

Preparation/Set-Up
Have all materials available, including predrawn circles in each color for each child. Some precut circles can also be made available.

Procedures

1. Arrange the children in a small group and tell them that they are going to make a stoplight.

2. Have the children sit at a table around you.

3. Show the children pictures of stoplights.

4. Next, have the children cut out three circles: red, yellow, and green. Provide precut circles for children who need less cutting.

5. Using a prepared rectangular frame, have the children glue the circles to make a stoplight, with lights in proper order from top to bottom.

6. Talk about what the different colored lights mean (red = stop, yellow = slow down, green = go).

7. Point out concepts of top, bottom, and middle.

8. Review counting number of lights using one-to-one correspondence. Have children tell how many, what color, and what each light means.

9. Hang the stoplights on the walls around the room.

10. Save these for use in other activities.

Adaptations for Children With Disabilities

Adaptive scissors may be needed for children with physical impairments. Hand-over-hand assistance may be necessary. See the mural activities in the Fine Motor chapter for an extension to this activity. Shorten the cutting task by precutting half of the circle or circles for them.

Directed Play 330

(188) Crossing the Street

Target Objectives
Safety; awareness of dangers; following directions; left and right; demonstrate understanding of stop, look, and listen

Developmental Domains
Cognitive, Language, Self-Help

Multiple Intelligences
Linguistic, Bodily, Musical, Intrapersonal

Materials
Pictures of streets, crossings, stoplights, crossing guards, crossing guard vests, chair, signs.

Preparation/Set-Up
Have materials available in a large area free of obstacles. Use chairs to set up the street.

Procedures

1. Show a small group of children pictures of streets, crosswalks, crossing guards, and stoplights.

2. Talk about safety in crossing the street.

3. Make a "street" out of two rows of small chairs.

4. Have two children stand beside the street and have the other children pretend to be cars or trucks.

5. Have the children crawl along the street making car sounds. As a variation, another child can be a crossing guard.

6. Children should practice looking both ways before they cross the street and waiting for the crossing guard to assist them when crossing to safety. Practice stop, look, and listen before crossing.

7. Conclude the activity by singing "Safety."

Adaptations for Children With Disabilities

Give children extra time and practice as needed. Have them identify all objects, events and people in the pictures. Another variation would be to visit with a crossing guard and observe him or her at work. Take the opportunity to practice crossing the street frequently.

Safety

Red says stop

And green says go.

Yellow says wait,

You'd better go slow.

When I reach a crossing place,

To left and right I turn my face.

I walk, not run, across the street,

And use my head to guide by feet.

Bus Safety

189 School Bus

Target Objectives
Following directions; bus safety;
complete school bus routine;
review stop, look, and listen
when crossing the street

Developmental Domains
Cognitive, Language, Personal-
Social

Multiple Intelligences
Linguistic, Interpersonal, Musical,
Intrapersonal

Materials
None.

Preparation/Set-Up
Prior arrangements with bus drivers.

Procedures

1. Make arrangements for a school bus to visit the school.

2. With children arranged in a group tell them that they are going to learn about bus safety.

3. Escort the children outside to the bus.

4. Have the children talk to the bus driver about how the bus works.

5. Have the bus driver demonstrate how the doors open, the sign comes out, etc.

6. Children should have an opportunity to walk around the bus.

7. Count the wheels and make note of how big they are.

8. Practice getting on and off the bus and waiting at the bus stop.

9. Have the children sit on the bus as if they were riding to school.

10. Practice getting off the bus and crossing the street. Review the stop, look, and listen procedure before crossing.

11. Show the children where to sit and stress how important it is that they stay in their seats while the bus is moving.

12. Bring the children back inside and have them discuss what they learned about the bus and bus safety.

13. Conclude the activity by singing "Wheels on the Bus."

Adaptations for Children With Disabilities

Physically assist children as necessary. Provide a picture schedule of the routine. Revisit this activity later in the school year.

School Bus Act Out

Target Objectives
Appropriate bus behaviors, completing a sustained play routine, dramatic play with peers

Developmental Domains
Social, Language, Cognitive

Multiple Intelligences
Interpersonal, Linguistic, Bodily

Materials
Chairs, hat, disc-shaped object for steering wheel, blocks for pedals, cane for gear shift, and backpacks for children to take on the bus.

Preparation/Set-Up
Have all materials available so that children can help set up the bus easily.

Procedures

1. With children in a small group, arrange chairs to look like a school bus. Tell them they are going to play riding the school bus.

2. Have a separate driver's chair and three to four rows of double seats as on a school bus.

3. Assign roles of bus driver and passengers to children.

4. Pretend the bus driver drives to pick up children for school.

5. Have children wait until the bus "comes to get them" and then the children board and sit on the bus while other children are picked up.

6. An adult should ride on the bus as one of the passengers.

7. Let children take turns being the bus driver.

8. Review school bus safety rules with the group.

Adaptations for Children With Disabilities

Some children may have a difficult time following directions or sitting as if riding the bus. Stay close to these children and provide direction as needed. Provide practiced or scripted dialogue. Offer suggestions or redirection as needed.

Bus Song—"Wheels on the Bus"

Target Objectives
Bus awareness, identification of objects and people, bus safety

Developmental Domains
Social, Language, Fine Motor

Multiple Intelligences
Linguistic, Musical, Bodily

Materials
Book, music (optional).

Preparation/Set-Up
Have book(s) and music ready.

Procedures

1. In a small group of children, read the story "Wheels on the Bus" or some similar book.

2. Sing the song "Wheels on the Bus" with children doing the appropriate actions.

3. Have children perform actions sitting on the floor then in chairs set up as the school bus with the bus driver serving as the song leader.

Adaptations for Children With Disabilities

Assist children as needed with the movements. Repeat the song daily for two weeks and revisit it again later in the school year.

Fire Safety

The activities associated with this play theme should be conducted over a period of two to three weeks. Various activities that cross developmental domains and multiple intelligences will be presented to children. Materials used are dependent on the specific activity. As part of the activities during the week, arrangements should be made for children to visit a fire station.

Fire

Target Objectives
Fire safety, concepts of heat and hot, dangers

Developmental Domains
Cognitive, Language, Personal-Social

Multiple Intelligences
Linguistic, Bodily, Naturalist

Materials
Candle; matches; pictures of firepersons, campfires, fire truck, stove, forest fires.

Preparation/Set-Up
Have all materials available in the group area.

Procedures

1. Arrange a small group of children in a semicircle on the floor.
2. Tell the children that you are going to talk about fire, fire safety, and firefighters.
3. Show the children pictures of fire and firefighters fighting fires.
4. Light a candle and let the children watch the flame. Point out that fire and matches are dangerous.
5. Point out the shape and colors of the fire.
6. Have children put their hands close enough to the fire that they feel the heat.
7. Tell the children that fire is dangerous and can hurt them and that they should never play with fire. Blow out the candle.
8. Discuss fire safety.

Adaptations for Children With Disabilities

Supervise children closely during this activity and be sure to properly put away materials when finished.

Drawing Campfires

Target Objectives
Identification of colors, increase fine motor, increase awareness of fire

Developmental Domains
Cognitive, Fine Motor

Multiple Intelligences
Spatial, Bodily, Intrapersonal

Materials
Blank paper; red, yellow, and orange crayons or finger paints.

Preparation/Set-Up
Have all materials available at a table or easel.

Procedures

1. Have children sit at a table around you or at an easel.
2. Provide the children paper and red, orange, and yellow crayons.
3. Have the same pictures of fire and firefighters from the first fire activity available for reference.
4. Have the children draw pictures of fire or use finger paints instead of crayons. Encourage children to complete the entire picture.
5. Let children show one another their drawings or paintings.
6. Save the drawings or paintings for later use.

Adaptations for Children With Disabilities

It may be helpful to tape the paper to the table or easel using masking tape. Have predrawn or prepainted pictures of fires available for children to imitate. Encourage children to talk about what they are drawing or painting.

Things That Are Hot

Target Objectives
Identification and use of objects, dangers, hot

Developmental Domains
Cognitive, Language, Self-Help

Multiple Intelligences
Linguistic, Bodily, Interpersonal

Materials
Hair dryer, curling iron, electric heater, picture of a stove, candle.

Preparation/Set-Up
Have all materials available, including access to electricity.

Procedures

1. Have the children arranged in a semicircle around you.

2. Show the children pictures or real objects that become hot. Plug in the hair dryer and blow hot air. Allow children to feel the air using caution. Have them name what they feel.

3. Discuss how these things are used and why they can be dangerous.

4. Review name, function, and safety rules for each object.

Adaptations for Children With Disabilities

Have children repeat the names of the objects and what they are used for. Review safety with hot objects often.

195 Firefighter Act Out

Target Objectives
Increase cooperative play, socialization, increase use of language

Developmental Domains
Language, Social

Multiple Intelligences
Intrapersonal, Interpersonal, Linguistic, Bodily

Materials
Toy firefighting equipment, hose, helmets, gloves, telephone, chairs arranged as a fire truck.

Note: Make an "ax" out of cardboard by cutting out the pattern and using some paint. The ax can be used in the fire fighter activities or the camping activities.

Preparation/Set-Up
Prepare the setting and have all play materials ready.

Procedures

1. Provide a small group of children with firefighting materials in a dramatic play setting.

2. Each child should have a fire helmet and other necessary equipment. It is essential that each child have the necessary props.

3. Assign each child a role—fire chief, firefighter(s), and fire truck driver.

4. Review as a group the role of each of these "characters."

5. Give children time to become familiar with the various props that are provided.

6. Identify the names of all the props and describe something about their importance or use.

7. Please note that this activity will be repeated several times.

8. Arrange chairs to look like a fire truck and have children ride the fire truck to a "fire."

9. Once the play episode is underway the adult can assume a role or step out to observe.

10. It may be helpful to set up a building that is "on fire."

11. If possible try to provide a long enough hose so that two or three children can hold it at one time. Let the children pretend to put out the fire.

12. After approximately 20 minutes, bring the children back together as a group and talk about what it is like to be a firefighter.

Directed Play 338

Adaptations for Children With Disabilities

Assist children in what to do and say. Assume a role in the play as a firefighter or as a citizen who needs assistance. Provide practice and scripted language. Provide a picture schedule telling the events in the pretend play (e.g., dress, board the fire truck, ride to fire, unload, put fire out). Role playing is an important activity for children with autism, mental retardation, and behavior disorders.

196 Fire Station Visit

Target Objectives
Increase community awareness, recognition of people and objects, retelling of events and recalling facts about firefighters.

Developmental Domains
Language, Cognitive, Social

Multiple Intelligences
Linguistic, Intrapersonal, Interpersonal

Materials
Name tags.

Preparation/Set-Up
Prior planning for field trip, including permission slips, transportation, emergency phone numbers, and class lists.

Procedures

1. Arrange to visit a fire station. Before visiting the station, discuss with children what they are going to see and who they will be talking with.

2. Identify and name objects and people found at the fire station.

3. Have the firefighters show children the various types of equipment they use, where they work, and the fire truck.

4. Be aware that some children may be afraid of seeing firefighters with all their equipment on.

5. After the visit, gather the children into a group and discuss with the children what they saw. Encourage children to retell the events and sequence of what they saw. Encourage them to list as many facts as they can.

Adaptations for Children With Disabilities

Provide assistance as needed. Help children identify and name objects and people. Use picture cards to help children retell what and who they saw. Make arrangements to repeat this activity later in the year.

339 Chapter 10

197 Fire Safety Review

Target Objectives
Increase understanding of fire safety; dial 911; answer questions about name and address; review Stop, Drop, and Roll

Developmental Domains
Language, Cognitive, Social

Multiple Intelligences
Linguistic, Bodily, Interpersonal, Intrapersonal

Materials
Telephones, blanket, pictures of fire and fire-fighting, drawings/paintings children made earlier, tumbling mats, toy telephones for each child, number cards with 911 for each child.

Preparation/Set-Up
Large area that is free of obstacles and with materials available.

Procedures

1. Arrange children into a small group seated in a semicircle around you.

2. Discuss the visit to the fire station with the children and review new words or concepts.

3. Use the "fire" pictures children made earlier to build a larger fire by wadding them up and putting them in a pile. Practice putting the fire out by smothering it with a blanket.

4. Review and practice fire safety; discuss calling 911, and practice Stop, Drop, and Roll.

5. Talk about when to call 911. Practice dialing the number.

6. Role play calling 911, with one child being the operator and one calling. Have the children ask and answer questions such as "What is your name?" and "What is your daddy's name?"

7. Talk about Stop, Drop, and Roll.

8. Using prepared tumbling mats, have children practice this by saying "In case of fire."

9. Point out why it is important not to run.

10. Children take turns running, stopping, dropping, and rolling on the mats to smother the fire.

11. Provide blankets or small rugs that children can use to cover a person whose clothes are "on fire."

Directed Play

Adaptations for Children With Disabilities

Assist children with finding the numbers 911. Let them practice dialing 911 many times. Provide physical assistance with Stop, Drop, and Roll.

 ## Fire Station

Target Objectives
Community awareness, social skills, dramatic play

Developmental Domains
Gross Motor, Fine Motor, Language, Social

Multiple Intelligences
Spatial, Interpersonal, Bodily

Materials
Large cardboard box, paints, pictures of fire stations, paint smocks, various sizes of paintbrushes. Have a cardboard box for every two or three children.

Preparation/Set-Up
Drop cloth or paper on floor. Paints readily available.

Procedures

1. Give a group of two or three children a large empty cardboard box and tell them that they are going to paint it to look like a fire station. Have pictures of fire stations available for reference.

2. Assist the children in painting the box to look like a fire station.

3. "Doors" can be cut into the side of the box to give children access to the inside of the "fire station." Allow to dry before engaging in dramatic play.

4. Let children engage in dramatic play by assuming firefighter roles.

5. Save the cut and painted cardboard box for other activities.

Adaptations for Children With Disabilities

Children who do not yet have well-developed symbolic play skills will have difficulty pretending with objects that are not real. Take advantage of peers to promote imitation. Assist children by using both verbal and physical prompts. Help them with what to say and do. Provide guidance and redirection throughout the activity as needed.

199 Drawing Ladders

Target Objectives
Prewriting, one-to-one correspondence, counting

Developmental Domains
Fine Motor, Cognitive

Multiple Intelligences
Spatial, Logical, Bodily

Materials
Paper or chalkboard, crayons or chalk, pictures of ladders, pictures of fire trucks with ladders extended.

Preparation/Set-Up
Have all materials available at a table, on the floor, or at an easel.

Procedures

1. Show children pictures of ladders, especially fire ladders. Tell children that they are going to draw pictures of ladders.

2. Children draw "ladders" with horizontal and vertical lines. Supervise children to be sure their lines are appropriate.

3. Demonstrate for them how to draw the ladders and then have them imitate it.

4. Horizontal and vertical lines are an important prewriting skill. This activity offers many opportunities to stop and start the drawing utensil on the spot. It promotes eye-hand coordination and strength.

5. Have children count the rungs on the ladder up and down using one-to-one correspondence and point out top and bottom.

Adaptations for Children With Disabilities

Tape the paper onto the table to assist children who may have trouble holding it. Provide physical assistance in drawing as needed. Take advantage of the environment. Let children do this activity standing, lying on their stomach, or sitting at a table.

Directed Play

Climbing Ladders

Target Objectives
Increase gross motor coordination, counting

Developmental Domains
Gross Motor, Cognitive

Multiple Intelligences
Spatial, Bodily, Logical

Materials
Climbing equipment.

Preparation/Set-Up
Schedule time to use a large motor area with equipment.

Procedures

1. Using indoor or playground climbing equipment, have children climb ladders.

2. Have the children count the steps as they climb.

3. Have children slide down a pole if one is available. Have firefighter props available to add to the play.

Adaptations for Children With Disabilities

Children with balance and coordination problems will probably have trouble climbing. Provide as much support as they need. Climbing is an extremely important activity for children. Make sure they are supervised and supported and that there is a soft surface underneath the climbing equipment.

Three-in-One Fire Safety Movement Activities

Target Objectives
Increase awareness of fire safety, following directions, movement and cooperation

Developmental Domains
Gross Motor, Social, Language, Self-Help

Multiple Intelligences
Bodily, Musical, Linguistic, Interpersonal

Materials
Fire hose, pictures, music

Preparation/Set-Up
Have materials available in a large motor area.

Procedures

1. Several movement activities can be combined into one session.
2. Have children "dance" to music like the flames of a fire.
3. Next, have children move in rhythm to music as they pull a fire hose, moving when the music is on, stopping when the music stops.
4. Finally, show children pictures of someone crawling under the smoke to get out of a room and have children crawl on the floor as if they were staying under the smoke.

Adaptations for Children With Disabilities

Assist with motor movements and social interactions as needed.

Put Out the Fire

Target Objectives
Increase coordination, cooperation

Developmental Domains
Language, Social, Gross Motor

Multiple Intelligences
Interpersonal, Naturalist, Logical, Bodily

Materials
Hose; water; towels; change of clothes, including socks and shoes.

Preparation/Set-Up
A large outside area that can get wet and prior planning for change of clothes.

Procedures

1. As weather permits, have children use the water hose outside.

2. Have them practice "putting out fires."

3. Let two or three children hold the hose at the same time to promote cooperation.

4. Children can take turns being at the front of the hose. Emphasize the concepts of front, middle, and back.

Adaptations for Children With Disabilities

Assist children with turn-taking and sharing. Praise children for taking turns. Review and repeat the positions and concepts.

(203) Fire Truck Visit

Target Objectives
Identification of objects, fire safety, awareness of people, following directions

Developmental Domains
Cognitive, Language, Social

Multiple Intelligences
Linguistic, Intrapersonal

Materials
None.

Preparation/Set-Up
Prior planning with fire department.

Procedures

1. Make arrangements for a fire truck and firefighters to visit the school.

2. Encourage the firefighters to put on and take off their firefighting equipment in front of the children.

3. Children can sometimes be afraid of individuals with costumes or different types of clothing, such as the masks firefighters wear.

4. Let children touch the clothing and equipment.

5. This activity is to help children become familiar with what firefighters look like.

6. Ask the firefighters to put out a prepared fire with a fire extinguisher if possible.

7. Children should also practice going to the firefighter when requested.

8. If possible, let children explore the truck while supervised.

Adaptations for Children With Disabilities

Children may be afraid of the firefighters if they are in full uniform. Introduce them gradually to the people and equipment. This is a nice activity to do later in the theme. Visiting the fire station, looking at pictures, and pretending to be a firefighter before seeing firefighters fully dressed is a good way to prepare children for this experience.

Directed Play   346

Firefighters

Target Objectives
Use of objects, dramatic play, personal/social skills, cooperation

Developmental Domains
Social, Cognitive, Language

Multiple Intelligences
Interpersonal, Linguistic, Intrapersonal

Materials
Fire equipment, chairs, cardboard box fire station, telephone.

Preparation/Set-Up
Set up the environment with the chairs and props to make a fire station.

Procedures

1. Repeat the firefighter dramatic play after the visit from the fire truck and fire fighters.
2. Have children assume the same roles as before.
3. Make use of the cardboard box fire station and arrange chairs as a fire truck.
4. The teacher should assume a role as a firefighter and guide children through the play episode.
5. Roles can be switched after children understand the routine.

Adaptations for Children With Disabilities

Help children with what to do and what to say. Assume a role in the play. Review social scripts and provide a picture sequence of the play events as needed. Supervise children with behavior disorders and autism and redirect them as needed. Give children lots of opportunities to touch and feel the objects.

205 Ladder Fun

Target Objectives
Increase balance and coordination, fire safety, first and last

Developmental Domains
Cognitive, Social, Gross Motor

Multiple Intelligences
Linguistic, Interpersonal, Bodily, Spatial, Intrapersonal

Materials
Ladders, blindfolds.

Preparation/Set-Up
Large, open area with two or three wooden ladders, each approximately 6 feet long.

Procedures

1. Have a small group of children practice walking through the rungs of a ladder that is lying on the floor.

2. Children should take turns walking over the rungs or on the rungs depending on the instruction.

3. Teachers should emphasize the concepts of first and last and count the rungs as children walk through.

4. Once children have walked through the ladder several times have them choose a partner.

5. Assist with putting on blindfolds.

6. The partner is to help the blindfolded child walk through the rungs of the ladder as if helping them to safety. Encourage the children to talk about what they are doing.

7. Have the children reverse roles and repeat.

Adaptations for Children With Disabilities

Watch children carefully. Children having problems with balance or coordination will need extra assistance. Promote positive peer interactions. Allow for children not to be blindfolded if scared or uncomfortable. If balance is a major concern a blindfold should not be used. As an alternative, children can carry something as they are walking to safety.

Directed Play

Water Safety and Boats

The Directed Play approach puts an emphasis on exposing children to real objects, places, etc. To the extent possible, children should be exposed to real boats. It is recognized, however, that this may be difficult in some settings. It would be ideal if children could be taken on a field trip to see boats at a river or lake or perhaps a parent with a boat would be willing to bring the boat to school for show and tell. Children will benefit from seeing all aspects of the boat, including motor, anchor, oars, life jackets, etc., and from having boating/water safety explained.

Water Play

Target Objectives
Sensory stimulation, show understanding of concepts of float and sink, wet and dry, heavy and light, full and empty

Developmental Domains
Fine Motor, Gross Motor, Personal-Social

Multiple Intelligences
Bodily, Spatial, Linguistic, Naturalist, Logical

Materials
Water table or small outside swimming pool; various water play items, including cups, boats, and pitchers; towels; change of clothing.

Preparation/Set-Up
Be sure children have a change of clothes or have children change into a swimsuit in warm weather. Fill the water table or pool early and let it warm up.

Procedures

1. Let children play with the water toys at the water table or pool. Bring only two or three children to the water table or pool at one time.

2. Point out what children are doing (e.g., "You are pouring the water in the cup").

3. Emphasize concepts such as empty and full, heavy and light, and float and sink.

4. Drain the pool at the end of the day and let it dry.

Adaptations for Children With Disabilities

Supervise and provide assistance as needed.

207 Water, Water, Everywhere

Target Objectives
Understand the importance of water; recognition of objects; understand age-level concepts of heavy/light, hot/cold, empty/full, full/half

Developmental Domains
Cognitive, Language, Social, Gross Motor

Multiple Intelligences
Linguistic, Naturalist, Logical

Materials
Pictures of various water sources, such as lakes, rivers, oceans, water fountains, bathtubs, sinks, faucets, rain, snow, steam, ice, or a boiling kettle; pictures of animals drinking and plants being watered.

Preparation/Set-Up
Have all materials available.

Procedures

1. Arrange children in a small group and tell them that you are going to talk about water.

2. Show them the various pictures of water sources and uses. Have the children repeat the name, source, and function.

3. Discuss with the children that water is everywhere and is necessary for animals and plants to live.

4. Show and discuss that water can change if very hot or cold (steam and ice).

5. Demonstrate that water can also weigh a great deal. Have children pick up gallon jugs with different amounts of water in them. Even a one-gallon jug will be heavy enough for some children. Have them practice passing and carrying the jugs with one another. Identify the concepts for children to repeat.

6. Ask children to tell you what they have learned about water.

Adaptations for Children With Disabilities

Repeat the names of water sources. Give children extra time and practice. Guide as needed during social interactions with peers.

Directed Play

Water Safety

Target Objectives
Understand what is involved in water safety, recognition and use of objects, hot

Developmental Domains
Cognitive, Language

Multiple Intelligences
Linguistic, Intrapersonal

Materials
Pictures of water sources used in the "Water, Water Everywhere" activity; pictures of, or actual, life jackets. A family may have some life jackets that can be borrowed.

Preparation/Set-Up
Materials readily available.

Procedures

1. Arrange children in a small group and tell them that they are going to learn about water safety. Stress that water can be dangerous and that people or animals can drown.

2. Show the children the pictures of the various water sources.

3. Discuss how important it is that there is always an adult around when children are near water.

4. Stress that children should never put their heads under water unless an adult is nearby.

5. For the bathtub picture, discuss that the water may be hot, as well as the danger of drowning. Stress that it is important to have an adult nearby. Children should approach bathwater cautiously when getting in and be careful when the water is running.

6. Have children practice putting on the life jackets if they are available. While in a boat or in deep water they should wear life jackets at all times.

Adaptations for Children With Disabilities

Repeat key concepts, especially the danger of water. Repeat that hot water can make other things hot, like faucets.

Chapter 10

209   Float and Sink

Target Objectives
Identify concepts and items that float and sink, categorization, sorting, predicting what will happen next.

Developmental Domains
Cognitive, Language

Multiple Intelligences
Bodily, Logical, Linguistic, Naturalist

Materials
Toy boats and other things that will float or sink (e.g., plastic and regular golf balls, rocks, sticks, leaves, popped and unpopped popcorn or other foods, plastic toys, shoes), tub of water, towels.

Preparation/Set-Up
Tile floored area or plastic mat and all materials readily available.

Procedures

1. Gather a small group of children together. Explain to the children that you are going to talk about things that float and sink.

2. Using a tub of water, have the small group of children experiment by placing objects in the water and have children predict if they will float or sink.

3. Discuss the concept of heavy and light.

4. Review with the children about how some things will float in water and other things will sink. For example, "Did the popcorn float or sink?" or "Did the wood float or sink?"

5. Children should also be asked if people float or sink, and teachers should address water safety.

6. Take turns trying out their predictions.

7. Assist children in sorting items into piles of things that float or sink.

Adaptations for Children With Disabilities

Give children a considerable amount of time to experiment. Provide assistance as needed.

Directed *Play*   352

2|0 Different Boats

Target Objectives
Identification and use of objects, size differences, counting, same and different classifications

Developmental Domains
Cognitive, Language

Multiple Intelligences
Linguistic, Naturalist, Logical

Materials
Pictures and toys of different kinds of boats and ships.

Preparation/Set-Up
Have materials available.

Procedures

1. Show a small group of children pictures of different boats and talk about how many kinds there are.

2. The pictures should include as many different types of boats as possible, including large ships, sailboats, etc.

3. Discuss with the children what the boats do (e.g., some boats carry cargo, others are for fun or military uses) and note differences (large/small, color and number of windows).

4. Let children count the number of sails or windows on boats.

5. Children should also be encouraged to identify what is the same and different when comparing the pictures of the boats.

6. Ask the children to tell you what they have learned about boats.

Adaptations for Children With Disabilities

Point out differences in size and color of the different boats. Focus on one concept at a time. Change concepts as children demonstrate understanding. Model and imitate vocabulary.

211 Build a Boat

Target Objectives
Increase cooperative play, understanding of how things move, concepts of front and back, increase language and vocabulary

Developmental Domains
Cognitive, Social, Language, Gross Motor

Multiple Intelligences
Linguistic, Spatial, Bodily, Interpersonal, Naturalist

Materials
Large cardboard blocks, long wooden blocks for oars, cloth tied to poles for sails.

Preparation/Set-Up
Clear a large area of obstacles and have blocks and other materials ready.

Procedures

1. Arrange children in a small group and tell them that they are going to work together to build a boat out of blocks. Let the children decide what kind of boat they are going to build.

2. Give each child some blocks and have the group build a "boat" with blocks. Provide assistance and encourage turn-taking as needed.

3. Discuss how the boat may be "powered" (sail, motor, oars; person, machine, nature) and discuss concepts of front and back.

4. Let children have an opportunity to act out sailing the boat.

5. Bring the children back into a small group and discuss the building of the boat and what could be done differently.

Adaptations for Children With Disabilities

Children with speech/language concerns may not be easily understood when speaking. Make sure all children can understand one another. Have pictures available for pointing and encourage gestures to assist in understanding. Give children a chance to resolve any conflicts before you intervene.

Directed Play

212 Gone Fishing

Target Objectives
Counting, sorting, size differences

Developmental Domains
Cognitive, Language, Social

Multiple Intelligences
Bodily, Naturalist, Logical, Linguistic

Materials
Laminated precut fish pictures of different sizes and colors with paper clips attached; fishing poles made of sticks, string, and magnets; three different-sized buckets (large, medium, small); a "boat" made of chairs or blocks (see previous activity).

Preparation/Set-Up
Have all materials available. Fish should be precut and "fishing poles" ready with sticks strung with string and magnets tied to the end.

Procedures

1. If possible leave the "boat" block construction set up overnight. Tell the children that they are "going fishing."

2. Have precut fish and fishing poles made of sticks, string, and magnets ready.

3. Arrange the fish in the "water" around the boat.

4. Have the children sit in the boat and "fish."

5. Children should name different sizes (large, medium, small) and colors of the fish they catch.

6. Have the children count how many fish they caught to promote one-to-one correspondence.

7. Children can also sort the fish into piles of large, medium, and small and then sort those piles by color.

Adaptations for Children With Disabilities

Have children repeat the size and color of the fish. Ensure that children are taking turns. Repeat the activity again at a later date. Work on sorting by shape and color at a table or on the floor in a one-to-one setting.

213 Row Your Boat

Target Objectives Cooperation, memory	**Materials** Books on boats, music (optional).
Developmental Domains Language, Personal/Social, Gross Motor	**Preparation/Set-Up** Large motor area.
Multiple Intelligences Musical, Linguistic, Bodily, Spatial, Interpersonal	

Procedures

1. In a small group, read a book about boats or sailing and discuss what boats do for us.

2. Next, have the children choose a partner.

3. The children should sit on the floor and face each other with feet touching and arms outstretched to hold hands.

4. Have the children sing "Row, Row, Row Your Boat" while moving back and forth to simulate rowing.

5. Then sing "Rock, Rock, Rock Your Boat" while moving from side to side. Sing songs two or three times and let children change partners.

6. Have children alternate voice by becoming a "giant" in a boat using a big voice or an "elf" with a small voice. Get creative and add different voices and characters.

7. Assist with peers as needed. Pair students by size and needed assistance.

Adaptations for Children With Disabilities

Provide assistance as needed.

Directed Play 356

Veterinarians

 ## Veterinarians

Target Objectives
Recognition of objects and professions, taking care of animals, increase vocabulary

Developmental Domains
Language, Social, Self-Help

Multiple Intelligences
Linguistic, Intrapersonal, Bodily, Interpersonal

Materials
Pictures of a veterinarian's office, toy veterinarian materials, children's storybooks about veterinarians.

Preparation/Set-Up
Have materials readily available in a group setting.

Procedures

1. Show a small group of children pictures and objects associated with a veterinarian's office, including equipment and people.

2. Discuss why we have veterinarians and the purpose of some of the equipment.

3. Have children name objects and pictures and answer simple who, what, where questions.

4. Read a book or books about visiting a veterinarian's office and have children discuss their past visits to the veterinarian.

Adaptations for Children With Disabilities

Have realistic-looking animals or toys to match with pictures. Repeat the activity in a one-to-one setting, reviewing identifying objects and vocabulary. Target "wh" questions for certain students.

Veterinarian's Office Dramatic Play

Target Objectives
Identification, use and function of objects, cooperative play, empathy

Developmental Domains
Social, Cognitive, Language, Fine Motor

Multiple Intelligences
Linguistic, Interpersonal, Spatial, Bodily

Materials
Commercial medical toys, blocks (optional).

Preparation/Set-Up
Clear the play area of obstacles. Have materials available for play.

Procedures

1. Divide children into small groups of not more than four members and present them with veterinarian toys.

2. Tell the children they are going to make-believe that they are animal doctors.

3. Blocks can be added to allow children to build parts of the office.

4. Be sure to have enough toys for all the children in the group.

5. Assist children by helping them to set up the veterinarian play and make sure that each child has a role to play. Roles can include veterinarian, nurse, assistants, and pet owners.

6. Help children understand how or why equipment or people do what they do.

7. Make simple statements such as "The bird looks hurt" to help guide the play.

Adaptations for Children With Disabilities

Scripted language or conversation between characters; picture schedule of sequenced events when visiting a veterinarian's office. Avoid overcrowding. Let children try to resolve conflicts before you intervene. Working with and taking care of animals is a good way to promote empathy. This would be a good activity for children with autism or behavior disorders.

216   Visit the Veterinarian

Target Objectives
Increase community awareness, recognition of objects, increase vocabulary

Developmental Domains
Language, Social

Multiple Intelligences
Linguistic, Intrapersonal, Interpersonal

Materials
Name tags.

Preparation/Set-Up
Prior arrangements for field trip, transportation, permission slips, class lists, cell phone.

Procedures

1. Arrange a field trip to a veterinarian's office.

2. Have the veterinarian explain his or her job and the equipment used.

3. Encourage children to ask and answer questions.

4. Practice naming new objects.

Adaptations for Children With Disabilities

Children with speech or language problems may be reluctant to ask questions. Help them think of a question to ask. Provide a visual schedule and picture of animals being examined in a veterinarian's office. Provide prior preparation for the visit to reduce any anxiety. This will also improve the appropriateness of social behaviors in a new or unfamiliar environment.

217 Veterinarian Play

Target Objectives
Identification, use, and function of objects, increase social language use, cooperative play, recall facts and events from previous experience

Developmental Domains
Cognitive, Language, Social

Multiple Intelligences
Linguistic, Interpersonal, Spatial, Bodily

Materials
Commercial medical toys, blocks (optional), ace or cloth bandages, various stuffed or plastic animals.

Preparation/Set-Up
Clear the play area and let children assist in setting up the play environment.

Procedures

1. After the visit with a veterinarian, repeat the dramatic play activity.

2. Have the children again play with the veterinarian toys and assign roles for each child.

3. The adult should point out things seen on the field trip and children should be encouraged to incorporate this information into their play.

Adaptations for Children With Disabilities

Use scripted dialogue, more teacher-directed play with physical assists as necessary, and a picture schedule of events.

Veterinarian Puzzles and Drawing

218

Target Objectives
Identification and use of objects, fine motor, problem solving, turn-taking

Developmental Domains
Cognitive, Fine Motor

Multiple Intelligences
Spatial, Logical, Linguistic

Materials
Veterinarian/hospital puzzles, paper, crayons.

Preparation/Set-Up
Have materials ready.

Procedures

1. Give small groups of children puzzles that have a veterinarian theme or a theme about taking care of animals or animals in general.

2. In addition, give children pictures of veterinarians and animals to color.

3. Conclude by singing "I'm a Veterinarian."

Adaptations for Children With Disabilities

Puzzles adapted with pegs or knobs; a variety of puzzles ranging in size from 6–20 pieces for use with children of different developmental ages; adapted coloring materials, such as paper taped to table and larger crayons or markers.

I'm a Veterinarian

I take care of animals,

I treat them one by one.

I take care of animals,

I'm a veterinarian.

I give shots,

And sometimes operate.

I take care of animals,

'Cause I think they're great.

Farms and Animals

Farm activities are often very enjoyable for children. Like other community awareness themes, the farm activities should be continued over the course of two to three weeks.

219   Farm Life

Target Objectives
Recognition and use of objects, naming animals, pretending in a group, singing paired with actions

Developmental Domains
Language, Social, Gross Motor

Multiple Intelligences
Linguistic, Musical, Intrapersonal, Bodily, Naturalist

Materials
Farm pictures, including animals and equipment; music (optional).

Preparation/Set-Up
Large area free of barriers.

Procedures

1. In a small group, show children seated on the floor around you pictures of farm life, including animals, crops, equipment, people, etc.

2. Discuss why we have farms, what kinds of animals are on farms, and the purpose of some of the equipment.

3. Have children name objects in pictures and answer simple "wh" questions.

4. Next, have the children pretend to be farm animals, such as cows, chickens, or horses.

5. Let them crawl around and make the appropriate sounds.

6. A child could be selected to be the farmer and direct all the cows into one area and all the horses into another.

7. Several children can be the same animals.

8. Conclude by singing "Old McDonald Had a Farm."

Adaptations for Children With Disabilities

Have realistic farm objects or toys to match with pictures. Commercially available toys that make farm animal sounds can also be used. Repeat the pretend play in a one-to-one setting, working on animal sounds and actions. Identify and name farm animals and objects during the play for additional practice. See the listing of different animals in Appendix A.

220 Build the Farm

Target Objectives
Identification and naming of farm animals, buildings, and objects, telling use of tools and equipment

Developmental Domains
Social, Cognitive, Language, Fine Motor

Multiple Intelligences
Linguistic, Interpersonal, Spatial, Bodily, Naturalist, Musical

Materials
Commercial farm toys, blocks (optional).

Preparation/Set-Up
Have materials ready.

Procedures

1. Present a small group of children with farm toys, including animals, buildings, and equipment (e.g., barn, silo, fence). Tell them they are going to make-believe that they are on a farm.

2. Blocks can be added to let children build fences, roads, or buildings.

3. Be sure to have enough toys for all the children in the group.

4. Tell the children to build a farm.

5. Assist them by helping set up the farm and organizing the play.

6. Adults should provide children with considerable freedom in this activity.

7. Help with understanding what sounds different animals make or how they move or point out how equipment is used.

8. Make simple statements such as "The cows look hungry" to help guide the play.

9. With the farm play still set up, bring the group of children back together again and identify something that each child contributed to the farm (e.g., "Billy built the fence" or "Megan has all the cows together").

10. At the conclusion, bring children together in a group to sing "The Farmyard."

Adaptations for Children With Disabilities

Watch children to be sure that they are talking to one another during play. Provide language and sentences for children to model. Demonstrate appropriate play with the animals. Caring for animals is a good way to promote empathy. This would be a good activity for children with autism or emotional disorders.

The Farmyard

In the farmyard at the end of the day,

All the animals politely say,

"Thank you for my food today."

The cow says, "Moo,"

The pigeon says, "Coo,"

The sheep says, "Baa,"

The lamb says, "Maa."

The hen goes "Cluck, cluck, cluck,"

The pig grunts, "Oink."

Then the barn is locked up tight

And the farmer says, "Good Night."

Farm Animals

Target Objectives
Identify and name differences in animals

Developmental Domains
Language, Gross Motor, Cognitive

Multiple Intelligences
Naturalist, Linguistic, Bodily, Musical

Materials
Pictures and toys of common farm animals, including cows, horses, ducks, sheep, goats, chickens, pigs, and birds. Try to have pictures of both adult and baby animals.

Preparation/Set-Up
Have all materials available in the group setting.

Procedures

1. Show and discuss these animals. Include how they move, what they eat, what sounds they make, their size or color, where they live, differences in adults and babies, and if they are dangerous.

2. Have children identify and name sounds, then act out movements of the animals.

3. Encourage them to tell what they have learned about these animals.

4. Conclude by singing "Animals."

Adaptations for Children With Disabilities

Provide adequate opportunities for practice in making sounds or movement. Model and imitate as needed. Review names with pictures of animals in a one-to-one setting.

> ### Animals
>
> Can you hop like a rabbit?
>
> Can you jump like a frog?
>
> Can you walk like a duck?
>
> Can you run like a dog?
>
> Can you fly like a bird?
>
> Can you swim like a fish?
>
> And be still like a good child,
>
> As still as this?
>
> *(Suit actions to words)*

 Planting Seeds

Target Objectives
Awareness of objects and nature, sequence of events, increase vocabulary, sing with peers

Developmental Domains
Cognitive, Fine Motor

Multiple Intelligences
Naturalist, Bodily, Linguistic

Materials
Dirt, two to three kinds of seeds of different types/sizes, small shovels (optional) or spoons, containers.

Preparation/Set-Up
Have seeds in labeled containers.

Procedures

1. In the spring or fall, as weather permits, prepare an area of ground for the planting of seeds. Common crops such as peas or beans would be good.

2. Give children an opportunity to dig in the dirt and to plant the seeds.

3. Children take turns watering the seeds everyday. Check to see if the seeds are growing and document the observations.

4. If the weather gets cold, have the children assist in transplanting the seedlings into small pots to bring inside.

5. If it is necessary to do this activity indoors, use a large tub with dirt.

6. Have children fill two to three cups with dirt and plant their seeds. Label the cups with each child's name.

7. Place the cups in a warm place and have the children water their cups to keep the dirt moist.

8. Seeds should sprout in seven to ten days. Make sure to explain to children that it takes time for seeds to sprout and grow.

9. Conclude the activity by having children sing "Farmer and His Seed" to the tune of "Farmer in the Dell."

Adaptations for Children With Disabilities

Some children will not like to get their hands dirty, so assist as needed. Reward these children even if they only get a little dirt on their hands. Encourage these children to help dig with small shovels. Repeat the names of the seeds and plants. Repeat the song often over a two-week period.

Farmer and His Seed

The farmer plants his seeds,

The farmer plants his seeds,

Hi, ho, the dairy-o,

The farmer plants his seeds.

The rain begins to fall,

The seeds begin to grow,

The farmer cuts them down,

He binds them into sheaves,

And now we'll have some bread.

223 Matching Seeds to Plants and Trees

Target Objectives
Associate objects with other objects, sequencing, cause and effect, classification

Developmental Domains
Cognitive, Language

Multiple Intelligences
Naturalist, Logical, Linguistic, Musical

Materials
Seeds can be acquired commercially or from families. Have a variety of seeds that differ in size and color and by what is grown. Pictures of plants and trees will also be needed. The selection of seeds can include peas, pumpkins, marigolds, acorns, spinach, maple trees, potatoes, or corn. Pictures that show a sequence of planting a seed, a seedling, and a full plant will also be helpful.

Preparation/Set-Up
Materials readily available.

Procedures

1. Arrange children in a small group and tell them that you are going to talk about seeds that grow into plants.

2. Show the children seeds and pictures of what the seeds grow into. Identify the names of the plants.

3. Point out differences in the size, color, and shapes of the seeds.

4. Discuss the plants or trees that are grown and what we can do with them (e.g., we eat peas, birds live in trees).

5. Have children match seeds to the corresponding plants.

6. In a related activity, children can make a seed collage by gluing different seeds to paper with labels or pictures for the plants.

7. Have the children return to a small group area and ask them what they have learned about seeds and plants.

8. Conclude by singing "A Little Seed."

Adaptations for Children With Disabilities

Seeds are small. Make sure children do not put these in their mouths. Assist children in making a seed collage. Model new vocabulary for children to imitate.

> **A Little Seed**
>
> A little seed is planted
> In the dark, dark ground.
> Out comes the yellow sun,
> Big and round.
> Down comes the cool rain,
> Soft and slow.
> Up sprouts the little seed,
> Grow, grow, grow.

224 Visit the Farm

Target Objectives
Increase community awareness, recognition of objects and events

Developmental Domains
Language, Social

Multiple Intelligences
Linguistic, Intrapersonal, Naturalist, Interpersonal

Materials
Transportation, emergency phone numbers, class lists, cell phone, cleaning materials for hands, first aid bag.

Preparation/Set-Up
Prior arrangements for field trip, transportation, permission slips, emergency phone numbers, parent volunteers.

Procedures

1. Arrange a field trip to a farm.

2. If a farm visit is not possible, a local nursery might be a good option.

3. Have the farmer or nursery staff explain their job, the tools they use, and how things grow.

4. Encourage children to ask and answer questions.

5. Practice naming new plants, crops, animals, insects, or tools.

Adaptations for Children With Disabilities

Children with speech or language needs may be reluctant to ask questions. You may want to help them think of a question to ask. Assist them also with answers to questions. Review new vocabulary.

225 Farm Play

Target Objectives
Identification and use of objects, language, personal/social

Developmental Domains
Cognitive, Language, Social

Multiple Intelligences
Linguistic, Interpersonal, Spatial, Bodily

Materials
Commercial farm toys, blocks (optional), paper for drawing or constructing flowers or plants.

Preparation/Set-Up
Have enough toys and materials for all children.

Procedures

1. After the visit to a farm or nursery, repeat the farm dramatic play.

2. Have the children again play with the farm toys, animals, etc.

3. The adult should point out things seen on the field trip and children should be encouraged to incorporate this information into their play.

Adaptations for Children With Disabilities

Assume a role in the play. Assist children in what to do or say as needed. Promote social interactions between peers. Let them try to resolve conflicts on their own.

Farm Puzzles and Drawing

Target Objectives
Identification and use of objects, drawing and constructing, problem solving, turn-taking, counting

Developmental Domains
Cognitive, Fine Motor

Multiple Intelligences
Spatial, Logical, Naturalist

Materials
Farm puzzles of various difficulty levels, paper, crayons, farm pictures.

Preparation/Set-Up
None.

Procedures

1. Small groups of children complete puzzles that have a farm theme.
2. Also, give children pictures of farms or farm animals to color.
3. Adults should point out qualities, such as size, color, sounds, or how many legs on farm animals.
4. Children can take turns drawing farm animals and completing farm puzzles.

Adaptations for Children With Disabilities

Provide assistance as needed. Tape paper to the table or drill small holes in puzzle pieces and insert small dowel rods for pegs.

227 # Butterfly Shapes

Target Objectives
Use scissors to cut on lines, concepts of half/whole, completing a task with several steps

Developmental Domains
Fine Motor, Cognitive, Language

Multiple Intelligences
Bodily, Spatial, Naturalist, Musical, Logical

Materials
Paper, scissors, crayons or paints.

Preparation/Set-Up
Have standard-size paper folded in half. Predraw the outline of the butterfly on one side of the paper so that after cutting the paper and opening it a "whole" butterfly shape will appear. Have a completed example ready to show the children.

Procedures

1. Have children sit in a small group at the table. Tell the children they are going to make butterflies.

2. Show the children pictures of butterflies and an example of the butterfly they are going to make.

3. Give the children the prepared butterfly outline and scissors and have them cut out the butterfly shape.

4. The children use crayons or paints to decorate the opened butterfly.

5. Hang the butterflies from the ceiling when finished.

6. Conclude by singing "The Caterpillar."

Adaptations for Children With Disabilities

Adaptive scissors may be needed for some children. Lines should be drawn thicker or wider for some children. Some children will need physical assistance in cutting, or some of the butterfly can be precut. See the Fine Motor chapter for other construction activities.

The Caterpillar

A caterpillar crawled to the top of a tree

"I think I'll take a nap," said he.

So, under a leaf he began to creep

To spin his cocoon, and he fell asleep.

All winter he slept in his cocoon bed,

'Till spring came along one day and said,

"Wake up, wake up, little sleepyhead.

Wake up; it's time to get out of bed."

So, he opened his eyes that sunshiny day,

Lo, he was a butterfly, and flew away.

Directed Play

⟨228⟩ Ladybugs

Target Objectives
Increase fine motor manipulation, color recognition, increase vocabulary

Developmental Domains
Fine Motor, Cognitive

Multiple Intelligences
Naturalist, Spatial

Materials
Hardening clay; picture of ladybugs or real ladybugs, if available; red and yellow paints.

Preparation/Set-Up
Have enough materials for all children.

Procedures

1. Have each child sit at a table with clay available. Tell the children they are going to make ladybugs out of the play-dough.

2. Show the children a picture of a ladybug or real ladybugs if available.

3. Have the children make ladybugs out of the play-dough noting the different body parts.

4. Children may need to make their "bugs" fairly good size so that they are easy to paint.

5. Put the name of the child on the bottom and set the "ladybugs" to harden overnight.

6. The next day give children their bugs.

7. Show the children an example and the pictures of the ladybugs and have the children paint their ladybugs. Set aside to dry.

8. On the third day, children can take their ladybugs home or they can be placed around the classroom.

Adaptations for Children With Disabilities

Give children time and assistance but let them make these themselves. Identify how many legs, colors, and shapes.

229 Aquarium

Target Objectives
Increase fine motor, use of scissors, identification of objects, number concepts, concept of like and different, task completion

Developmental Domains
Fine Motor, Social, Language, Cognitive

Multiple Intelligences
Linguistic, Spatial, Musical, Interpersonal, Naturalist

Materials
Construction paper of various colors, glue sticks, scissors, clear plastic kitchen wrap cut to size, stapler.

Preparation/Set-Up
The amount of preparation/set-up can be dependent on how much the children are able to do for themselves. Construction paper fish, plants, and border can be precut for some children. Lines should be drawn to outline fish and water plants or straight rectangles drawn for the frame of the aquarium if children cut the pieces themselves.

Procedures

1. Children can do this activity individually, in pairs, or as a small group. Tell children that they are going to make an aquarium and show them a picture of one.

2. Show the children an example of a completed "aquarium" before beginning.

3. Have the children cut out three or four different sizes or colors of "fish."

4. Children should also cut out some various "water plants" and the frame for the outside of the aquarium.

5. The frame will be made with four strips of paper—two long and two short—to make a rectangle.

6. Have the children glue their fish and plants to a blank piece of paper.

7. Next, have them use a blue crayon to rub across the paper sideways to give more of a "water" effect.

8. Once the fish and plants are glued on and the background is colored, wrap the clear or blue plastic wrap over the glued items and tape or glue it down in the back.

9. Glue or staple the four straight rectangle pieces around the border over the plastic wrap to complete the aquarium.

10. Let children show their aquariums to the other children and discuss how they are similar or different. Encourage children to compliment one another.

Directed Play

11. Conclude the activity by singing "Five Little Fishes."

Adaptations for Children With Disabilities

Provide precut shapes and assistance with gluing. Guide through the activity one step at a time.

> ### *Five Little Fishes*
>
> Five little fishes were swimming by the shore,
> One took a dive and then there were four.
> Four little fishes were swimming in the sea,
> One went for food and then there were three.
> Three little fishes said "Now what shall we do?"
> One swam away, and then there were two.
> Two little fishes were having great fun,
> But one took a plunge, then there was one.
> One little fish said, "I like the warm sun."
> Away he went and then there were none.

230 Spiderwebs

Target Objectives
Recognition of objects, increase fine motor skills, cause and effect, counting

Developmental Domains
Cognitive, Language, Fine Motor

Multiple Intelligences
Bodily, Spatial, Naturalist

Materials
String or yarn, paper, pipe cleaners, glue, pictures of spiders and spiderwebs, Styrofoam balls or pom-poms.

Preparation/Set-Up
Have all supplies ready at a table.

Procedures

1. Have children sit at the table with supplies available. Tell them they are going to make spiderwebs.

2. Show children pictures of real spiderwebs. Have them name what they see and count the number of legs on a spider.

3. Let children create their own spiderwebs using the string or yarn and gluing the finished web to paper.

4. "Spiders" are created using the pipe cleaners and Styrofoam balls and these can be placed on the spiderwebs.

5. Hang the spiderwebs around the room.

6. Conclude by singing "Eency, Weency Spider".

Adaptations for Children With Disabilities

Assist with cutting and stringing the yarn or string. Provide an outline of a web that children can glue and trace with yarn or string. Reward children for task completion. Encourage children to compliment one another.

Animals

There are many different kinds of animals—farm, pets, wild, zoo, and insects/reptiles—that children can learn about. An abundance of books and puzzles about animals are available. There are also a variety of songs and movements that can be incorporated into animal activities. Some songs and music that involve animals include: "Mary Had a Little Lamb," "Old MacDonald," "Baa, Baa Black Sheep," and "Farmer in the Dell." See Appendix A for additional descriptions and comparisons of animals. See the Motor and Movement chapter for yoga exercises based on animals.

Table 10.1

Simple Animal Compare and Contrast

Animals that have **four legs**	dogs, cats, bears, lions, rabbits, horses, elephants, pigs, sheep, giraffes, hamsters, turtles, squirrels, alligators
Animals that **run fast**	dogs, cats, bears, lions, rabbits, horses
Animals that **live in trees**	monkeys, birds, squirrels
Animals that **move slowly**	turtles, hamsters
Animals that **give us food**	cows, pigs, bees, lamb, chickens
Animals that **live near water**	ducks, snakes, alligators
Animals with **two legs**	ducks, birds, chickens, monkeys
Animals that **climb**	squirrels, monkeys, cats, spiders

Directed Play   374

Multiple Intelligences and Play

Common Toys and Play Materials Appropriate for Different Intelligences

Intrapersonal	Interpersonal	Logical-Mathematical	Linguistic	Spatial	Bodily-Kinesthetic	Musical	Naturalist
Blocks	Blocks	Blocks	Blocks	Blocks	Blocks	Blocks	Sticks, leaves
Mirrors	Toy telephones	Nesting cups	Books	Easel painting	Swings, Merry-go-rounds	Rhyming words	Sand and water
Puppets	Puppets	Pattern games	Toy telephones	Chalkboards	Finger paint	Tapes of music	Farm toys
Dress-up clothes	Dress-up clothes	Puzzles	Walkie-talkie	Puzzles	Beanbags	Musical instruments	Toy garden tools
Dolls	Balls	Paper and crayons	Microphones	Toy trains and tracks	Sand and water	Some computer programs	Toy animals
Doctor's kit (promotes empathy)	Card or board games	Card or board games	Card or board games	Some computer programs	Trikes and wheeled toys	Records CD's	Wood, hammer, and nails
Thematic materials	Thematic materials	Toy money	Some computer programs		Balls		Pet animals
Stuffed animals	Dolls	Number cards	Listening to book tapes		Stuffed animals		Mud pies

375

Common Games and Activities to Promote Different Intelligences

Intrapersonal	Interpersonal	Logical-Mathematical	Linguistic	Spatial	Bodily-Kinesthetic	Musical	Naturalist
Body tracing	Group projects	Sorting objects	Jokes	Drawing	Water play	Musical chairs	Climbing trees
Role playing	Role playing	Counting objects	Read books	Painting	"Freely" bags	Rhythmic patterns	Sand and water
"Missing person"	Family-style snacks	Counting backwards	Lotto games	Beanbag toss	Dancing	Dancing	Planting seeds
Body parts game	Creating cartoons	Nesting and stacking	House play	Bowling	Dodge ball	Singing	Taking care of pets
Different occupations	Card and board games	Concentration	Poetry	Carrying heavy and light	Easel painting	Listening to music	Hiking in park
Familystyle snacks	Thematic play	Hide and seek	Finger plays	Sculpture	Swings	Parades	Cooking

Words of the Alphabet Associated With the Multiple Intelligences

Letters	Intrapersonal	Interpersonal	Logical-Mathematical	Linguistic	Spatial	Bodily-Kinesthetic	Musical	Naturalist
A	Anger, alone, able	Adopt, agree, ancestor	Add, age, after	Act, address, alphabet	Around, above, angle	Arms, around, active	Allegro, accordion	Ape, alligator, apple
B	Body, beauty, birth	Baby, boyfriend, beside	Bank, budget, balance	Books, bookmark, Braille	Blue, backward	Body, ballet, bat	Bagpipe, beat, band	Bird, boa, bamboo
C	Calm, careful, clever	Charity, caretaker, cartoon	Count, chess, calendar	Catalog, chatty, cell phone	Circle, curve, camera	Crawl, carry, catch	Clarinet, chorus, CD player	Clouds, cat, chicken
D	Decide, delight	Dad, daughter, direct	Dice, decode, dime	Debate, discuss, disctionary	Diamond, draw, design	Dance, drop, dive	Drum, dance	Dirt, duck, daisy
E	Effort, embarrass	Each other, enjoy, emotion	Equal, early, even, end	Echo, envelope, express	East, empty	Eyes, ears, eat		Elephant, eggs, earth
F	Fear, frown, feel	Friend, father, funny	First, five, fact	Fairytale, French	Figure, flat, form	Feet, fly, fast	Flute, fiddle	Fire, frog, flood

Directed Play   376

Letters	Intrapersonal	Interpersonal	Logical-Mathematical	Linguistic	Spatial	Bodily-Kinesthetic	Musical	Naturalist
G	Gentle, glee	Group, get along	Graph, gram	Gag, gesture	Green, globe	Grab, give, go	Guitar	Germs, grass, garden
H	Happy, hermit, honest	Help, hero, hate	Height	Hear, handwriting	Half, high, hollow	Hop, hike, hit	Horn, harp	Horse, hill, hawk
I	Idea, identity, imagine	Include, injure	Inch, invent	Intercom, interrupt	Incline, inside	Itch, inhale	Instrument	Ice, igloo, insect
J	Joy, jolly, jealous	Join, judge, jest	June, July	Joke, jargon, journal	Jigsaw puzzle, jumbo	Jump, jerk, jog	Jazz, jingle bells	Jellyfish, jungle
K	Keep, keen, karma	Kind, kiss	Kilogram	Knowledge	Kite, knot	Knee, kick	Keyboard, kazoo, key	Kangaroos, kitten, kid
L	Laugh, lazy, love	Love, like, listen	Last, late, length	List, library, letters, listen	Large, left, length	Leap, lift, limp	Lute, lyrics	Leaves, lamb, lemon, land
M	Me, mad, make-believe	Marriage, mate, mercy	Many, match, math, measure	Magazine, message	Map, machine	Mouth, muscle, motion	March, melody, music	Mountain, monkey, macaw
N	Name, nervous	Niece, neighbor	Number, nickel, nine	Name, novel, newspaper	Near, narrow	Nose, neck	Note	Night, nectar, nuts
O	Oneself, openminded	Offend	Organize	Outline	Over, oval		Oboe, orchestra	Ocean, opossum, oak tree
P	Patience, polite	Parents, party, person	Pattern, piece, price	Phrase, poem, phonics	Picture, paint, parallel	Push, pull, pedal	Play, piano, parade	Park, pine tree, pond
Q	Quit	Quarrel	Quarter, quantity	Quack, question		Quick	Quiet	Quack
R	Ready, relax	Relative, rude, respect	Rocket	Read, riddle, rhyme	Rectangle, right, round	Reach, roll, run, ride	Record, radio, recorder	Rose, rabbit, rain, river
S	Smile, surprise, sad	Scared, smile	Six	Secret	Square, straight	Snap, slide, soccer	Sing, song	Sheep, spinach, sky
T	Timid	Talk, telephone	Time, three, two, ten	Talk, telephone	Triangle, tool, tiny	Tumble, toes	Trumpet, tango, tempo	Thunder, toad, tree
U	Upset, unique, understand	Unity, uncle, us	Unit	Uppercase	Underline, under, up	Upstairs, upper, umpire	Ukulele	Universe, undertow

Letters	Intrapersonal	Interpersonal	Logical-Mathematical	Linguistic	Spatial	Bodily-Kinesthetic	Musical	Naturalist
V	Violent, virtue, vote	Visit, victory, volunteer	Volume	Voice, verb, vowel	Visual, vertical, violet	Volley, voice	Volume, violin	Vet, vegetable, volcano
W	Win, wait, wave	Worry, wacky, warm	Watch	Words, write	Work, white, wash	Walk, wrestle	Whistle, warble	Water, wind, wasp, weather
X					X-Ray		Xylophone	
Y	You	Yawn	Year, yesterday	Yippee	Yellow	Yoga		Yard
Z		Zany	Zero, zip code			Zigzag, zip		Zoo, zebra

Comparisons of Farm Animals

Animals	Movement	Eat	Sounds	Size/Color	Live	Adults/Babies
Cows	Walk/run on all 4's	Grain, hay, grass	Moo	Large, brown, black, and white	Farms, pastures	Calves
Horses	Walk/run on all 4's	Grain, straw	Whinny	Large, black, brown, white	Farms, pastures	Foals, colts
Ducks	Walk, swim, waddle	Grain, fish	Quack	Small, white, yellow	Ponds, water areas	Goslings
Sheep/goats	Walk, run on all 4's	Grain, grass	Baa baa	Medium, white	Pastures, barns	Lamb, kid
Chickens	Walk on 2 legs	Grain	Cluck	Small, white, red	Pens	Chicks
Pigs	Walk on all 4's	Grain	Oink	Small, medium, pink, gray	Pens, barns	Piglets

Comparisons of Zoo/Wild Animals

Animals	Movement	What Eat	Sounds	Size/Color	Where Live	Adults/Babies
Lions	Run, walk on all 4's	Small animals	Roar	Large, yellow	Forests, jungles, zoos, clans	Cubs
Bears	Walk, run on all 4's	Nuts, animals, fish	Roar	Large, brown, black	Forests, zoos	Cubs
Monkeys	Climb, walk	Fruit	Eek	Small, medium, brown	Jungles, forests, zoos	
Giraffes	Walk, run on all 4's	Leaves		Large, yellow with spots	Jungles, herds	Fawns
Alligators	Walk, swim	Fish	Chop, snap	Large, green, brown	Water	Eggs
Elephants	Walk, run on all 4's	Grass, nuts, fruit	Roar, trumpeting	Very large, gray	Jungles, forests, zoos	Calf

Comparisons of Insects and Reptiles

Animals	Movement	What Eat	Sounds	Size/Color	Where Live	Adults/Babies
Spiders	Climb, walk	Insects		Small, brown, gray	Webs	Eggs
Ants	Walk	Anything		Very small, black, red	Ant hills	Eggs
Snakes	Slither	Small animals	Hiss	Long, yellow, brown	Holes	Eggs
Butterflies	Fly	Nectar		Very small, various colors	Tight places	Caterpillars
Frogs	Jump, swim	Insects	Ribbit	Small, green	Near water	Eggs, tadpoles
Bees	Fly	Pollen	Buzz	Very small	Hives	Eggs, larvae

State Technology Projects

Federal law has established technology assistance projects in every state to serve as a resource for assistive technology. Information, materials, support services, or equipment may be available from these sources. This resource listing includes contact information for all 50 states and several outlying areas.

Resource Listing for State Technology Assistance Projects

ALABAMA STATEWIDE TECHNOLOGY ACCESS AND RESPONSE
PROJECT (STAR) SYSTEM FOR ALABAMIANS WITH DISABILITIES
Montgomery, AL
(334) 613-3480
(800) STAR656 (In-State)
tbridges@rehab.state.al.us
http://www.rehab.state.al.us/star

ALASKA DIVISION OF VOCATIONAL REHABILITATION ASSISTIVE
TECHNOLOGY PROGRAM
Anchorage, AK
(907) 563-0138 (V/TDD)
(907) 269-3569 (V/TDD)
jim_beck@labor.state.ak.us
http://www.labor.state.ak.us/at/index.htm

ARIZONA TECHNOLOGY ACCESS PROGRAM (AZTAP)
Phoenix, AZ
(602) 728-9532
(800) 477-9921
jill.oberstein@nau.edu
http://www.nau.edu/ihd/aztap/

ARKANSAS INCREASING CAPABILITIES ACCESS NETWORK (ICAN)
Little Rock, AR
(501) 666-8868 (V/TDD)
(800) 828-2799 (V/TDD, In-State)
sogaskin@ars.state.ar.us
http://www.arkansas-ican.org

CALIFORNIA ASSISTIVE TECHNOLOGY SYSTEM (CATS)
Sacramento, CA
(916) 263-8687
dorcats@dor.ca.gov
http://www.atnet.org

ASSISTIVE TECHNOLOGY PARTNERS
Denver, CO (303) 315-1280
cathy.bodine@uchsc.edu
http://www.uchsc.edu/atp/

CONNECTICUT ASSISTIVE TECHNOLOGY PROJECT
Hartford, CT
(860) 424-4839
(860) 424-4850
cttap@aol.com
http://www.techact.uconn.edu/

DELAWARE ASSISTIVE TECHNOLOGY INITIATIVE (DATI)
Wilmington, DE
(302) 651-6794
(800) 870-DATI (3284) (In-State)
dati@asel.udel.edu
http://www.asel.udel.edu/dati/

UNIVERSITY LEGAL SERVICES AT PROGRAM FOR THE DISTRICT
OF COLUMBIA
Washington, DC
(202) 547-0198
ajohns@uls-dc.com
http://www.atpdc.org

FLORIDA ALLIANCE FOR ASSISTIVE SERVICE AND TECHNOLOGY
Tallahassee, FL
(850) 487-3278 (V/TDD)
faast@faast.org
http://faast.org

GEORGIA TOOLS FOR LIFE
Division of Rehabilitation Services
Atlanta, GA
(404) 657-3084
(800) 479-8665 (In-State)
toolsforlife@mindspring.com
http://www.gatfl.org

ASSISTIVE TECHNOLOGY RESOURCE CENTERS OF HAWAII (ATRC)
Honolulu, HI
(888) 532-7110 (V/TTY)
(800) 645-3007 (V/TTY, In-State)
atrc@atrc.org
http://www.atrc.org

IDAHO ASSISTIVE TECHNOLOGY PROJECT
Moscow, ID
(208) 885-3771
(208) 885-3559 (V/TDD)
seile861@uidaho.edu
http://www.ets.uidaho.edu/idatech

ILLINOIS ASSISTIVE TECHNOLOGY PROJECT
Springfield, IL
(217) 522-7985
iatp@iltech.org
http://www.iltech.org

ASSISTIVE TECHNOLOGY THROUGH AWARENESS IN INDIANA
ATTAIN PROJECT
Indianapolis, IN
(317) 486-8808
(800) 528-8246 (In-State)
attain@attaininc.org
http://www.attaininc.org

IOWA PROGRAM FOR ASSISTIVE TECHNOLOGY (IPAT)
Iowa City, IA
(319) 356-0766
(800) 331-3207 (V/TDD, National)
Infotech@uiowa.edu
http://www.uiowa.edu/infotech

ASSISTIVE TECHNOLOGY FOR KANSAS PROJECT
Parsons, KS
(316) 421-6550 x1890
(800) KAN DO IT
ssack@ku.edu
http://www.atk.Isi.ukans.edu

KENTUCKY ASSISTIVE TECHNOLOGY SERVICE (KATS) NETWORK
Louisville, KY
(502) 327-0022
(800) 327-5287 (V/TDD, In-State)
katsnet@iglou.com
http://www.katsnet.org

LOUISIANA ASSISTIVE TECHNOLOGY ACCESS NETWORK (LATAN)
Baton Rouge, LA
(225) 925-9500 (V/TDD)
(800) 270-6185 (V/TDD)
jnesbit@latan.org
http://www.latan.org

MAINE CONSUMER INFORMATION AND TECHNOLOGY TRAINING
EXCHANGE (CITE)
Augusta, ME 04330
(207) 621-3195 (V/TDD)
kpowers@maine.edu
http://www.mainecite.org

MARYLAND TECHNOLOGY ASSISTANCE PROGRAM (TAP)
Baltimore, MD
(800) 832-4827
(410) 554-9230 (V/TDD)
rasinski@clark.net
http://www.mdtap.org

MASSACHUSETTS ASSISTIVE TECHNOLOGY PARTNERSHIP (MATP)
Boston, MA
(617) 355-7820 (V)
(800) 848-8867 (V/TDD, In-State)
(617) 355-7301
matp@matp.org
http://www.matp.org

Directed *Play*

MINNESOTA STAR PROGRAM
St. Paul, MN
(800) 657-3862 (In-State)
(651) 296-8478
star.program@state.mn.us
www.state.mn.us/ebranch/admin/assistivetechnology/index.html

MISSISSIPPI PROJECT START
Jackson, MS
(601) 987-4872
(800) 852-8328 (V/TDD, In-State)
spower@mdrs.state.ms.us

MISSOURI ASSISTIVE TECHNOLOGY PROJECT
Independence, MO
(800) 647-8557 (In-State)
(816) 373-5193
dcgolden@swbell.net
http://www.dolir.state.mo.us/matp/

MONTECH
Missoula, MT
(406) 243-5676
montech@selway.umt.edu
http://ruralinstitute.umt.edu/HDC/montech.htm/a >

NEBRASKA ASSISTIVE TECHNOLOGY PARTNERSHIP
Lincoln, NE
(888) 806-6287 (V/TDD, In-State)
(402) 471-0734 (V/TDD)
atp@atp.state.ne.us
http://www.nde.state.ne.us/ATPI

NEVADA ASSISTIVE TECHNOLOGY COLLABORATIVE
Carson City, NV
(775) 687-4452
pgowins@govmail.state.nv.us
http://www.state.nv.us/detr/rehab/reh_pgbs.htm#State

NEW HAMPSHIRE TECHNOLOGY PARTNERSHIP PROJECT
Concord, NH
(603) 862-4320
(603) 224-0630 (V/TDD)
(800) 427-3338 (V/TDD, In-State)
twillkomm@nhaat.mv.com
http://iod.unh.edu/projects/assist.htm#nhatpp

NEW JERSEY TECHNOLOGY ASSISTIVE RESOURCE PROGRAM (TARP)
Trenton, NJ
(609) 777-0945
(800) 342-5832 (In-State)
rringh@njpanda.org
http://www.njpanda.org

NEW MEXICO TECHNOLOGY ASSISTANCE PROGRAM
Santa Fe, NM
(800) 866-2253
(505) 954-8539 (TDD)
aklaus@state.nm.us
http://www.nmtap.com

NEW YORK STATE TRAID PROJECT
Albany, NY
(518) 474-2825
(800) 522-4369 (V/TDD, In-State)
traid@emi.com
http://www.advoc4disabled.state.ny.us/TRAID_Project/technlog.htm

NORTH CAROLINA ASSISTIVE TECHNOLOGY PROJECT
Raleigh, NC
(919) 850-2787 (V/TDD)
ncatp@mindspring.com
www.mindspring.com/-ncatp

NORTH DAKOTA INTERAGENCY PROGRAM FOR ASSISTIVE
TECHNOLOGY (IPAT)
Cavalier, ND
(701) 265-4807 (V/TDD)
jlee@polarcomm.com
http://www.ndipat.org

ASSISTIVE TECHNOLOGY OF OHIO
Columbus, OH
(614) 292-3158
(614) 292-2426 (V/TDD)
(800) 784-3425 (V/TDD, In-State)
huntt.1@osu.edu
http://www.atohio.org

Directed *Play*

OKLAHOMA ABLE TECH
Stillwater, OK
(405) 744-9864
(800) 257-1705 (V/TDD)
mljwell@okstate.edu
http://okabletech.okstate.edu

OREGON TECHNOLOGY ACCESS FOR LIFE NEEDS PROJECT (TALN)
Salem, OR
(800) 677-7512 (V/TTD, In-State)
(503) 370-4530
ati@oregonvos.net
http://www.taln.org

PENNSYLVANIA'S INITIATIVE ON ASSISTIVE TECHNOLOGY (PIAT)
Philadelphia, PA
(800) 204-PIAT (7428) (National)
(800) 750-PIAT (National)
piat@astro.temple.edu
http://www.temple.edu/inst_disabilities/piat

RHODE ISLAND ASSISTIVE TECHNOLOGY ACCESS PARTNERSHIP (ATAP)
Providence, RI
(401) 421-7005 x390
(800) 752-8088 x2608 (In-State)
reginac@ors.state.ri.us
http://www.atap.stat.ri.us

SOUTH CAROLINA ASSISTIVE TECHNOLOGY PROGRAM
Columbia, SC
(803) 935-5263
(803) 935-5263 (V/TDD)
jjendron@usit.net
http://www.public.usit.net/jjendron

SOUTH DAKOTA ASSISTIVE TECHNOLOGY PROJECT (DAKOTALINK)
Rapid City, SD
(605) 224-5336 (V/TDD)
(800) 224-5336 (V/TDD, In-State)
dvogel@tie.net
http://dakotalink.tie.net

TENNESSEE TECHNOLOGY ACCESS PROJECT (TTAP)
Nashville, TN
(615) 532-3122
(800) 732-5059
(615) 741-4566 (TDD)
kwright@mail.state.tn.us
http://www.state.tn.us/mental/ttap.html

TEXAS TECHNOLOGY ACCESS PROJECT
Austin, TX
(800) 828-7839
(512) 471-7621
s.elrod@mail.utexas.edu
http://techaccess.edb.utexas.edu

UTAH ASSISTIVE TECHNOLOGY PROGRAM
Logan, UT
(435) 797-7157
(435) 797-3824
(435) 797-7089 (V/TDD)
Judith@cpd.usu.edu
http://www.uatpat.org

VERMONT ASSISTIVE TECHNOLOGY PROJECT
Waterbury, VT
(800) 750-6355 (V/TDD, In-State)
(802) 241-2620 (V/TDD
Mikell@dad.state.vt.us
http://www.dad.state.vt.us/atp/

VIRGINIA ASSISTIVE TECHNOLOGY SYSTEM
Richmond, VA
(800) 552-5019 (In-State/VATS)
(804) 662-9990 (V/TDD)
KnorrKH@krs.state.va.us
http://www.vats.org

WASHINGTON ASSISTIVE TECHNOLOGY ALLIANCE
Seattle, WA
(800) 841-8345 (V/TTD, In-State)
(800) 214-8731
(206) 685-4181
uwat@u.washington.edu
http://wata.org

Directed *Play*

WEST VIRGINIA ASSISTIVE TECHNOLOGY SYSTEM (WVATS)
Morgantown, WV
(304) 293-4692 (V/TDD)
(800) 841-8436 (In-State)
jstewart@wvu.edu
http://www.ced.wvu.edu/wvats

WISTECH
Madison, WI
(608) 266-1794
abbeysu@dhfs.state.wi.us
http://www.wistech.org

WYOMING'S NEW OPTIONS IN TECHNOLOGY (WYNOT)
Laramie, WY
(307) 766-2084 (V/TTY)
klaurin@uwyo.edu
wynot.uw@uwyo.edu
http://wind.uwyo.edu/wynot/wynot.htm

AMERICAN SAMOA ASSISTIVE TECHNOLOGY SERVICE PROJECT (ASATS)
Pago Pago, American Samoa
(684) 699-1529
edperei@yahoo.com

COMMONWEALTH OF THE NORTHERN MARIANA ISLANDS
ASSISTIVE TECHNOLOGY PROJECT
Saipan, MP 96950
straid@cnmiddcouncil.org
http://www.cnmiddcouncil.org/atstraid/atflash.htm

GUAM SYSTEM FOR ASSISTIVE TECHNOLOGY (GSAT)
University Affiliated Program-Developmental Disabilities
University of Guam
Mangilao, Guam
(671) 735-2490
gsat@ite.net
http://uog2.uog.edu/uap/gsat.html

U.S. VIRGIN ISLAND TECHNOLOGY-RELATED ASSISTANCE
FOR INDIVIDUALS WITH DISABILITIES (TRAID)
St. Thomas, VI 00801
(340) 693-1323
yhabtey@uvi.edu

Activity List

Alphabet Letters	.279
Animal Body Parts	.72
Apple Tree	.215
Aquarium	.372
Back Stand	.164
Bad Weather Mural (3 Days)	.243
Bad Words Gone Forever	.100
Balloon Bounce	.148
Balloon Relay Game	.161
Balloon Tennis	.158
Basketball and Soccer	.169
Bead Stringing	.189
Beanbag Fun	.140
Beanbag Toss	.155
Big Feet, Little Feet	.293
Block Sorting	.184
Body Part Game	.71
Body Part Movement	.75
Bounce and Catch	.156
Bowling	.166
Broom Push	.149
Brooms	.208
Brushing Teeth	.84
Buddy Balance Ball	.147
Buddy Drawing	.124
Buddy Dress-Up	.81
Buddy Sandwich	.91
Build a Boat	.354
Build the Farm	.363
Bus Song—"Wheels on the Bus"	.334

Butterfly Shapes	.370
Camera and Camcorder Fun	.77
Camp Out	.118
Castle Play	.119
Climbing Ladders	.343
Clothespin Shapes	.205
Cognitive Mapping	.130
Cold	.264
Color/Shape Sorting	.253
Colorful Trees—Fall	.216
Constructing a Person	.76
Constructing a Stoplight	.330
Crossing the Street	.331
Day and Night	.297
Deliver the Mail	.317
Describe Common Objects	.259
Difference Hats	.312
Different Boats	.353
Different Sounds	.273
Different Voices	.128
Doctor Play	.321
Doctor Puzzles and Drawing	.322
Doctor's Office	.319
Doctors and Nurses	.318
Draw a Person	.196
Drawing Campfires	.336
Drawing Dot-to-Dot	.282
Drawing Ladders	.342
Drawing My Family	.107
Drawing Self	.105
Dress-Up Play	.79
Emotion Sort and Move	.98
Emotions in Action	.96
Eye Doctor, Glasses	.125
Face Construction—Jack-O-Lantern	.217
Family Pictures	.106
Farm Animals	.364

Farm Life	362
Farm Play	368
Farm Puzzles and Drawing	369
Feeling Faces	93
Feelings and Emotions Mural (4 Days)	245
Feet Pick Up	141
Figure Construction—Dancing Jack-O-Lantern	218
Find What's Missing	268
Fire	335
Firefighter Act Out	338
Firefighters	347
Fire Safety Review	340
Fire Station	341
Fire Station Visit	339
Fire Truck Visit	346
Flag Color Tag	168
Float and Sink	352
Flower Garden Mural—Flower and Bugs	220
Flying Kites	144
Form Boards	190
Free For All	150
Furniture Sorting	109
Garden Mural—Corn, Tomatoes, and Watermelon (4 Days)	241
Get Ready to Write	280
Getting Ready for Scissors	206
Girls and Boys	101
Go Fish	271
Gone Fishing	355
Grocery Store	116
Group Story	278
Guess Who It Is	103
Hair Care	83
Happy Face Collage	95
Happy Teeth Picture	85
Healthy Teeth Mural (3 Days)	222
Hear Not	127
Helping Me Be Safe	324

Holiday Placemats 213

House 212

House Collage 111

House Play 110

How Many Spoonfuls? 295

I Am Special 104

I Can't, but We Can 121

I'm Lost 325

Instrument Memory 260

Ladder Fun 348

Ladder Walk 138

Ladybugs 371

Large and Small 265

Leaf Cutting 214

Let's Make a Mess and Clean It Up 204

Lock It Up 192

Make Me Laugh 94

Making Faces 97

Matching Faces 73

Matching Objects to Pictures 276

Matching Seeds to Plants and Trees 366

Measuring Things 292

Memory Game 261

Miniature House 112

Mirror, Mirror 70

Move Like a Turtle 157

Moving With Directions 269

Musical Chairs 163

My Mailbox 316

Number Clap 288

Number Hunt 291

Number Rabbits 289

Nuts and Bolts 191

Ocean Mural (4 Days) 234

One Piece at a Time 122

One-to-One 286

Our Day 298

Paintbrush Fun	151
Paint Mix-Up	199
Paper Strip Collage	209
Partner Kick Ball	165
Pass the Ball	162
People Who Build and Fix Things	311
People Who Keep Us Safe	312
Pick Up and Hold	287
Planting Seeds	365
Pop Beads	188
Preposition Directions	262
Preposition Obstacle Course	146
Pumpkin Patch Mural (3 Days)	228
Put Out the Fire	345
Puzzle Fun	290
Raking Leaves	153
Red Light, Green Light	329
Refrigerator Mural (4 Days)	230
Ring Around the Rosie	167
River Jump	139
Rocket Ship	120
Roller Ball	160
Rooms of the House	108
Row Your Boat	356
Safe and Dangerous	323
Safe With Scissors	207
Same and Different	256
Same and Different People	102
Sandpaper Letters	282
Scavenger Hunt	270
School Bus	332
School Bus Act Out	333
School Mural (3 Days)	239
Sequencing Pictures	277
Shape Cutting Practice	211
Shape Matching	252
Shape, Color, or Emotion Bingo	255

395 Appendix C

Shoe Game	82
Shoe Store	117
Sign Language	129
Simple Balance Beam	136
Simple Calendar	296
Simple Kick Ball	145
Smallest to Largest	266
Smelly Art	201
Snaky Moves	154
Snipping Practice	210
Something About Mail	315
Space Mural (4 Days)	232
Spiderwebs	373
Sponge Fun	200
Standing on One Foot	137
Stone Drop	193
Stop and Go	263
Stop Sign	328
Target Throw	142
Texture Pictures	197
Things That Are Hot	337
This Goes With This—Classification	258
Three-in-One Fire Safety Movement Activities	344
Thumbprint Picture	202
Together Mural—People of the World (3 Days)	248
Tower Ball	194
Towers Together	123
Traffic Signs and Safety Mural (3 Days)	237
Tricycle Fun	143
Trust Walk	126
Veterinarian Play	360
Veterinarian Puzzles and Drawing	361
Veterinarian's Office Dramatic Play	358
Veterinarians	357
Visit the Doctor	320
Visit the Farm	367
Visit the Veterinarian	359

Warm Weather Land and Sea Mural (3 Days) 224

Warning Signs 327

Warning Sounds 326

Washing Babies 86

Water Play 349

Water Safety 351

Water, Water, Everywhere 350

Weighted Blocks 152

What You Wear—What's Different? 80

What's That Sound? 274

What's Wrong With This Picture? 267

Which Holds More? 294

Who Am I? 92

Why Are Bad Words Bad? 99

Winter Mural (3 Days) 226

References

Axline, V. (1947). *Play therapy*. New York: Ballantine Books.

Barnett, L. A., & Fiscella, J. (1985). A child by any other name: A comparison of the playfulness of gifted and nongifted children. *Gifted Child Quarterly, 29*(2), 61–66.

Beckman, P., & Kohl, F. (1984). The effects of social and isolate toys on the interactions and play of integrated and nonintegrated groups of preschoolers. *Education and Training of the Mentally Retarded, 19*, 169–174.

Bender, J. (1978). Large hollow blocks: Relationship of quantity to block building behaviors. *Young Children, 33*(6), 17–23.

Boutte, G., Van Scoy, I., & Hendley, S. (1996). Multicultural and nonsexist prop boxes. *Young Children, 52*(1), 34–39.

Bronfenbrenner, U. (1977, July). Toward an experimental ecology of human development. *American Psychologist*, 513–531.

Brown, E. R. (1996). Effects of resource availability on children's behavior and conflict management. *Early Education and Development, 7*(2), 149–166.

Christie, J. F., Johnson, E. P., & Peckover, R. (1988). The effects of play period duration on children's play patterns. *Journal of Research in Childhood Education, 3*(2), 123–131.

Crittenden, P. M. (1989). Teaching maltreated children in the preschool. Topics in *Early Childhood Special Education, 9*(2), 16–32.

Doll, B., & Elliott, S. (1994). Representativeness of observed preschool social behaviors: How many data are enough? *Journal of Early Intervention, 18*(2), 227-238.

Dunn, O. (2000). *Acka Backa Boo! Playground games from around the world*. New York: Henry Holt and Company.

Erikson, E. (1963). *Childhood and society*. New York: Norton.

Feeney, S., & Magarick, M. (1984, Nov.). Choosing good toys for young children. *Young Children*, 21–25.

Fewell, R. R., & Glick, M. (1993). Observing play: An appropriate process for learning and assessment. *Infants and Young Children, 5*(4), 35–43.

Foreman, G. F. (1982). A search for the origins of equivalence concepts through a microanalysis of block play. In G. Foreman (Ed.), *Action and thought: From sensorimotor schemes to symbolic operations*. New York: Academic Press.

Froebel, F. (1894). *The Education of Man*. New York: D. Appleton and Co.

Gardner, H. (1993). *Multiple intelligences: The theory in practice*. A Reader. (ERIC Document Reproduction Service No. ED 446124)

Gowen, J. W. (1995). The early development of symbolic play. *Young Children, 50*(3), 75–84.

Greenwood, C. R., Carta, J. J., Kamps, D., Terry, B., & Delquadri, J. (1994). Development and validation of standard classroom observation systems for school practitioners: Ecobehavioral assessment systems software (EBASS). *Exceptional Children, 61*(2), 197–210.

Harris, P. L., & Kavanaugh, R. (1993). Young children's understanding of pretense. *Monographs of the Society for Research in Child Development, 58*(1), 1–92.

Hirsch, E. S. (1984). *The Block Book*. Washington, DC: National Association for the Education of Young Children.

Howe, N., Moller, L., Chambers, B., & Petrakos, H. (1993). The ecology of dramatic play centers and children's social and cognitive play. *Early Childhood Research Quarterly, 8*, 235–251.

Johnson, H. M. (1984). The art of block building. In E. S. Hirsch (Ed.), *The Block Book*. Washington, DC: National Association for the Education of Young Children (pp. 8–23). (Reprinted from an article originally published in 1933).

Johnson, J. E., Christie, J. F., & Yawkey, T. D. (1987). *Play and early childhood development*. Glenview, IL: Scott, Foresman and Co.

Johnson, J. E., & Ershler, J. (1985). Social and cognitive play forms and toy use by non-handicapped and handicapped preschoolers. *Topics in Early Childhood Special Education, 5*(3), 69–82.

Johnson, J. E., Ershler, J., & Lawton, J. T., (1982). Intellective correlates of preschoolers' spontaneous play. *The Journal of General Psychology, 106*, 115–122.

Kamii, C., & DeVries, R. (1980). *Group games in early education: Implications of Piaget's theory*. (ERIC Document Reproduction Service No. ED 221294)

Kohl, M. F. (1989). *Mudworks*. Bellingham, WA: Bright Ring Publishing.

Kohl. M. F. (1994). *Preschool Art*. Beltsville, MD: Gryphon House.

Kohl, M. F., & Gainer, C. (1991). *Good Earth Art*. Bellingham, WA: Bright Ring Publishing.

Krantz, P. J., & Risley, T. R. (1972). *The organization of group care environments: Behavioral ecology in the classroom.* Paper presented at the annual American Psychological Association, Honolulu, HI, Sept. 1972 (ERIC Document Reproduction Service No. ED 078915)

Linder, T. (1990). *Transdisciplinary play-based assessment.* Baltimore, MD: Paul Brooks Publishing Co.

Mann, B. L. (1984). Effects of realistic and unrealistic props in symbolic play. In T. Yawkey & A. Pellegrini (Eds.), *Child's play: Developmental and advanced.* Hillsdale, NJ: Lawrence Erlbaum Associates.

Mayes, S. D. (1991). Play assessment of preschool hyperactivity. In C. E. Schaefer, K. Gitlin, & A. Sandgrund (Eds.), *Play diagnosis and assessment.* New York: Wiley.

Montessori, M. (1967). *The discovery of the child.* New York: Ballantine Books.

Musselwhite, C. R. (1986). *Adaptive play for special needs children: Strategies to enhance communication and learning.* San Diego, CA: College-Hill Press.

Myhre, S. M. (1993). Enhancing your dramatic play area through the use of prop boxes. *Young Children, 48*(5), 6–11.

Nelson, W., & Glass, H. (1992). *International playtime: Classroom games and dances from around the world.* New York: Simon and Schuster Education Group.

Odom, S., Bender, M., Stein, M., Doran, L., Houden, P., McInnes, M., Gilbert, M., Deklyen, M., Speltz, M., & Jenkins, J. (1988). *The Integrated Preschool Curriculum.* Seattle: University of Washington Press.

Orlando, L. (1993). *The multicultural game book.* New York: Scholastic Professional Books.

Parsons, S. (1986). Function of play in low vision children (Part 1): A review of the research and literature. *Journal of Visual Impairment and Blindness, 80*(3), 627–630.

Parten, M. (1932). Social participation among preschool children. *Journal of Abnormal and Social Psychology, 27,* 243–269.

Peterson, N., & Haralick, J. (1977). Integration and handicapped and nonhandicapped preschoolers: An analysis of play behavior and social interaction. *Education and Training of the Mentally Retarded, 12,* 235–245.

Peterson, N. L., & Rettig, M. A. (1982). Social interactions among Downs Syndrome and nonhandicapped preschoolers on the playground. *Final Report, Kansas Early Childhood Research Institute,* Lawrence: University of Kansas Press (pp. 175–178).

Piaget, J. (1962). *Play, dreams, and imitation in childhood.* New York: Norton.

Reifel, S. (1984, Nov.). Block construction: Children's developmental landmarks in representation of space. *Young Children,* 61–67.

Repp, A. C., Karsh, K. G., Acker, R., Felce, D., & Harman, M. (1989). A computer-based system for collecting and analyzing observational data. *Journal of Special Education Technology, 9*(4), 207–217.

Rettig, M. (1986, December). Computer access for young handicapped children: Touch screens. *Closing the Gap, 5*(5), 19–37.

Rettig, M. (1995). *Effects of different quantity of toys on the play of young children.* Unpublished manuscript, Washburn University: Topeka, KS.

Rettig, M. A. (1998). Environmental influences on the play of young children with disabilities. *Education and Training in Mental Retardation and Developmental Disabilities, 33*(2), 189–194.

Rettig, M. A., Kallam, M., & McCarthy, K. A. (1993). The effect of social and isolate toys on the social interactions of preschool-aged children. *Education and Training in Mental Retardation, 28*(5), 252–256.

Rubin, K., & Howe, N. (1985). Toys and play behaviors: An overview. *Topics in Early Childhood Special Education, 5*(3), 1–9.

Saudargas, R. A., & Bunn, R. D. (1989). A handheld computer system for classroom observation. *Journal of Special Education Technology, 9*(4), 200–206.

Schneekloth, L. H. (1989). Play environments for visually impaired children. *Journal of Visual Impairment and Blindness, 83,* 196–201.

Smilansky, S. (1968). *The effects of sociodramatic play on disadvantaged preschool children.* New York: John Wiley.

Smith, C. A. (1993). *The peaceful curriculum.* Beltsville, MD: Gryphon House.

Smith P., & Connolly K. (1980). *The ecology of preschool behavior.* Cambridge, England: Cambridge University Press.

Snyder-McLean, L., Solomonson, B., McLean, J., & Sack, S. (1984). Structuring joint action routines: A strategy for facilitating communication and language development in the classroom. *Seminars in Speech and Language, 5*(3). New York: Thieme-Stratton, Inc.

Strain, P. (1985). Social and nonsocial determinants of acceptability in handicapped preschool children. *Topics in Early Childhood Special Education, 4*(4), 47–58.

Tegano, D. W., & Burdette, M. (1991). Length of activity periods and play behaviors of preschool children. *Journal of Research in Childhood Education, 5*(2), 93–99.

Vanderheiden, G., Bradenberg, S., Brown, B., & Botterf, C. (1988). *Toy modification note.* Revised. Trace Center, University of Wisconsin-Madison, (ERIC Document Reproduction Service No. ED 297498)

Vygotsky, L. (1976). Play and its role in the mental development of the child. In J. S. Bruner, A. Jolly, & K. Sylva (Eds.), *Play: Its role in development and evolution.* New York: Basic Books.

Waterhouse, L., & Fein, D. (1997). Perspectives on social impairment. In D. J. Cohen & F. R. Volkman (Eds.), *Handbook of autism and pervasive developmental disorders* (2nd ed., pp. 901–918). New York: Wiley.

Westby, C. (1980). Assessment of cognitive and language abilities through play. *Language, Speech, and Hearing Services in Schools, 11,* 154–168.

Wolery, M., & Bailey, D. (1989). Assessing Play Skills. In D. Bailey & M. Wolery (Eds), *Assessing infants and preschoolers with handicaps.* Columbus, OH: Merrill Publishing.

Children's Books Mentioned in the Text

Andy and His Yellow Frisbee by Mary Thompson, 1996, Woodbine House.

Children of the World by Thomas Bracken, 1999, Chelsea House.

Doctor Desoto by William Steig, 1997, Demco.

Elbert's Bad Word by Audrey Wood, 1996, Harcourt Child Books.

Elmer the Elephant by Georgeanne Irvine, 1983, Ideals Pub.

Fall Harvest by Gail Saunders-Smith, Children's Books.

Froggy Goes to School by Jonathan London, 1996, Viking Penguin.

Lee, the Rabbit With Epilepsy by Deborah Moss, 1989, Woodbine House.

The Pumpkin Patch by Elizabeth King, 1996, Viking Penquin.

Pumpkin Pumpkin by Jeanne Titherington, 1986, Demco.

Shelly, the Hyperactive Turtle by Deborah Moss, 1989, Woodbine House.

A Snowy Day by Ezra Jack Keats, 1996, Penguin Putnam Young Readers.

Storm Book by Charlotte Zolotow, 1952, Hale.

There's a Nightmare in My Closet by Mercer Mayer, 1968, Demco.